Poor John Fitch

By THOMAS BOYD

Fiction

THROUGH THE WHEAT

THE DARK CLOUD

POINTS OF HONOR

SAMUEL DRUMMOND

SHADOW OF THE LONG KNIVES
(Charles Scribner's Sons)

IN TIME OF PEACE
(Minton, Balch & Company)

Biography

MAD ANTHONY WAYNE

LIGHT-HORSE HARRY LEE
(Charles Scribner's Sons)

SIMON GIRTY: THE WHITE SAVAGE

POOR JOHN FITCH
(Minton, Balch & Company)

POOR JOHN FITCH

Inventor of the Steamboat

By
THOMAS BOYD

A
MINTON BALCH
BOOK

G·P·PUTNAM'S SONS
NEW YORK

Copyright, 1935, by Ruth Fitch Boyd

Printed in the United States of America
THE VAN REES PRESS, New York

For **GRANT FITCH**

FOREWORD

WHEN John Fitch was a lonely, disheartened man with an over-mastering sense of injustice, his friend, the Rev. Nathaniel Irwin, urged him to set down the history of his steamboat invention and a "detail" of his curious and singular life. This Fitch did in a completely frank, queerly mis-spelled document, which he deposited with the Library Company of Philadelphia. With it he left an injunction that it must not be opened until thirty years after his death. It was his plea to posterity.

He would have been amazed to discover that the journals he kept when surveying in the Ohio and Kentucky wilderness are now treasured in the Library of Congress.

As most of the quotations in this work are from these and other original sources, it seemed unwise to impede the narrative with numerous footnotes. Other quotations are all from reliable sources mentioned in the Bibliography, and have been specifically indicated only when a statement might appear controversial.

For the late Thomas Boyd I wish to thank for courteous and kindly assistance Bunford Samuel of the Ridgeway Branch, Library Company of Philadelphia; M. A. DeWolfe Howe; C. W. Garrison of the Library of Congress; H. R. McIlwaine of the Virginia State Library; Harold Rug of the Dartmouth College Library; Helen Woodward and Granville Hicks, and to express my apologies for the omission of any one whom he would have remembered.

RUTH FITCH BOYD

NEW YORK,
July, 1935.

CONTENTS

CONNECTICUT YANKEE   3

WESTERN SURVEYOR   59

STEAMBOAT INVENTOR   131

BIBLIOGRAPHY   303

INDEX   309

ILLUSTRATIONS

The Model of Sept., 1785, with Endless Chain and Floats and Paddle-boards   185

The *Perseverance*, Philadelphia, 1786-'87   185

The Steamboat, Philadelphia, 1788-'90   185

Fitch's Screw-propeller Steamboat on the Collect, New York, 1796   287

Fitch's Model Steamboat, Bardstown, Kentucky, 1797-'98   287

Connecticut Yankee

I

W HEN John Fitch was eleven years old he was "nearly crazey after learning."

He was already better educated than the average child of poor parents who lived in Connecticut in the middle of the eighteenth century. He had learned the New England Primer, that dour gloss on original sin, "all by heart from Adam's Fall to the end of the Catichism," in the Windsor town school. And at home he had studied his father's worn copy of Hodder's Arithmetic till he had mastered "the true Principles of Addition, substraction, multiplycation & Division."

Like most impoverished parents of Windsor parish, John's father assumed that "the extent of his duty" towards his son "was to learn me to read the Bible that I might find the way to Heaven and when he had done that felt perfectly easy; and if I could earn him 2 pennies per day it ought not to be lost." So for the benefit of the "pitiful, trifleling Labour" John could perform around their run-down Connecticut farm, Mr. Fitch had taken him out of school and he had not been given regular instruction since he was five, the year his mother died.

But when he was eleven John heard of a book that would illuminate "the whole world." The book was Salmon's Geography. It cost ten or twelve shillings and was not procurable nearer than New York. John had never owned a shilling in his life and had been no farther from home than East Hartford, but compared to the wonders of enlightenment Salmon promised, these obstacles were small. With the same determination that had kept him at Hodder until, at nine, he was able to compute "how many minutes I should be when I should be ten years old," he now schemed to get Salmon's Geography.

He first demanded the book of his father.

Joseph Fitch was not prejudiced against knowledge. At night, coming from the barnyard toward the candle-lighted kitchen where his wife was getting supper over the open hearth, he would sometimes stop to look up at the stars and speculate on astronomy. He also had an interest in mathematics and natural philosophy. But he had begun life as a poor orphan, and he was stiff from the struggle for existence. He was "always at work when he was not a Sleep or at his Prayors or meals" and he "never spent five shillings at a Tavern in his life." Money was scarce in Windsor. A few families like the Ellsworths and Stoughtons, who had land enough to make it pay, shipped long leaf tobacco to the West Indies in return for Spanish milled dollars; and old Governor Wolcott grew wealthy through his position as head of the Connecticut colony, but the small farmers and journeymen lived chiefly by barter. To such men taxes were high even at a penny on the pound. Joseph Fitch saved his shillings for the tax collector and ignored the pleading of his youngest son.

John nagged with almost hysterical anxiety. His father didn't understand—the book was Salmon's Geography—it would tell him all about the whole *world!* He turned for support to his stepmother, but as usual she sided with his father. John persisted. It was winter, the winter of 1754. There was no chance of earning ten shillings while the ground was hard. But soon it would be spring. There was that headland at the end of the cornfield which had never been used. If his father wouldn't buy him the book, he began to bargain, would he please give him that headland; it was no good for anything else and would make a small potato patch. He would plant and cultivate it, he promised, only on holidays and in that way his father would not be the loser by a minute of his service!

Joseph Fitch grumbled his consent and John waited patiently to carry out his campaign. He helped his father until the first spring holiday, which came on the first Monday in May, when all the men, except those who were rich enough to pay for substitutes, assembled on the commons and drilled with pike and musket to be ready to fight the French and Indians. That morning John got up before sunrise and while the men were drilling and the children were playing he spaded up the sod between the fence and the cornfield.

Borrowing seed from his father, John planted the potato patch and cutivated the vines, working at noontime during the summer. When he dug them in the fall he had several bushels left after repaying his father for the seed. The potatoes brought ten shillings at a Windsor store. Taking the money to another merchant, who "delt to New York" occasionally, he at last, after a year of work and scheming, got hold of Salmon's Geography. Using "the small oppurtunities I had of studying, which was only in the inter vails of hard labour and times for Rest," he kept at the book as he had kept at Hodder's Arithmetic until "no question could be asked me of any Nation, but I could tell their numbers, Religion, what part of the Globe their Latitude and Longitude and [also] turn at once to any town marked down in the Maps." And before he was thirteen he had become "the best Geographer of the World that Connecticut could produce, according to Salmon."

John's sense of security had been buried with his mother. She had been "one Sarah Shaler" from the neighboring town of Bolton "and from the Rest of the familey, which were very numerous, and from the progress" his father "made during her life compaired with that afterward and from what I have heard of her, I am inclined to believe that she was the most active and enterprising of the two and [I] believe her death to be the greatest loss which I ever met with, which happened when I was about four years and Eight months old." That was in

September, 1747. The time lodged unforgettably in his mind because all that summer his teacher, Mistress Rockwell, had inquired about his mother's health and because it was the last year he went to school regularly.

John had four brothers and sisters: Joseph, Augustus, Sarah Anne and Chloe. He was the last child and he was born the night of January 21, 1743, old style, when "all nature seemed to Shrink at the Convulsed Elliments" and his father struggled through four miles of deeply drifted snow to fetch the midwife. When the roads cleared the neighbors came and there were "the same Cerimonies, Meryment and invidious tales as is common on such occasions." But if there was merriment, its moment was brief. Behind it lay a lifetime of silent striving for existence.

The death of Sarah Fitch increased the rigor of their household economy. All the drudgery fell on young Sarah Anne. She cooked the Indian puddings and simmered the pots of broth, swept the wide-planked floors, carried water, made the beds and milked the cows. Joseph and Augustus labored steadily in the fields and took their turns at road-mending. Sometimes the falling dusk showed a candlelight through the kitchen window, but often the house was dark except for a faint stain from the smoldering hearth, like the vestige of light from a sun that has set. As Johnny and Chloe were too young to share in any of the important tasks, they were both regarded as unavoidable nuisances to be cuffed out of the path of their elders. Along with their feeling of stress and cheerlessness came the sense of disturbing change. John's father had begun to court Miss Abigail Church of Hartford. But before she came to take charge of the motherless home "a most extreordany circumstance happened" which John thought "worth the notice of a Roman Soldier."

Joseph and Augustus had spent the day dressing flax and had stored two bundles in the kitchen. When John came home "in the dusk of the evening," after walking a mile and a half from school, the house was dark. His father had "gone a courting." Joseph was feeding the stock. Augustus was in the barnyard holding "a Wicked cow" for Sarah Anne to milk. But Chloe called from the kitchen in high excitement. Somebody had given her a present, a kind of trinket, and she wanted John to look at it. She lighted a candle and he stood watching her carry the flaring wick toward a far corner of the room where she began searching along the floor. In her eager preoccupation she let the candle dip close to the two bundles of flax which Joseph and Augustus had spent the day dressing. Fire rustled the stalks like an autumn wind. Chloe screamed and ran in a panic to the barnyard.

John was frightened but he went forward "and seased one Bundle." It weighed eight pounds or more and was too bulky for his six-year-old arms, so that he had to support it with his knees as he carried it to the hearth, which "set my hair all in a Blaze and burned my hands in Blisters. I then with my hands quinched the fire on my head and ran and seased the other Bundle and brought it to the same place and lighted my head the 2nd time and extinguished it in the same manner and then with my feet extinguished the flames of the two bundles of Flax.... And when I had the fire Extinguished, notwithstanding my painful hands and smarting face, which was then covered in blisters, I went to relate the tale to my elder Bretheran."

But the scared Chloe had already stammered "some improper Story" to Augustus, and John "no sooner arrived at the yard than my brother fell foul of me, boxing my Ears and beating me beyond reason for the greatest fault and would not give me leave to say a word in my behalf. And as my father had that evening gone a Courting, I had no whear to apply to for redress, therefore was obliged to submit not only to the greatest indignities, but to the greatest injustice." His sense of grievance was increased when "on the Return of my Father, I made my complaints, but without any satisfaction or redress."

There was much to resent in the years of his childhood. His father was a "Riged Christian" and was "a bigot and one of the most Strenios of the sect of Prisberterions and carried it to such excess that I dare not go into the gardain to Pick Currants or into the Orchad to Pick up an Apple on the Saboth." Though John was weak as a child, when he was eight or nine his father set him to work "in the most serious and deligent manner" and prevented him "from going to school any more than one month in the dead of winter" and even then John was obliged to leave school before it was out to "come to help him fodder."

There was no place on a New England farm for a spindly, narrow-chested child who was "nearly crazey after Learning." The land had been tilled for a hundred years and was wearing out. Insufficient livestock made a continual scarcity of manure for replenishing the soil. While a few farmers experimented with peat and various other substitutes for fertilizer their discoveries were never known among the poor. The town commons, in which all the inhabitants were permitted to graze their cattle, were in the hands of the selectmen and rapidly disappearing. Then as now, the poor farmer was bound to the land he had bought or inherited from his father, for the Colonial laws prohibited men from clearing the forests beyond the town lines. And the farmer's children, unless he allowed them to be apprenticed to a trade, were required to serve him until they were twenty-one.

Thus Joseph, John's oldest brother, after working a year for a cooper, came back to work as his father's farmhand until he was of age. At twenty Joseph was small but "the smartest man in the township and none able for him at wrestling or any kind of work." It irritated him to labor for his father when he could have been earning money as a cooper and he spent his resentment on John, who was only ten, by making him "hoe Row and Row about with him" in the cornfield on Jamestown Plain which was overgrown with sorrel and bluegrass, till John was "ready to faint and fall down in the field but dare not stop for one minute to rest myself, as knowing his cruil hand." Frequently leaving John "three or four Poles behind," Joseph would "go under the Bush to rest and cool himself and as soon as I was out he would set in again."

Haying was even harder, for Mr. Fitch had agreed to mow one of Governor Wolcott's meadows on shares. It was fine weather and the stout wiregrass dried so quickly that Joseph, his father and John worked incessantly to bring in two loads a day, one for the Governor and one for Mr. Fitch. Beginning before dawn and stopping after sundown, in two weeks they "halled twenty-four loads out of the meadow. The mowing of the hay was a Tremendious job for a person of my strength. The Hot Barn, the dust from the Hay, and the sevear labour whilst about it sometimes almost made me faint, yet was obliged to exert every nerve and stand it to the last." And to increase the hardship, his "Tyrant Brother strove to throw off the hay in such rowls and heaps to imbarrass me in breaking it to peaces and getting it away and at the same time he would speak to me in such a manner that I expected every minute he would jump on the Mow and give me a whipping for not doing what was impossible for me to do."

Physically weak and quickened by the sting of injustice, John struggled blindly against his environment. He had a dim sense that he could escape subjection to the meager soil by knowledge, so he kept at his Salmon and Hodder's Arithmetic until, at thirteen, he had studied as far as "Alligation Alternate" and when he managed to go for six weeks to school that winter his master told him "he could learn me no further in Arithmatic, but if I chose he would learn me Surveying."

This was the first practical encouragement John had received. And he "so earnestly solicited my father to indulge me in that that he could not resist my intreatys and went to Hartford and got me a Scale and dividers and on his return I never felt a greater sence of gratitude to mortal man than what I did to him at that time." While his master could teach him "nothing of Logarethms or of calculation by Latitude and departure, but only Geometrically," he "learned in two weekes what we call surveying in New England and knew no better, but thought myself Perfect master."

This brief course in surveying immediately led to an unexpected honor. During the next summer's haying John gained the recognition of Governor Wolcott. Beginning as an uneducated weaver, Wolcott had become a soldier and had risen to the rank of second in command to Sir William Peperill. After the campaign against the French he had been chosen Governor of the Connecticut Colony and in 1750 John used to see him "go to Hartford by my father's house dressed in a Scarlet Coat." One day "my oldest Brother, with many others, was mending the highway at Grindle Hill close by my father's and it was the custom at that time and since in them parts for roadmenders to keep a bottle of Rum and offer every traviler which passed a dram, from which they expected a generous price and frequantly received as much as would buy a whole quart. On this day Governour Woolcut passed that place, who was selected agreeable to custom and gave them one Copper only for the dram he drank. What makes me remember it so perfectly well was that my oldest Brother, who was possessed with quite as much meaness as either my father or Governeur Woolcut, brought the Copper to my Father's and punched a hole thro it and got a Piece of Scarlet Cloth and went out and sat a Post in the ground so near the Road that every traviler must see it. I stood by and see him punch the hole in the Copper and then went with him and see them Plant the Post and nail the Copper and Scarlet Rag to it and heard many invictives thrown out against him [Governor Wolcott] for his meaness."

But when the governor, visiting his meadows adjoining the Fitch farm and seeing John "a little, forward boy, one day requested my father to let me go and carry the Chain to measure some small Persals, his request was easily granted, as is common for Poor men to exert themselves to oblige the great."

They surveyed along "a Very crooked Creek called Podunck River." "The Governeur was exceedingly farmiliar with me and would consult me on the most minute part of the business as much as if I had been an able Counciler and he knew nothing of the business himself; and I was equally as Proud of his Company and as efficous as I could be to render him every service. And I must say that I was very Allert in proportioning the quanities left out and those taken into the Survey to reduce them to Squair measure; and I believe not an instance happened that day but he asked my opinion and abided by my judgment...."

"We could not finish surveying that evening... but left, I believe, Seven or Eight acres when we quit. He left the Chain with me and gave me directions how to lay it off for sundry People. I being proud of the office readily accepted it and executed it faithfully.

"Some short time after ward he called at my father's for the Chain. I fetched it to him with the greatest Expedition and Expectancy of some Pennies, when he took it, put it into his saddlebags and Rode of (f) without saying a word more to me."

Mortified at the discovery that he had made an eager young fool of himself for Wolcott's benefit, his "spirets depressed" by overwork and for "want of proper Books to studey," although he had "already attained a greater degree of Learning than any of my neighbours", John "imperceptibly left my Studies and fell into the common practices of the boyes in our neighbourhood and devoted myself to play when I could steal a minute, as much as I had before to my Books. This helped to sweeten life and from the time that I was between thirteen and fourteen years of age till I went Apprentice I enjoyed myself as well as most Virginia Slaves, who has liberty to go to a dance once a week."

Feeling himself "beloved by both old and young as I could speak Rationally to the old and was always foremost amongst my Play fellows," he looked upon himself "to be a man altho a Very little one, stunted by bodely labour" which kept him from growing until he was seventeen, when he "started up all at once without giving nature time to consult herself into my disproportion Shapes."

But he was continually worrying about his future, "fitted with a good deal of ambition" and "growing Very uneasy at home, and being desireous of learning some sort of business that I could make a living by when I came for myself." He represented his "situation to my father in as strong a manner as I could ... and beged of him to let me go to a Traid, or to sea, or some other imployment than a farmer. He saw the reasonableness of my request and the force of my reasoning and partly Consented."

John's first opportunity came when he was seventeen. A "new stately meeting House" was built at Windsor "by a tax laid on the Parrash." In September the "steaple was raised, when it seemed by the People going that all the men, woman & Children, both in Windsor & Hartford were determined to see the Sight except myself." As the Fitches had only "one horse fit for Use" Joseph and his wife, Abigail, set off with that. John had other plans. Although he had "ever a singular curiosity in seeing merchanical opperations," . . . he borrowed a Horse and went down to Rockey Hill, where there was a great number of Costers lay, to see to get me a Birth for a Short Voiage in order to settle my opinion whether I had best go to sea or Learn a Trade."

He agreed to ship with Captain Abbot to New York but as it was for a trial only did not ask any wages. However, when John went to obtain his father's consent Mr. Fitch with "unaccountible generosity" gave his son "Twenty Shilling Bill Lawful money, equal to three Dollars and one Third." This "raised the highest sence of gratitude in me to so kind a father and I sat out with plenty of Riches to try the Seas."

An unfortunate experience with a mate named Stan made John alter his plans. "When I came to lay myself down at night altho there were empty Births, and I went without either Bed or Blanket, he refused me one, and I was obliged to lay on a Chest which was much too short for me without any covering, which was extreamly hard for me as being used to a comfortable bead at home."

Furthermore, "the next day he began to treat me in the language as is common for Sea Captains to do to their hands at Sea, and found no amendment in my birth at night." So, "the following day I went to one Capt. James Ebens, of Providence, and instead of going to New York went to Rhodisisland." He was "treated Very well during the Voiage...as Capt. Ebens allowed me wages the whole time I was in Rhodisisland, altho he was not obliged to do it according to Contract. And I came home more Rich than I went, not being resolved against the Sea, nor much inamoured with it" and "being as much at a loss how to dispose of myself as ever." His youth had abruptly ended.

II

A FEW days after his return from sea, in November 1760, John Fitch was leading his father's mare to the mill where the bags of grain on her back were to be ground into flour. Still puzzling with the desperate earnestness of seventeen how to escape from farming and come by a trade for himself, he reached a crossroads where a chaise turned in his direction.

Perched high in the seat over the spindly wheels sat a middle-aged man and his young wife. The man had suffered from rickets in his youth and was all bulging head and stomach, but there was a crafty light in his eyes. Benjamin Cheney, the East Hartford clockmaker, knew what he wanted. Talking as they jogged the forty or fifty poles to the next crossroad, Cheney shrewdly appraised the boy and as they parted told John to call on him in a few days, "that they wanted just such a boy as I was as an apprentice to learn the Clockmaking business."

No trade could have been more to John's liking. Clockmakers were the most advanced craftsmen of the Eighteenth Century. Their shops were small storehouses of machine invention. Besides the usual tools for forge and foundry, they had equipment to draw wire and cut screws, machines to make gears and lathes to turn metal. They worked with wood, copper and brass. Between clocks, for which they charged from eighteen to forty-eight dollars in wood and from thirty-eight to sixty in brass, they were prepared to make buttons, buckles and screws, repair watches and clean the clocks already sold in the neighborhood.

Connecticut clockmakers were as technically advanced as their fellow craftsmen in Europe. Of the Connecticut clockmakers

Benjamin Cheney and his brother Timothy were among the most expert. Benjamin had learned his trade from Seth Young of Hartford, his still more famous predecessor, in 1739, and had carried it on in his own shop since 1745. In 1760, when he offered to take Fitch as an apprentice, he had limited himself to the manufacture of wooden clocks, but his shop was also equipped to make brass ones. And a young man who learned clockmaking under him could expect to become a competent craftsman.

When he visited Cheney in his shop at East Hartford John suspected that what Cheney wanted was not a helper in the use of intricate tools, but a farmhand to work his fields, split his wood and carry water for his wife. For it was one of the unfair hazards of the apprenticeship system that a youth was indentured for a specified purpose, but was actually employed at whatever most benefited his master. And as apprenticeship was tacitly accepted as a brief period of slavery, both laws and public opinion were in favor of the master instead of the youth.

The apprenticeship system in America was an unfortunate combination of education for minors and punishment for idlers and debtors. It was the earliest organized method of instruction for youth, supposedly involving supervision of religious and other studies as well as the teaching of a trade. But since apprenticeship was also used as a penal system for debtors, idlers and unemployed, and as a method of poor relief, the youthful apprentice found himself classed with delinquents. If a master went bankrupt he listed his apprentices among his assets. If the master died, the apprentice was often sold with the rest of the estate. Until he became of age he could be beaten and starved and he had to endure it so long as the period in his indentures ran. If the master was mean enough, the youth might gain his freedom as ignorant of his craft as he had been when he went to work.

When Fitch perceived that Cheney's object was not to teach

him a trade, but to get a hired hand without the expense of wages, he was considerably "allarmed." But there was no way out of the situation. He either risked the hazards of the system or he failed to learn a trade. And "being too conceited" that he "could learn a trade in a Short time if only he had the first Principles of it" he agreed to Cheney's one-sided bargain that until he was twenty-one he was to work in the shop seven months of the year, and five months at farming and household chores and that, in addition, he was to furnish his own clothing.

At home that night, when John informed his parents of the terms that were to be in the indentures, Mr. Fitch looked dour and disapproving. John was bound to him by law until he was twenty-one and he had not decided whether to give his son freedom or not, let alone the matter of clothing. Mrs. Fitch, who was a "Very orderly, easy tempered, good woman and a woman of some little property and an Old Maid of about forty years of Age" and ever concerned for her husband's interest, exchanged glances with Mr. Fitch and said smartly that it was very hard for John's father to part with him when he had raised him just big enough to earn him something; not only that, but to find him "in Cloaths into the Bargain" was too much! No, if John must learn a trade he should "go to one that would find him in Cloaths" and "for her part she would do nothing toward procureing them."

But John was determined to be a clockmaker. The conditions were unfair, but it was a superior trade and if he rejected Cheney's offer he might never get another chance to learn it. He had "some spirit" of his own "and some pride" and he told his parents "that a Trade [I] would have and would not be beholden to them for it." He had one hope left, which lay in his brother-in-law, Timothy King.

Timothy King, "a Poor, industerous man of Windsor," had married Sarah Anne when she was sixteen. Mr. Fitch "had great objections to the Match on account of his being poor," or rather because Sarah's marriage would make him "loose over two years of her services." Mrs. Fitch had sided with her husband, but Timothy had met their surliness with a quiet persistence till he forced them back of their last line of defense. This was that, since Timothy was a weaver and since he was robbing them of Sarah's labor, "he ought to do their weaving for nothing till she was Eighteen Years of Age." But as their first objection had been to Timothy's poverty and as their natures were not without logic they never could bring themselves to insist on this. Timothy and Sarah, who had "Spirit enough to treat his meanness with a becoming dignity and proper decency to a Parent," got married and Mr. Fitch, "poor man, had his weaving to pay for."

Since then Sarah and Timothy had modestly prospered. They did all their own work and had little expectation of ever depending upon the labor of others to increase their wealth. Timothy had pride in his craft and Sarah shared it. Out of the yarn the wives of Windsor brought to his shop he made good cloth and was generous with the payment he received. Sarah was "the most Manly, generous spirited woman [I] ever saw, not only to me but also to others." Together, she and Timothy "was the greatest orniment that ever adorned" the Fitch family. And when John arrived and explained the situation, Timothy, "who never waited to have the favour asked, said 'John, go and learn that trade and I will find you in Cloaths and pay me when you can!'"

But when he reached home John discovered that out of his morose meditations his father had evolved a new objection. Unless it was written in the agreement that he should have his son three weeks in harvest time he would not consent to the indentures! And again all the arguments and lamentations of his father and stepmother were brought forth to make him feel the force of his filial duty and to save his family a few shillings a year.

"Obstanately persisting" that the three weeks' extra time was not to be taken from the period of his shop work, John went back and forth between his father and prospective master until, just as the objection "had like to have broke off the bargain," Cheney agreed to subtract the three weeks from the period John was to work for him out of doors. So the indentures were finally executed and in January John set out with his few belongings for Cheney's house in East Hartford.

John "then found himself fixed with them People for three years." He was "Pleased at the Idea of getting a trade" and "had no dread of any hardships which" he "might indure in obtaining it." But as he had "strong suspicions that Cheney wanted" him "more to work his place than to learn him the Trade" he was "particularly cairful to minute down every day, half day, one third and quarter of the days" he was used as chore boy, "and this un be known to all the world but" himself.

From the beginning John was kept out of Cheney's workshop, except when his master sent him in to kindle a fire or to fetch wood. This increased his suspicions, for if he was to work outside the shop only five months of the year it would be during spring and summer, not in the middle of winter. But his master was "possessed with a great many odities" and John waited patiently.

His first employment was as Mrs. Cheney's houseboy. "This Deborer was a handsom, young, forward, foolish garl" who had been so ardently in search of a husband that she had conspired with her sister, the wife of Timothy Cheney in East Windsor to be invited there during one of Benjamin's visits and "one night after being at the house for near a week [she] attempted to frighten him out of his bedroom and went to bed before him in his bed." And though Benjamin had eluded matrimonial snares for forty years "his resolutions at that time was most certainly more than Common and he would not be drove out of his bead by a woman; and at that time or some other they jumbled up a smart, sensible, active boy who was about two years old" when John went to work there.

But after she had succeeded in marrying, Deborah began to reflect on the enormousness of her husband's head, "which was near double the size of common proportions." Rum was the only solace for her wry reflections and "she would get drunk as often as she would come accross Licquor and to such excess that it would purge her both ways and lay her helpless." Because of this John "put up with many things" he "might otherwise have Resinted. Thro her imprudence, imperiousness and mismanagement" the household "was frequantly without a maid, as she could not keep one for any length of time." Thus the housework fell on John, for her old bachelor husband fondly tolerated her whims and John, "being perfectly willing to serve them faithfully and to indulge her as far as possible, learned to milk the Cows and when learned and no maid at hand" he was ordered by her to do it as if he were the maid. Nay, he "did there demean" himself "to the washing of Dishes and never complained of it to mortal man."

Deborah was not only a "Very Silly woman," but a "Very lazy one as well as Proud and as bad as a housekeeper." Though she "loved the best the world afforded in Victuals" and "was extravigent in some things, she was rather penurious in others" and John's fare was "Very indifferent" except when he "eat with her ... at Dinner, but never at Brakefast and seldom at Suppur. ... In the fall of the year my Master bought four Sheep and salted them down and my Mistress had a large Iron Pott that would contain three or four Pails full. She picked out all the beans Suitable for Broath and boiled them all up together and made as good a Pot of Broth as perhaps was ever made in the Parash, of which I eat Very hartily for several days together. But when it came to be about one week old I began to grow Tired of it, eating it constant twice a day and sometimes three times, and began to complain of its being too salt. To this she found an immediat Remidy by adding Water. I stuck to it till it was nine days old without complaining, but finding no one eat of it but myself and that it rather increased upon my hands, I got almost disheartened and on the tenth day eat but a Very little and on the Eleventh eat none but a peace of Dry Bread only. And unfortunately on the 12th Day, after many complaints that no one would eat such fine Broth, and expatiating on the loss of its being thrown away, it was finally condemned to the hogwash, which sacrifice I thought but just, nor ever did I think that the Gods was offended at it."

At the end of the first year John had not yet seen a clock made and his private account book showed that nearly all his time in the Cheney household had been spent as their servant, washing dishes, carrying water, splitting wood, plowing, hoeing, planting, haying and harvesting. His alarm increased. Waiting until a holiday, he tramped back to Windsor in search of advice from Sarah and Timothy.

Timothy King was surprised. He soberly studied John's account book and approved his prudence in keeping it. Upright and generous himself, he gave John the best advice he could, which was for him to continue noting the days his master employed him as a hired man and to hope that Cheney would repent of his meanness or that John would learn the trade in spite of him. If he quit, Cheney could sue him for the time he still had to serve.

John went back and worked through the winter. Soon after his nineteenth birthday, as Cheney still ignored his requests to be allowed in the workshop, he confronted him, account book in hand. "I informed my master how the accounts stood and gave him my advice not to call me off on trifling business as it was probable that he would stand in real need of me when business was urgent in hay-time &c. He seemed somewhat affronted in the first place that I had done it, but as he was a pretty moderate man did not strike me on the occasion."

But John's protest "had not the desired effect, for before two years was out I had compleated all my outdoor work and after that still compelled to work abroad till it run over the agreement in my indenture about three months. I did not complain of anything else but the loss of my Trade, altho my fare was Very course and hard and many things imposed upon me which is ungenerous in masters to require or Mistresses to ask."

John stayed there till the summer after his twentieth birthday, wearing out clothes for which he was indebted to his brother-in-law and getting nothing for it. In June, when Cheney could find no other tasks to put him to, he called him into the shop to help with brasswork. This fulfilled a part of the agreement and, incidentally, acquainted John with an important handicraft, for the cheaper buttons and buckles were made of brass and there was a ready sale for them throughout the Colonies.

Though Cheney taught him the rudiments of brassfoundering, he continued to keep the mysteries of clockmaking secret. Bending over the workbench at his "pottering brass," or moving to and from the forge with tools for his master, John could merely look at the row of ticking works on the shelf and wonder how they had been put together. Each morning started another cheated day of his life and in June he began to "hector" Cheney even at the risk of a beating. With his steady, accusing eye he would stare at his master, charging him with double-dealing, and when Cheney sent him into the fields to hoe he defied him, reminding him that he had finished his outside work long ago and saying stubbornly that he would learn clockmaking or nothing.

Cheney quietly pondered over this rebellion. Obviously, nothing further could be gained from an apprentice who had struck work. But his brother Timothy also made clocks. His brother Timothy could use just such a willing apprentice as John had shown himself the first year. And the boy was still anxious to learn clockmaking. Benjamin spoke to Timothy. Together, "they concerted another plan" and Timothy came over to East Hartford to see John.

Timothy Cheney was one of the most respectable freemen of Windsor parish. He held the honorable commission of Captain of the Five-Mile Trainband, which was formed to protect the settlement from Indian marauders who had been driven from their land. He also occupied the honorable position of Grand Juror, settling the affairs of the community in squabbles over property and morals. He was shrewd, active, acquisitive, stingy and an excellent clockmaker. His tools were even finer than Benjamin's and when he offered John the chance to work for him John was overjoyed and "sure of geting a trade whereby I might subsist myself in a Genteel way when I came for myself."

It was June. As John would be twenty-one the following January and as the agreement was for a year, he had to get a property owner of the parish to sign a bond insuring his faithful service after he was of age. Since he had already spent so much time at clockmaking and was still anxious to continue, his father agreed to become his surety "and the indentures was Executed on the 6th of June . . . and the Specifications was Very particular that [Cheney] was to learn me the Art of making Brass and Wooden Clocks and also Watchwork."

As soon as John's "situation was changed" he "sat into work with high Spirits." His new mistress did not get drunk like her sister Deborah, but was "a Pretty sensible, good sort of a Woman as far as the duty of women extends to their Husbands and in all cases [she] endeavoured to recommend herself to him by complying with his humers," including his griping miserliness, which was severely classic.

"The usage I met with in that House perhaps was as Singular as is to be found in the United States. The true state of the matter was this: my master was always absent out of the Shop before Breakfast, Dinner and Supper and was the smallest eater at those meals of any man I ever Saw. He seldom if ever sat down to a meal without exclaiming against gluttoney. The family, who knew him and who had Victuals, eat as quick as him and whenever I had eaten the peace he had cut for me he always Started up and returned God thanks for what we had eaten, or I believe I may say because I had eat no more.

"I have ever esteemed myself a Very small eater and there learned to Eat very fast and finally to cut for myself and now Challinge any man to eat a meal as quick as I can. Yet notwithstanding, I never got a Belly full with him at any one time unless it was one evening when my master was from home and my Mistress Sat me down to a Dish of Tost and Cyder with a large Dish of boiled Potatoes, when I nearly eat my fill."

Perpetually hungry, John was roused each morning before sunrise. In the darkness he stumbled down the stairs and lighted a fire in the workshop where he spun brass for his master. From "the 20 of September to the 20 of March" he was made to work every week night till ten o'clock, sixteen hours of drudgery.

One afternoon that winter, a raw day of intermingling snow and rain, Cheney came into the shop and sent John for the doctor. His small child, who had been ill for some time, had grown desperately worse. John set out through six miles of sleet, sloshing over the snowy country roads. When he returned with the doctor it was dark. In the shop the fire had gone out. He took off his hat and was about to rekindle it and work till ten o'clock as usual, but Cheney stopped him, explaining that "his Child lay at the Point of Death."

John waited in the dismal candlelight. He was wet and weary from his twelve-mile journey, but afraid to go to bed for fear his master would call him. At about eight o'clock a sense of stifled commotion pervaded the house. Then everything was quiet except for the rain and snow creeping over the shingled roof. After a while the doctor's tough boots pounded slowly down the stairs and the front door slammed in the gusty night. At nine o'clock Cheney came in to where John waited. He told him the child was dead and John got ready to go after some of the neighbors to sit up with the corpse and "keep the spirits," as was the custom. But it was also the custom to spread a feast for the watchers who were called in; and whether Cheney "thought it would be less expence to him for" John "to set it up with it than to call in some of the Neighbours," he told him he "must set up with the Child that Night." "So it was," Fitch wrote bitterly, thirty years later, "I sat up with the Child all Night alone and no Soul to assist me in keeping of Spirits and a dismal, lonely night I had; and that without any expence to him, only the water I got out of his Will."

In the morning Cheney came in and sent John to the cemetery to dig the grave. Sleepless, and without changing his clothes, which were still damp from his journey for the doctor, John took a spade from the shed and went to the graveyard, about a quarter of a mile from the house. "Whether the Saxton was pleased with it or not," he "never made inquiry, but after much difficulty in getting thro the frost," he finished digging the grave in time for the funeral, which "Happened toward Evening."

When they returned from the graveyard John "kindled up a fire in the Shop in order to go to work," but for the second time during his apprenticeship Cheney was lenient and did not make him work till ten o'clock, for "whether he considered my being broke of my rest the night before or fear of the Neighbours taking notice of it, I do not know, but he came into the Shop and told me not to work that Evening."

But it was not against such hardships and humiliations as these that Fitch complained. They were a part of the apprenticeship system and he had prepared himself to face any difficulties without dread in order to learn a valuable trade. He could have lain hungry at night and thought of the "Pickle pork, Pork and Beans, Codfish and Potatoes, milk, Hasty Pudding or a Good stought Indian pudding" at his father's house and stoically endured his emptiness if only Cheney had given him a chance to learn clockmaking. But like his brother Benjamin, Timothy took no chances in instructing a future competitor and John was kept at small brass work "from week to week and month to month without any change, except going out once in a while to work his place or to his Shop which he was building that Summer, Tending on Masons, Carpenters &c."

As for the intricacies of watchwork, which the articles of his indenture required Cheney to teach him "I never saw one put together during my apprenticeship and when I attempted to stand by him to see him put one together I was always ordered to my work. And what was the most singular of all, it was but seldom I could get to see any of his tooles for watchwork, as he had a drawor where he was particularly cairful always to lock them up as if he was affraid that I should know their use and by that means gain some information of the business. And he never would nor ever did tell me the different parts of a Watch and to this day I am ignorant of the names of many parts of a watch and do not know the parts by name. The reason is: I served my apprenticeship to Clock and Watch work and am ashaimed to shew my Ignorance of the business by inquiring. Had it not been that I had served my time to the business I probably might have been a considerably proficient in that traid, but I never was permitted to turn a peace of Brass or Iron in his Shop. Of course, I was ever ashamed to attempt it in company afterward; my apprenticeship, in fact, was much worse to me than if I had taken the traid entirely out of my own head."

Cheney was not only "wicked, unjust and intolerably mean," he was a "proud, imperious, hasty man." John had kept an account book as he had done at Benjamin's; though he spent half the first eight months as a hired hand and though he "was not put to one single clock, neither wood nor Brass during that time," he dreaded to face his master and demand his rights. Until he was twenty-one Cheney had legal protection in beating him, so he "worried thro" until three or four days after his twenty-first birthday and then charged Cheney with ignoring his side of the bargain. "I informed him that he had bound himself to learn me clockmaking and that he could not expect to do it in a day and I thought from that time [the end of January] to June was a Short space enough to learn me that business, considering I was at that time ignorant of it."

This was a useless warning. Clockmaking was a scientific mystery. If a master turned out an unskilled apprentice through his refusal to instruct him, he had always the alibi that the apprentice was too stupid to learn; and not all the apprentices lived to prove the lie by inventing steamboats. Weeks passed and Fitch repeated his request, telling Cheney "if he did refuse me I certainly would seeke redress by the law after my father's Bond had expired."

At this "insolence" Cheney "thretened to Strike" John "and made an attempt as if he ment to put his Threts in Exicution."

"I rose off my seat and faced him and said 'Mr. Cheany, do not strike me now, for I am no longer your apprentice. But if I do not serve you faithfully sue out the Bond you have against my Father!'"

Recollecting his dignity as Grand Juror and realizing that since John was of age he "was a subject on an equal footing with him," Cheney dropped his hand and John "escaped punishment for so heinous an offence" as demanding his rights.

But Cheney had ways other than violence to show his authority. As there was no third brother to benefit from John's education in disillusionment, he began to starve him in earnest, to find continual fault with his work, to speed up his tasks until John became so miserable that he would rather "loose everything than to continue four months longer in such Tortures." Cheney then told him he would take eight Pounds, lawful money for the time John still had to serve. More, John could have the day off to see if he could raise the money among his father and brothers!

John knew it was futile to stay longer. He would never learn clockmaking no matter how long he remained with Timothy Cheney. But if he left now he would have to pretend that he had learned the trade; otherwise none of his relatives would risk lending him the eight Pounds necessary for his freedom. And yet his "usage in the House" had become so "intollerable" that rather than endure it four months longer he was willing to pretend that the Cheneys had taught him all he needed to know.

"I saw the cruilties with which I was treated; the wickedness of the man; the dilema which I had brought myself into by running myself in debt three years to wear out them Cloaths for monsters, and a demand of Eight Pounds more added to it" and "sat out for home and Cryed the whole distance...."

III

JOHN FITCH was now a freeman of Windsor parish in the Colony of Connecticut. He was at liberty to vote if he could pay the poll tax, support himself if he could earn the money and marry when he could provide for a wife and family. Cheney had taken the notes of Augustus and Timothy King in place of old Mr. Fitch's bond and John was indebted to them for eight pounds. He also owed Timothy for the clothes he had worn the last three years, which increased the amount to "upwards of twenty Pounds." He was ragged, penniless, in debt—"which in New England where money is so hard to be acquired was a pretty serious thing"—and he "dare not go to work journey work for fear" he should show his "ignorance in the business."

But New England was breeding resourceful men. Living on small farms instead of on large plantations, the majority pieced out their livelihood with handicrafts. Rivers and streams furnished water power for a mill in nearly every village. There were iron mines at Salisbury, Enfield and Canaan. Forges were numerous. Copper and brass were replacing wood. Weaving had grown from the earliest days until, as far back as 1705, Lord Cornbury had anxiously reported to the British manufacturers "that upon Long Island and Connecticut they are setting upon a woolen manufacture and I myself have seen serge made upon Long Island that any man may wear."

The spirit of metal was in the air. But the British Government kept it floating there by laws confining the Colonies to the production of raw materials. It was an outrage for the Americans to make finished articles; "all these Colloneys ... ought to be kept entirely dependent upon and subservient to England, and that they can never be if they set up the same manufactures here as they do in England." And in 1718 a bill was introduced in Parliament prohibiting the erection of forges and iron mills in America.

By Navigation Acts passed by Parliament British business men enriched themselves at the expense of America almost from the beginning. They monopolized the shipping industry by making it illegal for American merchants to receive cargoes "but such as are laden and put on board in England... and in English-built shipping, whereof master and three-fourths of the crew are English." To curtail American trade with the West Indies, France and Holland they prohibited the Colonies from shipping their chief produce "to any land, island, territory, dominion, port or place whatsoever other than to such other English Plantations as do belong to his Majesty." And to raise revenue and prevent capital from forming in America they imposed duties on a variety of goods, including sugar, coffee, indigo, wines and running from silks to calicoes, to be collected by British customs officers in hard silver.

This last revenue law, which was called the Sugar Act, was passed by Parliament in April, 1764, the year Fitch ended his apprenticeship with the Cheneys. Nearly destroying America's trade with the Spanish and French possessions, it checked the flow of modoires, half-johanneses and Spanish-milled dollars which had furnished coin and bullion for use in America and remittance to England. As the duties were payable in silver this scarcity was greatly increased and trade was still more stifled by the lack of paper currency, which had been prohibited in 1751.

Searching for a few dollars "to set up the business of small brass work," which was the only activity his apprenticeship had fitted him for, Fitch had the good luck to be offered twenty shillings by "one Reuben Burnham who had a strong Passion" for his sister Chloe. Chloe was "of a haughty, imperious disposition as well as Very ill natured." She had fought with her stepmother until she had been sent off to live with her uncle, "John Fitch in the Massichusitts." But she had recently come home and John was also at his father's, having been "made a preasant of one month's Board;" and Reuben, "as he was in much fear of loosing Chloe as she treated him with a great deal of indifference," lent John the money to secure his interest in the match.

With "Twenty Shillings and some little Credit," a great deal of determination and more ingenuity than any man in Windsor, Fitch began his small brasswork. He applied himself "as close as perhaps ever man did and being Very active and lively as well as industerous turned a great deal of work off my hands and made money fast, considering my situation."

It took Fitch only two years to pay his debts. By that time he had established credit in the neighborhood, had "got money beforehand" and was worth about fifty pounds. But he was not engrossed by "trifleling, pottering brass," he was still brooding because he had learned nothing of clocks. If his father or any of his friends with whom he felt on an equal footing had owned a clock he would have taken it apart long ago. But clocks were only in rich men's houses.

One day his "Tyrant Master Timothy Cheany" came over to Windsor and stopped at Fitch's shop. "Whether it was for an insult or out of Friendship," he let it be known with a fine attempt at casualness that he had come into John's neighborhood to clean a clock. It was a chance like this that John had been waiting for and he asked him if he could go along to see the clock taken apart and put together again. But Cheney had merely stopped to taunt him and his request was "ungeneriously refused."

When Cheney left Fitch was "much dissatisfied." Spurred by the arrogance of his former master, he "shortly after went to one Roger Woolcutt, Grandson to Governour Woolcutt whose clock was somewhat disordered and told him candidly that I had never taken apart or put together a Brass Clock, but requested I might do it to his." He was so earnest and sure of himself that young Wolcott "readily granted my request." Nor was Fitch overweening. "I did it. And after much trouble, got it together Right and the Clock went pretty well."

Afterward Fitch "attempted to clean Brass Clocks" wherever he found one in need of repair. Although he "run into many blunders," being "but a novis in that Business," he "met with tolerable good suckcess." He soon had two small trades at which he could work for his living. But he was still dissatisfied. Capital was scarce and the possession of fifty Pounds disturbed him. Feeling that the money should be productive and being "anxious to increase" his "fortune," he engineered a partnership with two young men of Windsor to erect a potash works at Hartland.

Hartland was a new settlement twenty-five miles northwest of Windsor. At that time it contained forty families at most. Fitch's arrangement with his partners was that he was to furnish the money and that they were to do the work. But before they had got their plant started, the partner he had chiefly relied upon "got Sick of the scheme" and Fitch, though it was contrary to his "judgment and inclination," had to buy his share. The other partner, "haveing som little lands to till and take cair of" in Windsor, "made many excuses about giving attention to the Potash works" because they were so far away. "I soon perceived I could have but little dependence upon him and that I should be obliged to go on with it myself; and haveing expended so much money, obliged me to turn my attention to it and being ignorant of the business, I thought it advisable to go and work in a Potash House for a short time. Accordingly, I ingaged in one for one month before we sat about working up our own ashes," with the result that he neglected his own business and earned only "small wages."

But whether the partners had coöperated or not, the potash works could only consume the money that was put into it. Fitch realized this after the first year when he was unable to get more than a thousand bushels of ashes "to salt down and calsigne." Forty families did not burn enough wood to make the basis of a profitable undertaking and when Fitch tried to increase the amount by burning logs for their ashes he found it cost more than the ashes were worth.

At the beginning of the third year the owner of the shop Fitch rented in Windsor told him he needed it himself and that Fitch would have to find another place. "The Potash Works had not quite ruined" him; he had "some loose Cash," several uncollected bills and "pretty extended Views," so he decided that when he came back from working up ashes at Hartland he would build a shop of his own. Being only twenty-four and expecting he had a lifetime of ingenious, profitable labor ahead of him, he planned to make the shop "three times as large" as his business required at the time even if he had to borrow the money. He had been in debt before and had paid his way out of it and in spite of the unproductive potash works he felt shrewd, capable and ambitious.

He went up to Hartland in the summer and "lodged at one Beamens," probably Jonathan Beamen of the Poquonnock district in Windsor, who had been a sergeant in the Connecticut militia. Beamen had married a girl named Roberts from Simsbury and after Fitch "had been there a short time her sister Lucy Roberts Came to pay a visit to her Sister at Hartland."

Lucy Roberts "was a decent woman enough and no ways ugly, but somewhat delicate in her make" and "rather inclining to be an Old Maid. Her father was a man of much repute in the Neighbourhood where he lived and a man of a considerable of an Estate." Whether Lucy came to Hartland "with a design of throwing herself in my way, I do not know, but I there got acquainted with her and finally married her after a short Courtship of about six months. I cannot say that I ever was passonately fond of the Woman, but for the Sake of some Promises I determined to marry her."

She was "a Very honest woman" so far as Fitch knew, but he later discovered he had not been "the first that Paid their addresses to her;" however, "she proved herself to be honest by the first Child she brought, which was ten months after" he and Lucy "had license for whoredom." And that was all right. What exasperated him was that he "might as well have taken her the first time I saw her" so far as any opportunities "of hearing her Character" were concerned.

That Lucy's "Character" was of the nagging sort he soon discovered. She nagged him continually and there was no way for him to quiet her. They should never have been married, but that was as much her fault as his. It is not strange, aside from her abrasive tongue, that he was not "passonately fond" of her. That she was "somewhat delicate in her make" and "rather inclined to be an Old maid" was hardly a recommendation for a happy marriage. And from the day of their wedding, December 29, 1767, "there was some Intestine Broils" in the young Fitch family.

Moreover, John's desire for women must have been somewhat faint, for later he managed to live in celibacy seven years without discomfort or regret. When he grew passionate it was because of some scientific invention or over some concept of religion. His heterodoxy increased Lucy's natural irritation. There were only Congregationalists and Presbyterians in Windsor and he was neither. In a village where the social life was governed from the Congregational pulpit and where the worth and prominence of subjects were registered by the pews they occupied in church, John's heretical notions made him a living scandal.

Also, he had lost the potash works and was struggling to pay for the shop he had built. Since his marriage his expenses had increased, but his business was no better than before. Lucy had been accustomed to more comfort than he could provide her with, especially since it "imbarassed" him "Very much" to be in debt and he was repaying his creditors with every penny he could spare.

When the dissatisfied Lucy sought to relieve herself by railing at him she was equipped with every basic argument she could have dreamed of. And all her charges, it was painfully demonstrable, were true. Though John was meek and "in all cases appeal [ed] to Heaven for the propriety of his Conduct," it was a weak defense against his wife's irritable attacks. She nagged him the first summer when she was pregnant. After the birth of their son, who was born on November 3, 1768 and named Shaler after John's mother's family, she continued to nag him. When he swore he would leave her, as he frequently did, she pushed his threats aside with scornful skepticism and went on nagging till John, "convinced that we could not live happy together, resolved to make both her and myself so as far as I could" by carrying out his threat. And this was "not the hasty passion of an hour, but the Cool determination of six months."

Leaving Lucy meant leaving Windsor, which had been the home of his family for more than a hundred years. When Thomas Fitch died on his estate at Bocking, Essex County, England, four of his sons and their mother came to America. Thomas, the oldest, was one of the original settlers of Norwalk, Connecticut. Samuel became a school-teacher in Hartford; James, the youngest, married the daughter of Major-General John Mason and with his father-in-law founded Norwich and Lebanon. And Joseph, to whom was entrusted his widowed mother and her hundred Pounds annuity, proceeded on up the Connecticut to Windsor, of which he became a proprietor by buying a twentieth part of the township.

This first Joseph was John's great-grandfather. He was Captain of the militia and one of the half-dozen ranking citizens of the new settlement. He married and had three sons—Joseph, Nathaniel and Samuel. Amidst the excursions against the Indians, the expense of building schools and churches and the persistent efforts needed to acquire money where the barest living was to be had, this second generation of the Fitch family in Windsor began to merge into the indistinguishable mass of early settlers. Old Joseph had been one of the three proprietors to negotiate with Timothy Edwards to take the Windsor parish, but his sons Nathaniel and Samuel, when they were grown men, were crowded up into the balcony with the nonentities while the Wolcotts, Ellsworths, Bissels and Stoughtons occupied the front pews. All three brothers died without leaving any property. In fact Joseph, the oldest brother, became insolvent before his death and his son, John Fitch's father, was brought up by "a Very industerous, Regular family in Hartford where," besides learning "to read, write and cypher," he abandoned the correct, Congregationalist tents of his fathers and boldly became a "Prisberterion."

All of John's ancestors during the past hundred years had been righteous subjects, churchgoers, volunteers in the militia and taxpayers. Excepting Samuel, who "died an old Bacheler," they had all married and lived respectably with their wives. Only one, John's uncle and namesake, "John Fitch in the Massichusitts," had ever moved away from Windsor.

It was left to John to make a complete break with tradition. And on January 18, 1769, having brought his "business into a narrow Compass" and urged by tardy fear of increasing his family —which had already occurred without his knowing it—he left his "native Country with a determination never to see it again."

That day, he recollected after a quarter of a century, "was the most dismal of any I ever saw." And it was only a goaded spirit that would "set off from home and leave my Friends and relations, Neighbours and acquaintances and a" three months old "Child which I valued as much as my own life and to go almost bare of money I knew not where—nor what distresses might come upon me when friendless and amongst Straingers." For six months he had told Lucy every day that he would leave her unless she held her distracted tongue, but "she never would believe me nor effect to believe me till about an hour before I sat out, when she appeared affected and distressed and in a most humble manner implored my stay and followed me about half a mile, where I stopped. This added double grieff and I really felt an inclination to try her once more, but my judgment informed me that it was my duty to go, notwithstanding the struggles with Nature I had to contend with."

"Haveing no fixed place where to Wander," with only seven or eight dollars in his pocket and "not an extravigent supply of Cloaths," he went up into Massachusetts as far as Pittsfield, then veered over toward Albany where, "finding no prospect of doing anything for" himself, he journeyed on down the Hudson, growing more homesick and discouraged every night. When he reached New York he tried to get passage to Jamaica, where his mother's brother, Timothy Shaler, had a plantation at Savannah la Mar, but when he "inquired amongst the shiping" he found he couldn't get a ready passage, so he wandered gloomily on into the Jerseys.

One night he lay awake in a strange house near Elizabethtown Point, in the "keenest distress." He could not sleep, but kept thinking "of my Child, my Parents and all my relations and connections and where I was and if Sickness should seaze me, what would become of me." And when morning came and he shouldered his "heavy budget of cloathes" he would undoubtedly have "there tacked about to New England had not the people at the Tavern known my journey was from the East." Rather than look foolish before a few strangers he "finally feablely walked on to the westward, having many thoughts of a Circuitous Rout" for his return to Windsor, "but still wandering slowly on to the westward" until he came to Rahway.

It was a hot day in May. The pack on his back made his shoulders ache. His will had been pushing him against his inclination and when he came to a comfortable looking house he turned in to rest. It was a small house and stood on the right of the road surrounded by a yard with a white, picket fence around it. Going through the gate and up the walk, Fitch raised the brass knocker on which was engraved the name, Benjamin Alford.

The front door was a double one and the upper part swung open. Fitch heard a woman's angry voice, but it was too late to retreat. Instead, he stood on the porch and looked through the open door. There were "an Old woman, a young Woman and an old man." The old man "was setting in a large Chimney Corner with his head against the back, smoking a short, black Pipe, whose face I never saw till near the End of my Visit. The old woman was so busily ingaged in reprimanding her Husband, she really had not time to bid me come in. The Daughter not takeing it upon herself and the man not dareing to turn his head, I was obliged to wait at the door. After they had treated me with such ill manners for about one minute I took the same freedom and walked in without biding."

The old woman stared at Fitch uncomprehendingly and continued to berate her husband, who still shrank in silence in the deep chimney corner.

Fitch asked abruptly why, if they couldn't live together peaceably, they didn't separate.

Old Mrs. Alford turned and filled the room with a loud description of the joys she would experience at living alone.

Mr. Alford said quietly he'd give her half the house.

Half, Mrs. Alford railed scornfully. Half?

Fitch said he would rather give away everything than live like poor Alford.

Mrs. Alford reached spryly into the hearth and jerked a brand from the fire under her iron pot. She turned on Fitch, who put his pack in front of his face and backed through the door. He ran down the steps as the brand flew over his head. Along the path Mrs. Alford came quickly after him, but he reached the gate and got out in the road again.

He tramped on westward, with a steadier, surer step, "quite out of any designs of returning to New England."

IV

SOBERLY cured of all desire to return to Windsor and live with Lucy, Fitch began in earnest to seek a new place for himself. On the road from Rahway to Brunswick he turned in lane after lane that led up to the broad, Georgian manor houses and asked the owners or superintendents for a job as a farmhand. They all rejected him. He was so thin and narrow-chested that he had "the appearance of one being considerably advanced in the Consumption." When he arrived at Brunswick, as he "could see no prospect of geting any imploy as a labourer on a Plantation," he went up to the British Garrison which was stationed there and asked the sergeant-major to enlist him in the service of the King. But war was six years off and the recruiting officers were choosing soldiers for their figures. The bright red jacket of the British service would have shown at a disadvantage on his lanky frame and the recruiting officer rejected him.

He had now been refused the only two kinds of employment which would have assured him a steady livelihood and he had to earn his living from day to day or starve. This was lucky. Comparatively cheap land cut down surplus labor in spite of immigration and among the jobless Fitch's understanding of mechanics gave him a great advantage over the rest. If he could once acquire a set of tools he would be his own master.

At Brunswick Fitch "lit off a wagon which brought" him "to Greggstown on Millstone Creek" where he "got a Clock to clean." And next day he "steared" his course to Princeton, past the residence of Dr. Witherspoon and huge, bare Nassau Hall with its four stories of glittering windows and a dozen tall chimneys where the sons of rich men from Virginia, Pennsylvania, Connecticut and New Jersey studied to take high places in public life. Princeton was the first college Fitch had ever seen and as he passed by the classrooms where the lace-cuffed, frilled and powdered youths were being taught all the things he had hoped to know and had been denied by poverty when he was "nearly crazey after learning" he must have been stabbed by envy and regret. But Harvard, William and Mary, Yale, Columbia, Dartmouth and Princeton were not for poor men's sons, except an occasional youth who worked his way through a course in Divinity; and Fitch was grimly satisfied, as he passed through Princeton, to get "two or three more clocks to clean and try fortune a little further."

He arrived at Trenton in the middle of May and met Matthew Clunn, a tinsmith and a "friend to Straingers." Clunn took him in and when he discovered his ingenious aptitude he gave Fitch an order "to make him three or four hundred pr. of Brass Buttons, nothwithstanding it was out of his line of business." Fitch "gladly accepted the offer and sat to work and in a short time compleated" the job despite a lack of proper tools. And when that was finished he borrowed Clunn's old watch, which he "took apart, cleaned and put together again after much difficulty." This gave him "confidence to under take watches in futer" and he began to make a small set of tools which would enable him to perform the business in a less bungling manner.

Fitch had a talent for making cronies among odd and active-minded characters. He lived in an age of mechanics and skepticism, a skepticism not of the future but of the past. Workmen still owned their means of production, and their small shops were hot-beds of invention, foreshadowing the development of machinery. Everything was accomplished with clever tools and the spirit of craftsmanship was a bond between the men who used them. And when Matthew Clunn, "the Tinman," saw the eagerness with which Fitch made use of tools, he decided to help him still further by getting him in with James Wilson, the silversmith, who lived next door.

James Wilson was not of the Clunn-Fitch category. His father had owned the South Amboy ferry and James, as his only son, was "left a man of fortune" at his death. As a youth he had been apprenticed to a silversmith in New York who had been given "a large fee" by the executors and had "had his Bord paid out of the Estate. And as his master could not be the looser by him, [he] gave but little attention about learning him the Trade and probably gave him his own way as to his Morrals." At any rate "He was a man not possessed with lively sensations of Honor and gave a loose to his passions, in particular in Drinking and was seldom if ever sober."

At the time Clunn "persuaded Wilson to give [me] imploy," Wilson had very little business, but an extraordinarily good set of tools, both for silversmithing and watch repairing. He gave his attention to drinking and gambling and was satisfied merely by "haveing the appearance of Carrying on business." And Fitch "being apprehensive that he had nearly run thro his estate and involved in debt, thought it best to agree with him for the half of his Earnings."

Fitch worked for Wilson until September, "but had Very little to do and neither him nor me any stock to do with. Amongst the rest, I had some few Watches to repair, but my business was so scant that I stinted my Expences at 3d. per day, which I laid out chiefly in fruit." Before he left, Wilson "had such serious Calls for money that he expected a seasure of all his goods and picked out the Choicest part of his tools and got me to help way with them, which I did by stilth in the night." But when Fitch went away there was a watch in the shop which belonged to one Daniel Pegg of Amwell. While he was gone Wilson "either Lost, sold or Gaved away" the watch. And this caused trouble.

Fitch had less than ten shillings and he had worn the same clothing since he left Windsor, but he had made up "fifty or 60 pr. of Brass Sleave Buttons" and when he "steared" his "course down in the Jerseys in order to find a Few Clocks to Clean" he carried the buttons in his budget.

"I went down into Springfield and Mansfield, which was the best Part I could have gone to; and in less than two weeks I Cleaned 12 Clocks and sold all my Buttons at 10d. pr. pair ... and found myself Rich." Returning to Trenton, he "bought an Old Brass Kittle and from tools which I had and som which I borrowed I worked it up into Sleave Buttons and in about Ten days Sat off a second journey down into Monmouth where I made out nearly as well [as before]. I, finding this business to answer very well, and growing at least one dollar a day Richer, took lodgings and a room with one William Smith at Trenton and made not only Brass but Silver Sleave Buttons and in about two weeks made my third trip to Raritan."

But when he came back from this last journey he was "much allarmed to hear that Daniel Pegg of Amwell had called on me for a watch I had repaired whilst I lived with James Wilson. Finding that I was likely to be served for the Same by the Authority of a Majistrate," and knowing that Wilson was responsible for the missing watch, Fitch took Wilson "as security" and threatened him with jail. Fitch was anxious to use Wilson's tools and made a bargain that he would pay Pegg for the watch and apply the money as rent on the tools.

"Rather than go to jail, Wilson delivered up his tooles which he had selected out for small work." But more suits were pending. "His other tools being Taken by the Sheriff and them not being sufficient to answer his Creditors, he was thrown into Gaol" anyway and Fitch contracted with him to buy the small tools outright for eighteen pounds.

This was more money than Fitch had earned from his buttons. Though he had paid all but the last forty shillings "with the greatest promptness," when he "beged two weeks' time to pay that," Wilson served him for the money and he too would have gone to jail or lost the tools if his landlord, William Smith, had not offered to become his surety.

But there was still the larger set of silversmith's tools, which were in the hands of Wilson's creditors. Fitch bargained for them and in six months raised twenty pounds and went in debt for ten more. And before he had been a year at Trenton he not only possessed "the best set of Silver smith's tools in america," he had increased his stock and in 1791 had taken their former owner as his first journeyman.

Fitch now had a chance to show his shrewdness as a business man. "My first attention was to establish my Credit and Paid every person with as much punctuality as the Bank of Philadelphia does now. I saught out the most monied people to borrow money of and borrowed from two, three and four weeks and gave Extravigent Interest and never failed of paying on the day. By that means I soon established my Credit with the Wido Pidgeon, William Pidgeon and John Bowes" until he could be intrusted with almost any sum. "And when I have been 150 Pounds in debt and could not answer for it, could Borrow from one to pay another and Borrow the same money back again to repay it.

"This enabled me to carry on business much more extensive than I otherwise could and with a small Stock was enabled to keep several Journeymen to work and continued to increase in Riches pretty Rapidly.

"I also found a great advantage in Traviling, for when I went out with one Load I generally had large quantities of work bespoke me. And I thought it as necessary in the Silversmith's business to establish a Character as an honest man as it was that of Punctual Pay. The best way that I could ever find to make the world believe me to be honest was to be the Very thing itself. However, I conducted myself in such a manner that all my customers believed me such and I believe soon got a greater run of business than any Silversmith in Philadelphia, or at least it was the opinion of my journeymen that I had. But I did not forsake my Traviling abroad with my budget of Silver on my Back, which has weighed not less than 30 lb. and worth 200 Pounds. Cleaned Clocks wherever they fell in my way."

By the end of the fifth year Fitch worked in Trenton he was worth eight hundred pounds. But that last year was 1775 and though he had been long undecided in his "opinion as to the dispute between the two Nations, as soon as the Parlement of Great Britan declared that they had a Right to bind us in all cases whatever," he "became a Violent opponent to that declaration."

It was the punitive phase of the growing struggle that made Fitch revolutionary. England's East India Company had accumulated an unsalable surplus of tea. With the connivance of the British Ministry the company tried to make America buy it. The American merchants dumped the cargoes of tea overboard. As punishment for this the American colonies, beginning with Massachusetts, were to have their ports closed, special town meetings prohibited and their public buildings used as barracks for British troops. Massachusetts, especially Boston, was to furnish an example of British vengeance to the rest of the colonies and the threat of being bound by force was plain enough for the smallest business man to understand.

But the basis of the revolution was not America's refusal to be bound "in all cases," it was the determination of the big merchants, manufacturers and shippers of America to break the strangle hold which the merchants, manufacturers and shippers of Great Britain had over them through their control of the British Parliament. The efforts of British capital to confine America to the production of raw materials, to limit her trade to England, in ships that were English built and manned, and to prevent American capital from forming, had met with retaliatory acts long before the revolution actually began.

In 1764, after the Sugar Act had stopped the flow of silver into the colonies and had increased America's dependence on British manufactured goods, the business men of Pennsylvania, New York and New England began to agitate for economic independence. "Nothing do they talk of but their own manufactures. The downfall of England and the rise of America is sung by the common ballad-singers about the streets, as if in a little time we should supply ourselves with most of the necessaries we used before to take from England." And to hasten the day, a group of small capitalists in New York formed a "Society for the Promotion of Arts, Agriculture and Economy" which offered cash prizes for the first iron stocking looms, for a water-powered flax mill, a bleaching field and "not less than five hundred yards of best quality 36-inch linen check, each color of highest perfection, white and blue" to be manufactured in the province.

Non-importation agreements were signed by the colonies against England; Committees of Correspondence sprang up in the cities to prepare the triumph of American business and the college students joined in by declaring they would wear no other cloth but what was manufactured in their own country. When in July, 1770, the students at Princeton learned that the business men of New York had weakened in their resolution and suggested to the business men of Philadelphia that they disregard the embargo which was stifling their trade, they seized the letter and "fired with a just indignation at its contents," they went into the village, hired a hangman, and in solemn black gowns marched out in front of Nassau Hall where, to the dismal tolling of the chapel bell, they presented the letter to the executioner.

Commencement exercises at both Harvard and Princeton in 1770 were attended by students dressed entirely in clothing of American manufacture and that same year sweat-shop spinning schools were opened up in Massachusetts by William Molyneaux who, besides using children from eight years old and upward to make his profit, was given a five hundred pound subsidy by the General Court on the basis of his humanitarianism.

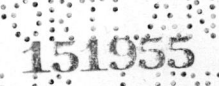

In the colonial towns where capital had begun to form there was a speed-up of manufactures in preparation for the approaching crisis. And this, to England, was the most provocative step of all, for it meant economic freedom for America and a sharp curtailment of British profits. But as the proprietary class of America had been subjugated by the capitalists of England, so the American workmen and small farmers were oppressed by the wealthy men of their own country. And as the brink of separation widened toward a field of battle it was the workers and small farmers who would have to do the fighting.

At the beginning of the war it was the masses who went into the attack. They were fighting against tyranny, fighting for liberty and human rights. In the first days after the battle of Bunker Hill there was a democratic spirit among the soldiers and officers. They were not a standing army, but volunteer militia, many of whom had elected their own commanders and if they were to be whipped and frightened into submission by the governing class it had to be done gradually. Thus Fitch, as "an avowed opponent against" Great Britain's declaration "that they had a right to bind us in all cases whatever," had the attitude of an independent individual at the beginning of the war. He petitioned for a commission in the Jersey Line, but when the Convention "ordered that the soldiers should furnish themselves with armes and Cloathing," he "refused to serve" and "made Bold declarations" that "soldiers were poorest class of People and could not equip themselves and put themselves on an equal footing with British troops."

After the authorities had made provision "not only for Armes but also for Cloathing," Fitch continued to give his opinions. When at the first election of officers at Trenton on June 17, he was "Chosen the first lieutenant under the High Sheriff of the County, who was elected Capt." and William Tucker was named Second Lieutenant, Fitch protested that Tucker "being so worthy and good a man and I but a Strainger, my Tounsmen did not do him justice and personally requested that his Commission might be for the first lieutenant and mine for the 2nd and they was made out accordingly."

Again, in the summer of 1776 when the company from Trenton marched to Maidenhead to join General Philemon Dickinson's regiment "with the full expectation of Seeing the Enemy at Amboy" and "there rose a muttering amongst the Soldiers who should serve as Lieutenant under Capt. Green," either John [Isaiah] Yard or John Fitch, the matter was decided by the soldiers themselves. And when the rank and file chose Yard by a majority of two votes Fitch felt at liberty to go back to Trenton.

During these few months when the army was swayed by mass discipline more than by the system of rank imposed by the governing class, which made the same chasm between officers and soldiers as between rich and poor, Fitch gave up his profitable business and worked as a gunsmith for the Committee of Safety. He collected all the muskets in the township and had twenty men at work repairing them and fitting the muzzles with bayonets. And from July till fall "troops came daily in from all quarters who wanted armes repaired," so that Fitch "worked sundays and all days alike" and "gave the Closest attention to business that summer as perhaps ever man did and from the first dawn of the day to 10, 11, 12 and one oClock at night he was always persuing it with unremited industry." And though it "gave great disgurst to the Methodists, of whose society" he was then a member, he worked "equally on sundays as on other days."

"Som time in the fall there was three Companies called for out of our Betallion and but two Captains that could be called upon to Serve. Of course Colonel Smith appointed me to command the 3rd Co. The officers of the Betallion being met, John Yard, one Green and some other streniously opposed my commanding the 3rd. and wanted to place one [Ralph] Jones over me, who was a younger officer." After the matter was seriously disputed for about two hours Conl Smith proposed to recall his appointment and submit it" not to the soldiers, but "to the officers."

For democracy was being hunted out of the army. "The heads of the mobility grow dangerous to the gentry," the wealthy Gouverneur Morris had noted disapprovingly the year before when, following the fight of Concord, an impromptu army of twenty thousand farmers in shirt sleeves surrounded Boston;[1] "and how to keep them down is the question." It was dangerous to equip poor farmers and journeymen with guns; they might not stop with driving the British off; once they understood the reasons for their oppression they might turn around and drive away the rich landholders, the wealthy merchants, shippers and manufacturers. Echoing the alarm of his class, Morris added, "The mob begin to think and to reason."

But Congress had chosen General Washington as Commander-in-chief of the American troops, a wealthy man, "an iron-willed conservative, a fighting aristocrat," and his first duty was to chastise democratic manners. He began with the poor man's army around Boston which "had held the British in close confinement for nearly three months, although the British troops were commanded by four of the most experienced generals in England's service"; which also "had given England's best troops a beating at Bunker Hill that they remember to this day. For some reason, not apparent in the military annals, the Continental Army, after having been trained and disciplined, never succeeded in doing so well on any other battlefield." But how well they fought was beside the point. Democracy was tried, convicted and executed in a series of courts-martial instituted by Washington and carried on every day. Lieutenant Whitney was convicted of "infamous conduct in degrading himself by voluntarily doing the duty of an orderly sergeant." A cavalry staff officer committed the atrocity of "unconcernedly shaving one of his men." And within a few weeks such outrages of fraternization had begun to disappear

[1] Woodward, Wm. E.—"Life of Washington," et seq.

and Washington was enabled to report with satisfaction, "I have made a pretty good slam among such kind of officers as the Massachusetts government abounds in." Flogging was better than fraternization; thirty, fifty, a hundred, two hundred lashes on a man's bare back while a physician stood by to revive him as often as he fainted. But that was not sadism, it was merely discipline. When Light-horse Harry Lee cut off one of his soldier's heads for desertion and sent the exemplary trophy to his Commander-in-chief, Washington had the object buried and reproved the executioner.

When Fitch's appointment was put in the hands of the battalion officers for decision he, "being ashaimed to contend the matter any further," submitted. Yet when they chose Ralph Jones as their fellow company commander, it struck Fitch as "a serious and designed affront committed by the Officers of the Rigiment and as an officer thought it my duty to resent it or that I should degrade the State for giving a Commission to one who was possessed with meanness." And when Colonel [Isaac] Smith asked him testily if he would serve, Fitch "told him positively that I would not.

"He asked me if I knew the consequences of my refusal. I informed him I did.

"However, I did not carry my resentment so far, but next day I went to Conl. Smith and told him altho I would not serve under those officers who had a design of affronting me, I would serve him as adjutant if he saw fit to accept me—when, in a Very short manner, he told me that he did not need my services."

The battalion marched and Fitch remained in his gunsmith shop, stubborn but exceedingly nervous. He had many friends in Trenton but they were not personages of authority. There were Richard Souse, the Cutler, and William White, the Brassfounder, who were fellow Methodists. There were John Clunn, Charles Clunn and Matthew Clunn, the Tinman; Samuel Tucker, Abraham Hunt and Thomas Yard, but they were all small craftsmen like himself, men who could make a set of tools out of a few old iron hoops and who liked nothing better than to sit for hours over a hot buttered dram or a noggin of whisky and hold forth on the mysteries of the universe, the fallacies of the Bible and the hope of reforming civil society by some kind of religion.

But meanwhile the war, which had been concentrated around Boston, was spreading toward the middle states. In April the British had evacuated Boston and both armies had moved in the direction of New York, Lord Howe by sea and Washington by marches. In August the Americans had retreated after the battle of Long Island to New York, had abandoned New York in September, had lost Fort Washington on the Hudson in November and began to retreat through New Jersey, with Lord Cornwallis following closely behind them. Washington reached Trenton on December 3rd and by the 7th had got enough boats from Philadelphia to carry his army over the Delaware. Only a few hours after the last ragged militiaman had clambered on board, Lord Cornwallis marched into the town with his redcoats.

Fitch hurriedly got together as much of his stock and tools as he could take with him and "fled over into Bucks County for Refuge." He was able to carry "only one small Waggon Load" and "the losses which he sustained by the British were great" and included "the destruction of my tools, Household furniture &c" with such havoc that it could not have been exceeded by "the most Savage Enemy. My Desk was split up for fuel and Windsor Chairs the armes and upper parts were cut off, I suppose for the same purpose, and nothing but the Stools left."

But the loss of most of his wealth was not so serious as the penalty for his refusal to serve under a junior officer. His battalion, "what there was of them," lay at Yardley's Ferry, which was also on the Pennsylvania shore of the Delaware not far from the Four Lanes' End, where he had taken refuge with John Mitchell. Colonel Rahl's Hessians were now in Trenton; most of his companions had been driven from their homes, and war, commissions, courts-martial and acts of carefree individualism were rolling over him like a cloudburst. "As I had been so active an Officer at Trenton my Enemies, who were not a few, called it a Desertion and did not fail to set me in the blackest light. And knowing if I returned I most certainly should have some disputes which would Terminate in a Very serious manner, and haveing the Vulgar against me ... I thought it most prudent to continue where I was."

But the officers of his battalion knew where he was staying and the question was whether he should go to them before they came for him. He "could not bair the thought of stealing into camp by" himself, yet he equally dreaded the arrival of a provost guard and in this fear he "remained constant at home for near two weeks, thinking every minute an officer would be sent for" him. But, "none comeing," he "wrote a petition to General Dickerson praying him to Arrest me and bring me to Trial." But John Cochran, whom he asked to deliver the message, "indeavoured" not without success "to persuade me I was doing wrong in doing it, alledging that I was always ready to do my duty and that as I was in the Neighbourhood of the Camp it was their duty to send for me and not me to them so long as I was forbid the Field."

Fitch accepted Cochran's counsel, but showed how much he thought it was worth by moving hurriedly inland, away from the battalion, across the peninsula toward the Schuylkill, where he lodged with Charles Garrison. Here, on Garrison's comfortable farm just outside Warminster, he began to make up his silver into buttons and had started a fairly profitable trade when the "British came the other way upon me over Schoolkiln" and he had to hide his property.

"When the British came over Schoolkiln I quit business and buried my Silver and Gold, which was to a very Considerable amount, on Charles Garrison's Place. It was a Very handsom stock to begin business upon" after the war was over or even after the British had left the neighborhood. But in the meantime he was worried over what would happen to him when he met the officers of the Jersey Line. Now that he no longer had work to occupy him, this fear goaded him until, on Christmas Eve, he began another petition to General Dickinson. He spent Christmas Day "writing it over and revising it," but while he was busy with his pen General Washington had at last taken the offensive and in a surprise attack on Trenton captured Colonel Rahl's Hessian garrison with about a thousand prisoners, six bronze cannon, four sets of colors, a thousand stand of arms, twelve drums, many blankets and other needed supplies. And when Fitch "heard the News of the defeat of the Hessians I again Suppressed" his petition as he "would not join our Army when flushed with Victory, but was resolved to do it if they should be reduced to the like again."

There was many an opportunity for Fitch to join an army *not* "flushed with Victory" during the next two years; and from Bucks County he had only a little way to go to join the bedraggled Continental columns. When spring came, Sir William Howe's army moved up along the Delaware toward Philadelphia, pushed Washington's divisions across the Brandywine and shoved them aside by a flanking movement. In September the Pennsylvania Line was surprised near the Paoli Tavern by Major-General Sir Charles Grey, who disposed of about two hundred Americans, killed, captured and wounded, in a night attack. In October, not more than ten miles from where Fitch was living, Washington began to mass his troops for an attack on Germantown where Generals Knyphausen and Grant guarded Sir William Howe in Philadelphia. Here again the Americans had to fall back. And in the middle of December Washington took his wearied army into winter quarters at Valley Forge.

When the British had captured Philadelphia and the Americans lay huddled on the slopes of the surrounding hills, Fitch "took my Horse and rode thro our army and inquired their

Wants and went to Baltimore and purchased two Load of Tobacko and a Considerable quantity of Dry goods. But before my loading returned, the Army was plentifully supplyed with Tobacko" and he had to keep his stock on hand a long time and finally to turn cigar manufacturer in order to dispose of it. But on the whole, he "did not loose much by the Voiage."

"I then found Several suttlers who wanted supplyes of different kinds and made it my business to supply them and ingage all the Beer from one Brew house in Bucks County, amounting to about 25 Barrils pr week and got one Team to take two Loads and another one Load pr week, on which Beer I cleared about five Pounds pr Barril. As soon as I had got that into a regular train I turned my attention to Whisky and had one Load or more brought every week to Camp, sent from Yorktown or Lancaster and what I could not sell in Camp I sent by my team to Bucks County and so to Trenton, on which I cleared from £50 to 150. This, with other supplys, Cleared me a large sum of money that winter."

Though this was profiteering, it was more laudable than the activities of many of the farmers and traders of the neighborhood, for the British were in need of supplies as well as the Americans and a large number of them dealt openly with the enemy, acquiring English Crowns in place of Continental paper. And the inhabitants were so unsympathetic to the suffering of the soldiers that one farmer of the vicinity, when he found one of Wayne's hungry soldiers milking his cow, shot him off the stool.

Moreover, Fitch put his profits in the Loan Office. And though he made about four thousand dollars "that Winter & spring our Army lay at the Valley Forge," the inflationary methods of Congress raised prices until ordinary commodities sold for many times what they had cost the year before and tea was worth twenty dollars a pound.

But he would not shoulder a musket at six dollars and a quarter a month and go up to lie in the windswept huts with the half-naked soldiers at Valley Forge He took part in a few forays with the Bucks County militia under his friend, Captain Jonathan Hart, in order to "incourage others" and so that he "might not have the word Tory imputed to" his "character," but he was "resolved never to appear in the field to expose" himself to his "own Betallion as a Private" until he "could have a hearing and either be degraded or acquitted and resign" his "Commission." Thus, he "never went out in the Militia Service, but paid his fines, and should have done so had it cost the last farthing; nay, would then have suffered imprisonment rather than degrade" his "Commission to act beneath it." So he "passed through the War in Disgrace," which he liked to think was a great pity, for if Heaven ever gave him "any Genius it was in that Science."

The British remained in Philadelphia and the Americans at Valley Forge until June, 1778. Then Sir Henry Clinton, the new British commander-in-chief, began to move toward New York and Washington followed him. And "as soon as our Army moved from the Valley Forge," Fitch disposed of his supply wagons and began to gather up his tools. It was safe now to resurrect his stock of silver and gold. He looked for his "Treasure, but could not find it, but in a few days got on the Track of it and discovered where it had gone." One of Charles Garrison's Negroes had found the hiding place and had given the stock to a young man of the neighborhood, the son of Squire Long, to sell. "So as to make certain proof," Fitch "had the young man taken by a Constable." The Squire, who was "respectable and pretty wealthy," became his son's security and when the "young man absconded, the father settled with" Fitch "in Continental money at 4 for one."

But most of his tools had disappeared; "and finding so many missing and out of order [I] thought it advisable to set to work in Bucks County where I could live cheap to put my tools in order again."

After the troops left the neighborhood, Bucks county settled down to its quiet, productive way of life. The six thousand acres of rolling fields in Warminster Township were all divided into fertile farms with large houses on them, and families of between five and six to each of the sixty-odd dwellings. There was a subscription library at Hatborough, a liberal Presbyterian pastor at Neshaminy and a number of craftsmen scattered among the villages. And Fitch, so far as associations were concerned, was in his element.

He lodged with Jacobus Scout, a fellow silversmith, who occupied a log house on Charles Garrison's land. He became acquainted with Rev. Nathaniel Irwin, who had graduated from Princeton and who maintained an interest in music, poetry, nature and mechanics on his salary of a hundred and thirty pounds a year which his Neshaminy congregation paid him. Fitch bought James Ogleby's membership in the Hatborough library and ransacked the histories and biographies, "The History of the Late French War," "The Life of Charles XII, King of Sweden," and "Du Pretz' 'History of Louisiana.'" He made cronies of Sutphen McDowell, the weaver; Daniel Longstreth, the well-to-do farmer whose house had been built by Philadelphia workmen and was considered the finest in that section of Pennsylvania; of James Ogleby, Charles Garrison and Squire Hart.

Making buttons and buckles, occasionally silver spoons and probably mugs, Fitch was contented to be at the workbench he shared with Cobe Scout. But all that year his four thousand dollars continued to depreciate. By September 1, 1779, Congress had issued one hundred and sixty millions of dollars and no taxes were coming into the Treasury. In June at Philadelphia a peck of green peas had been worth thirty-eight dollars, a pound of coffee, eight dollars, a pair of good shoes, one hundred and twenty dollars, while butter cost from seven to ten dollars a pound. In November the Hatborough library, "taking into consideration the depreciation of the currency," and "concluding that the fines on delinquent members are too small," appointed Fitch, Samuel Irwin and Daniel Longstreth to fix the fines accordingly, but as the value of the currency continued to slide they gave it up as a hopeless job.

By January, 1780, Fitch's "4000 Dollars, which was worth 1000 when I received them, became worth no more than 100." This made the "distresses" of his "mind, amazingly great." A comparatively rich man at the beginning of the war, he had lost the eight hundred pounds he had earned as a silversmith and also the money he had made as a suttler to the army. With the hope of saving as much as possible of the rapidly depreciating certificates he decided "to go to Virginia and lay the money out in Land Warrants and go to Kentucky and Lay those Warrants on the most Valuable Lands I could."

Western Surveyor

V

"THE Indians," as George Washington discovered when he ventured down the Ohio as far as the Great Kanawha, "view the settlement of the white people on this river with an uneasy and jealous eye, and do not scruple to say that they must be compensated for their right if the people settle thereon."

White individuals now owned all the land east of the Alleghenies which had once been the Indians' tribal hunting grounds; they also had begun as early as 1748 to acquire the Indian lands west of the Alleghenies, when a group of rich Virginians, including George Washington and his half-brothers, Lawrence and Augustine, had organized the Ohio Company under a grant of half a million acres from the Governor and Council of Virginia. The following year the same authorities granted a similar group, known as the Loyal Company, eight hundred thousand acres in the Indian territory.

But these large-scale speculations were shortly interrupted, first by the war with the French and Indians, then, in 1763, by the proclamation of King George the Third forbidding the colonial governors to grant land patents beyond the Alleghenies. Shrewd individuals, however, took advantage of both the war and the proclamation to acquire the choicest land in Kentucky. Virginia had paid off her soldiers with land warrants in this new territory, which was then a county of that state. Washington, along with other private speculators, was so successful in buying up these warrants cheaply that he "even entered upon plans of colonization and thought of importing Germans from the Palatinate as settlers."[1] As for King George's interdiction, Washington wrote to Colonel William Crawford, who was secretly acting as his agent in the western country:

"I can never look upon that proclamation in any other light (but this I say between ourselves) than as a temporary expedient to quiet the Indians. It must fall, of course, in a few years, especially when those Indians consent to our occupying the lands. Any person, therefore, who neglects the present opportunity of hunting out good lands ... will never regain it." Crawford, who was being paid to do the surveying, was meanwhile to "keep the whole matter a secret," for, as Washington explained, "I might be censured for the opinion I have given in respect to the King's proclamation, and then, if the scheme I am now proposing to you were known, it might give the alarm to others, and by putting them on a plan of the same nature before we could lay a proper foundation for success ourselves, set the different interests clashing and probably, in the end, overturn the whole."[2]

In 1770 Washington was still laying claims on the best lands of Kentucky through his agent, Crawford. That fall, while ostensibly on a hunting trip, he went forth to inspect the tracts Crawford had acquired for him and to mark out other parcels of cheaply acquired soldiers' warrants. Within three years he was advertising these lands as unsurpassed "in luxuriance of soil, or convenience of situation, all of them lying on the Ohio or Kanawha and abounding with fine fish and wild fowls of various kinds as also in most excellent meadows." They were to be settled, of course, under the old feudal quit-rent system, which meant that the tenant had to make all the improvements and do all the work and pay the absentee landlord so long as he lived.

But again war disrupted these easy schemes to acquire the western lands and resell them at great profit to small homesteaders. Meanwhile, the preëmption of all the land east of the

[1] Sakolski, "Great American Land Bubble."
[2] Sakolski, *et seq.*

Alleghenies had not only driven the Indians west of the mountains, it also forced the landless colonists to seek homesteads in the same direction. Braving the resentment of the Indians, ignoring the restrictive laws of both British and Colonial governments, these families in search of a home and a living pushed the frontier forward with their bare hands and defended it with their long squirrel rifles.

Until 1777 the Indians' anger at the encroaching pioneers made travel down the Ohio River a hazardous undertaking, and there were bloody raids through the clearings and cornfields along the Little Kanawha, the Great Kanawha, Mingo Bottom and the Big Sandy where the settlers had built their log cabins. They saw the threat to their hunting grounds and, since these represented their only means of subsistence, they fought to preserve them. The pioneers retaliated indiscriminately, killing braves, squaws and papooses, friends and enemies, which set many an Indian warrior on a murderous rampage. Thus when the family of Logan, the celebrated Mingo chief, were all killed by the whites, Logan went on the warpath because, as he said, "This called on me for revenge. I have sought it. I have killed many. I have fully glutted my vengeance."

But after the spring of 1777 journeying through the Indian country became acutely perilous. Since the Ohio forests abounded in resentful warriors, General Henry Hamilton, Lieutenant Governor of Canada, who was then stationed at Detroit, had suggested to Lord George Germain, the British war minister, that it would be a stroke for his Majesty if these braves were furnished with muskets, ball, powder and rations from the King's stores, guided by loyal Britishers and sent out to make "a diversion on the frontiers of Virginia and Pennsylvania." Receiving Germain's sanction, Hamilton called a council of the tribes at Detroit, the Shawanese, Senecas, Wyandots, Delawares, Ottawas and Pottawattomies who were crowding up in the Ohio wilderness.

The following winter, increasing numbers of Indians fell on lonely cabins and stockades up and down the frontier. In the spring General Edward Hand, American commandant at Fort Pitt, who had tried unsuccessfully to prevent the Indians from attending Hamilton's council at Detroit, led a small punitive expedition as far north as the Mahoning River where they signalized their mighty powers by killing one brave, one squaw and capturing another squaw. Guided by the slogan, "The only good Indian is a dead Indian," the inhabitants of a Kentucky stockade murdered old Chief Cornstalk who had come to warn them of a surprise attack. They also killed his son Ellimpsico and the warrior Red Hawk who had come in search of Cornstalk. Fighting for their tribal property, urged on by the British and infuriated by the haphazard revenge of the frontiersmen, the Indians made the Ohio's shores "the dark and bloody ground."

Fitch's first journey down the Ohio was in the spring of 1780, when he joined a convoy of flatboats and barges at Fort Pitt. A man of caution, Fitch had urged that they all lash their boats together, which would divide the work and night watches and provide greater security. Stone and Tumbleson, the owners of the largest and strongest manned boat, had refused, with the result that, when the Indians attacked, Tumbleson lost his "Lumber Boat" and several of the passengers were wounded. After this hard lesson in individualism the other boats "joined us about sunset and never parted with us more, but lashed fast to us till we came to the Rapids," which were at Louisville.

From the Rapids, Fitch went into Kentucky along Salt River, accompanied by the Rev. Barnard, "a Baptis preacher." Barnard and Fitch had been friendly toward each other since the beginning of the voyage, when Barnard had sided with him as to his coöperative scheme for staving off an Indian attack; and their esteem for each other had been mellowed by "numerious Drinks of grog." Barnard was a poor man, poorer even than Fitch, for "he had no land at that time nor any expectation of getting any."

There was no congregation he could saddle himself on, unless he became a missionary and imposed his presence on the indignant Indians. And though he was a good woodsman and "very capable of business," he was limited by the harsh conditions of the wilderness to a bare existence.

But Fitch, besides the warrants he had bought outright from the Virginia government, had a number of others from acquaintances which he had agreed to lay on shares. When he suggested to Barnard that they go into partnership with these shares he "never saw in man before the marks of gratitude which he expressed on the occation." They set to work building a cabin by a stream and from there they pushed into the forest with chain and compass. Fitch had brought a map of the district from the land office in Richmond and he laid his warrants "on the choicest land and in the heart of the country," thinking that some day he would sell part of the surveys and live comfortably on the rest. He and Barnard worked all that summer and fall. Before the first snow Fitch laid the last of his warrants and prepared to walk back over the mountains to Philadelphia, but cold weather set in and he remained in the cabin till early spring. Then, leaving Barnard to continue surveying for the warrants to be laid on shares, he started home by way of Richmond where he had the locations of his land recorded.

Fitch had been made a deputy surveyor for Virginia and from Richmond, "I returned to Bucks County, Sold all of my tools, settled all the business I could and collected 150 Pounds, Specie. But finding I could not settle all my affairs, but was obliged to come back again, I concluded to go to Fort Pitt, lay out my money in flower and go to New Orleans and to return to Philadelphia, which Voiag I concluded I could perform before any business should be done in the surveying way in Kentucky, as we had orders to cease on account of the Indians being so Troublesome."

It was the spring of 1782 when Fitch again reached the crumbling fortifications and crooked streets of Fort Pitt. Down at the wharf where the Allegheny and Youghiogheny meet, several rude cabined barges and flatboats with horses and cattle lay ready to be poled down the Ohio. In the unpainted tavern men in homespun and buckskin drank their whisky and talked meditatively about the trip they were to make downstream. Fitch came in and ordered grog. At the grist mill on the Monongahela he had bought all the flour his money would pay for and he was now in search of a boat which was going all the way to New Orleans. He had left his gun with Barnard in the cabin near Salt Creek, but he carried a heavy staff and wore "a noble Camblet cloak" lined with green baize. Joining easily in the tavern talk, he discovered that Joseph Parkerson was taking a large barge all the way down the Ohio to the Mississippi and on down to the Gulf. Parkerson had already stored two men's freight aboard besides his own, but his boat, he said, was big enough to hold Fitch's cargo of flour and he would be glad to accommodate him.

They made the bargain and prepared for the journey, waiting as usual until enough boats were ready to start so that they would be strong enough to repel an Indian attack. Parkerson introduced Fitch to Captain Magee and Thomas Bradley, to Sigwalt, Williams, Ely and to three others whose companionship he and Parkerson were to share for many hazardous months—Hopkins, Johnson and Jared.

On March 18, with three other boats, they pushed out into the river, rendezvoused one day at Wheeling and rowed on. Three days later they were opposite the Muskingum, which flowed down through eighty miles of Indian country and entered the Ohio from the side of the enemy shore. The Parkerson boat had "ten men on Bord, all well Armed" but Fitch. It was a "fine, still, pleasant morning," and wrapped in his camblet cloak Fitch was enjoying the weather and viewing the scenery from the quarterdeck when he began to realize that if the barge kept to her present course she would ram her bow full against the island below. Lining two trees to sight by, he made more certain of his observation. Then he called Parkerson and told him "I thought it prudent for me to get 3 or four hands and go under Deck and be ready to hawl off upon occation."

Parkerson nodded and Fitch took three men below to the oars, where they sat waiting in the hold for instructions. When they went down the boat was still a mile from the island and there was nothing for them to do but lie on their oars and listen for a command to row or back water. Except through a porthole on a level with their eyes when they stood up it was impossible for them to see ahead.

After about ten minutes somebody yelled from the deck, "Row!"

They pulled easily on the oars.

"Row harder!"

Stiffening their legs, Fitch and the three men with him pulled weightily.

"Harder!"

Now they rowed as rapidly as they could.

The bottom of the barge scraped ominously. The prow tilted up and settled down.

All at once the boat was completely motionless. Fitch ran up on deck and found they had driven her "as right on the Point of the Island as was Possible to place her."

The ten men aboard began cursing and blaming each other. They jumped down into the mud around the prow and tried to push her off. With its heavy cargo, the craft failed to budge.

A pirogue with a crew of three, which had been following them down the river, steered toward the island and the men gave their help. Tugging, sweating, in mud up to their knees, they struggled till noon. But the barge stayed firmly grounded by its heavy cargo. In the afternoon they all began the job of removing the flour in order to lighten the boat. Carrying it up from the hold, over a plank walk to a hillock where the ground was dry, it was sunset before they finished and they were all "exceedingly fateaged." The barge was afloat, but they decided to wait till morning before reloading. As the two other boats of the convoy had disappeared around a bend of the river, the pirogue with its crew of three remained with Fitch and Parkerson. Both crafts "fell down about 40 Pole," where the barge "made fast to a Saplin in an Eddy."

Fitch looked at the dark Ohio shore. From the mouth of the Muskingum, which they lay in sight of, there was not a white man in all that stretch of wilderness, excepting renegades and a few British traders, between them and the British garrison at Detroit. There were only Shawanese, Delawares, Mingoes and Miamis, hundreds of soft-footed, clear-eyed, dour braves who were guarding the Ohio as the frontier of their country.

Barely a month had passed since the men of the western settlements had committed the most provocative mass murder in the history of the old Northwest. Fitch, Parkerson and all the others had heard about it before they left Fort Pitt.

When the British and Americans each tried to gain the Ohio Indians as allies, half the Delaware tribe had remained determinedly neutral. They were the families which had been recently Christianized by three Moravian missionaries from Pennsylvania. These missionaries had instructed them in building tighter cabins, in better ways of cultivation and in increasing their winter stores. They established three towns—Gnadenhutten, Schonbrunn and Salem—which lay closest of all the Indian villages to the Pennsylvania border. And they impressed the Indians with enchanting pictures of a dwelling place called Heaven which could be inherited, they said, only by meekness on earth.

This Christianity neutralized the Delaware converts, but not their spiritual leaders. On the contrary, the Rev. John Heckewelder used his position as head of the mission to act as informer against the British and the rest of the Indians through a continuous correspondence with the American authorities at Fort

Pitt. It was Heckewelder who reported to Colonel Daniel Brodhead, who was then commandant at the Fort Pitt garrison, when the unchristianized brothers of the Delaware converts made a trading agreement with the British at Detroit. He also sent Brodhead the provocative statement, born out of his hysteria, that "the greater part of them [the Delawares] who had remained warriors will be upon you in a few days." And later he met and conferred with Brodhead as to ways and means when the Fort Pitt commandant arrived on the Tuscarawas near the Christianized towns with a punitive expedition of five hundred frontiersmen.

The neutral position of these Indians at Gnadenhutten, Schonbrunn and Salem was further imperiled by braves from the interior of the Ohio country who occasionally stopped there on their marauds against the Pennsylvania border. As Half King, one of the Delaware war-chiefs, warned his meek cousins, "Two powerful, merciless and angry tribes, the English and the Long Knives, stand ready, opening their jaws against each other like monstrous beasts. You are sitting down between them and are in danger of being devoured and ground to powder, if not in the jaws of one, then in the jaws of the other, or even both...." And he urged them, "Do not stand looking at your plantations, but arise and follow Half King" to a position of greater safety. "This is Half King's message and he has come solely for the purpose of delivering it."

Finally Major Arendt Schuyler de Peyster, the British commandant at Detroit, sent agents with orders to remove these Christianized Delawares from the Tuscarawas to the Upper Sandusky, where they would be safe from attacks along the border. To the indignation of Heckewelder, the removal was carried out in August, 1781. But several acres of unripened corn had been left standing in the bottomlands along the Tuscarawas. During their hungry winter in the marshy Wyandot country these hapless Delawares thought longingly of the fields of grain they had left behind. From the middle of January until nearly the end of February they stole back in small groups to gather the corn. Until the sixth of March, 1782, from Schonbrunn down through Gnadenhutten to Salem on the bend of the river, these meek, Christianized and exceedingly hungry Delawares were still husking in the bottomlands.

On the night of March 5, Colonel David Williamson and a hundred Fort Pitt militiamen arrived within a mile of Gnadenhutten. Next morning Williamson sent out two reconnoitering squads and followed with the main body into the village. All but two Indians, a buck and a squaw, had gone into the fields. Williamson's men promptly killed these two, then stood waiting for the scouting party to return.

The scouting party arrived in the middle of the morning behind a large group of unarmed Indians. They had come upon them in the bottomland and, being outnumbered, had assumed a friendly attitude, telling the Delawares that they had come to take them to a place of still greater safety, to some fine camp in Pennsylvania where the Americans would lavishly provide them with everything they needed.

This ruse was so effective that Williamson changed his tactics. He would not murder these Indians who had just been brought in; he would wait till he had assembled all the Indians of the neighborhood. He sent runners down to Schonbrunn and Salem with the message that a friendly White Captain was waiting to lead them into a new camp where they would be well supplied and protected from all enemies. Meanwhile, he and his men began to herd the Delawares into the Gnadenhutten cabins. When the others arrived, they also were thrust indoors, till the number stood at ninety-six.

"Boys," Williamson asked, "which shall we do, kill them or take them back to Fort Pitt?"

"Kill 'em!" The vote was eighty-two to eighteen. Indians were of no use to the white man; so long as there were unoccupied rivers with fish and uncaptured bottomlands for corn it was impossible to make them slaves.

Saving ball and powder, Williamson and the militiamen set to work with knives, clubs and tomahawks. Their ears rang from the screams of torture; their arms grew limp from bloodspattering blows and their feet slipped on the gory floors, but they continued with great perseverance until every one of the ninety-six Indians was a corpse.

At Fort Pitt Fitch had heard the alarming news of "Williamson's Massicree." This had sharpened his active sense of caution; and having "always thought that it was the worst kind of Courdice of being affraid that others should think us affraid," he had given his fellow travelers "several lessons of cautions on our passage, till they insulted me for being Timid."

Nevertheless, as the crews of the two boats prepared to spend the night so close to the Indian shore, Fitch raised his voice again, requesting Parkerson to post a sentry and urging Hopkins, Johnson, Sigwalt and the rest "to see their peaces was all in order and fresh Primed." And he also laid an ax conveniently near the bowfast so that in case of a surprise attack he could cut the rope loose from the sapling and pull out into midstream.

"The next morning about sunrise we sent out a man to scout on the Island, with orders not to fire at any sort of game whatever, that one gun should be an allarm to us." While he was gone they all strengthened themselves for the task of loading on the flour by going "up on deck Round the caboos and makeing a hot buttered dram till the sun was about an hour high."

But still there was no signal from the scout. Apprehensively, Fitch went to the bow to make sure the ax was there. Somebody had taken it. He made a nuisance of himself hunting "all the Boats for it," but the ax could not be found. As the scout failed to return he "grew exceedingly uneasy and got up and walked the deck and kept my Eye most constantly on Shore."

The sun rose higher. Everything was very bright, the budding twigs on the flooded saplings, the great heap of gray driftwood which the spring freshets had piled up on the island about twenty feet from shore, the bare branches of the great black walnuts, oaks and sycamores that lined the Ohio's banks. Around the cabin Captain Magee of Kentucky and several others of the crew were relishing the last of their hot buttered dram.

Suddenly there was an explosion of gunpowder, the whir and clatter of musket balls. All the men but Captain Magee, who had been knocked dead against the side of the caboose, leaped below deck.

"Indians!" somebody yelled.

The men snatched at their guns and went warily to the portholes in the hold, through which they began to peer at the pile of driftwood on the island. Fitch lamented the missing ax, but Thomas Bradley, a "man of more Courage than prudence," took his hunting knife in his hand and crawled up on deck to cut the boat loose from the sapling.

A single shot came from the pile of driftwood. Bradley winced as if stung by a mammoth insect. His legs and arms stiffened until he lay perfectly still.

Fitch grasped Bradley's gun and crouched by the porthole. There was nothing to be seen that hadn't been there before, no target of any kind. The Indians were so well hidden by the pile of driftwood that Fitch "could not discover a hair on their heads. In the same manner one Houston stood for about one half hour, but never discharged his peace." But none of the others "seemed to have any stomack for such a Breakfast. It is true that Parkerson, one Williams and Ealy did sometimes look out of a port hole, but as soon drew back again. The other four laid themselves down in the Bottom of the Boat and never thought of any resistance and if I ever felt myself angry or swor with a harty good will it was at that time." In fact Fitch had "the strongest Temptation to tommyhawk one Sigwalt who cringed down behind me that ever I had to do a wicked act."

"Standing at the port hole a spell and finding no prospect of driveing them off, as they was so strongly posted," Fitch turned his "attention to cutting the boat loose." Taking up a tomahawk, he dodged past the portholes to the bow, thinking that if he could cut a hole in the side he would be enabled to reach out with a knife and sever the rope that held the boat fast to the sapling. At the place in the hull nearest the bowfast he began to whack with swift precision and had "got a hole cut about three inches squair when there came a ball thro the bord about two inches from the hole I had cut," so close to hitting him that at the shot he "felt the wind of it fresh in my left eye and the splinters made my face smart many places where they struck it."

There were some pieces of plank nearby and he ran to get them as a shield to carry on his work in spite of the Indian's accurate fire. He went back and resumed chopping at the hole. Through the sound of his blows he heard a familiar voice. Peering through the opening, he saw the scout who had been sent out that morning on the island. The scout was standing at the side of the pile of driftwood, raising his arms and calling on the crew to surrender.

"Don't hear him!" Fitch yelled a warning to Parkerson, who was in the stern. "I'll have her loose and we've got nothing to fear from them till I do!"

But Parkerson had had enough. Lifting his hands above his head, he led the way up the steps to the deck. The rest followed. Fitch and Houston exchanged helpless glances. "If it must be so, we may as well go too," he said to Houston, when they both laid down their arms and followed Parkerson.

Hands over their heads, they straggled over the side, through the eddy and stood on the bank of the island. One, two, three, four—eight Indians appeared from behind the driftwood. "Them Indians was Very civil to us and behaved with the greatest coolness and deliberation and near half an hour elapsed before they went on Bord the Boat, when two of them went and scalped the two dead men and when they came back on Shore, Capt. Buffaloe, the commandant of the party, went on Bord and under deck and brought up considerable of Goods, when others in turns went down and brought up the chief of the Blankets, Guns, Ammunition &c. After which, Capt Crow, who spoke good English and [had been] brought up in the Jerseys, went on Bord and tide a war club to the Steering Oar and set her adrift. There being three or four Tons of Flower on Bord of Hopkins' Boat, we all went on bord of that and crossed to the Indian shore, took the flower out of the boat and rolled it on the top of the bank and some pains was taken to conceal it."

"After which, the Indians seemed to be in a state of suspence and cooly deliberateing amongst one another," till Fitch lost interest through weariness. Being "amazeingly fateaged from my day's work before, and doing near double centery duty" the previous night and feeling himself "fully resigned" to his fate, he became "perfectly easy" under the circumstances and lay down in his noble camblet cloak to sleep.

"But unfortunately Captain Buffaloe had made himself too free with our Whisky and I had not lain many minutes, I presume not more than one quarter of an hour, than I heard an Indian Speakeing in Broken Language, 'Teak! Teak!'

"I opened my Eyes and rose up on end and shook my head and said, 'No!'

"He said again, 'Teak!' and drew his tommyhawk a fair blow to sink it into my head."

But "I looked him full in the face and felt the greatest Composier to receive it that I ever felt to meet Death, unless it is since I began the Steam Boat. But Captain Crow, who gave me the permit, coming at the same instant of Time and catching Buffaloe's arm, stopped the fatal Blow."

"I then Rose and seated myself amongst the rest of the Captives, when the Indians sat to and made up Bundles for each of us to carry and in the most juditious manner, according to our appearance. The man who looked healthy and strong, they gave a heavy Load, but lighter ones to the weaker." Though some of the captives had to carry as much as thirty pounds on their backs, this was nothing "compaired to what they themselves" were burdened with. "I am confident that some of their packs would weigh 60 lb.

"After this was done we was all Tied, I think as a Badge of Captivity rather than for use. For some was pinioned with one single Ropeyarn out of a rope and I with a peace of bark not thicker than a Goos quill, which I could readily snaped with one fingure.

"We marched on till sun about an hour high, when we came to Camp where we all of us eat hearty and sat Very friendly about the Camp till Beadtime. As soon as they thought it was time to lie down we was all of us pinioned fast with good Cord which they had brought from the Boats. I believe I was closest tied than any of the rest, as I did not hear them complain, but my Armes in a Short time felt as if dead and I was obliged to call the Indians up to slacken the cords, which they did in some measure, but I suffered amazingly that night by the cords being too tight about my arms."

As they were the "first prisoners taken after Williamson's Massicree," Fitch and the others "expected nothing but a retaliation." Doubtless Captains Crow and Buffaloe had not heard of it, but the crime would certainly be known in the first Indian town they arrived at and this gave all of them a hang-dog fear in spite of the Indians' friendliness toward them. Hungry, weary, they would rather have gone on marching till doomsday than be brought into the Indians' council house. Talking fearfully among themselves, they concluded they had only one defense; and if it failed to mollify their captors, then they were doomed. They determined to deny that they had ever heard of the Williamson Massacre.

Every night Captains Buffalo and Crow marched their captives till an hour before sundown and then shared their provisions with them over the campfire. "They marched us moderate as they found we could hold out," so that "it was twelve days before we reached the Indian Towns," twelve days over a narrow footpath that wound northward along the Muskingum toward Wapomatica." Before they arrived their supplies were low and as they "drew near the Indian Towns the game was exceedingly scarse and we could not kill anything worth mentioning to support nineteen men," so that the Americans "suffered amazingly for provisions." But the next day one of the Indian hunters shot a deer and everybody "was brought to it and halted till it was skinned and cut up and every part of it saved except the intreals. "Captain Buffaloe took the tripe and scraped off the dung as clean as he could with a knife and rolled it up in a lump perhaps as big as a man's two fists and put it into his knapsack and, his body keeping it warm for several days, it became by that means Very mellow and when urgent necessity called he took the paunch out of his knapsack and laid it on the fire and warmed it thro. There was no occation of much rosting, as it was Tender without. After it was dressed he gave me a peace without either bread or salt. The smell of the dung was rather offensive, but my ravinous appetite overcame that squeamishness and I eat of it with the greatest eagerness, that the Juse and Dung ran down both corners of my mouth to my chin...."

Till the last day before they reached the Indian town their captors continued to treat them kindly. Having been "a Continental man in the War," Fitch was dressed "chiefly in homespun and had a striped Linsey Coattee and jacket with homade Silver buttons." And "the night before we got to the Town, Capt. Buffaloe called me to him and took his knife and cairfully cut off all the buttons of my coattee and put them in his knapsack, then cut the buttons off my jacket and showed me the way to my pocket. This peace of Generosity, I believe exceeds the most of Christian Nations." In fact it was not only generosity on Buffalo's part, "but humanity to save my cloaths."

The morning before they reached the first Indian town Captain Crow began to prepare for the ceremonial entrance. He "Cut a nice, Streight stick about the size of a large walking Cain and probably about 10 or 12 feet long, on which he tied the two scalps" of Captain Magee and Thomas Bradley. When he had first taken the scalps, Captain Crow had been "very envious to cut them round in a circle, then made two little hoops, perhaps about 3 inches diamiter and sewed the scalps in the inside of these Hoops and then painted them." Now he tied the hoops to the top of the pole and led the procession in Indian file with his scalp-pole raised high. And when they came within sight of the first town he gave a loud halloo.

From the collection of log houses and bark huts scattered along the river bank came one small boy. Racing down to meet the returning warriors, he grasped the pole from Captain Crow and hurried back to the village with it. But as all the braves and squaws had gone to the council house in the next village the ceremony was incomplete, for there was nobody to come out and form a gauntlet for the prisoners to run through.

By this luck, Fitch, Parkerson, Hopkins and the rest reached the first town safely. Toward afternoon when the Indians returned from the council "there came an abundance of Indians to see us and striped us of all our superflues cloathing and some of our Body Cloathing." That night the prisoners were more securely pinioned than at any time since they had been taken. They were tied both individually and together. But the Indians were neither threatening nor violent and after they had taken what they wanted they left the prisoners alone for the night.

Next day they were marched to the Delawares' council house where "there was a large Council sitting of several nations and an abundance of Indians. Before we came to the town our masters, knowing better than we did what was designed for us and, as we had been fellow travelers so long together, being kind and friendly toward us, halted us and took off all our Budgets and from myself, who had shoes on, they took them off and gave me a pr of Mogesons," but "we none of us knew the reason why or that we was to run the gantlot."

However, they were aware that something was up, for "we was told by our Captors that if any came out to abuse us, we must run for the long house and when we got into that nobody would hurt us." With these directions and preparations, "we marched coolly on till we came in sight of the Town," which was still about a quarter of a mile down the footpath.

Captain Crow raised his scalp-pole and gave the scalp halloo—once for the dead Captain Magee, once for Thomas Bradley, once for John Fitch, once for Parkerson, for Hopkins, for Jared, for Johnson, Sigwalt, for Ely, for Williams and for still three more, thirteen sharp scalp halloos capped by an exultant war shout.

"When this last was performed there came a Stout Indian, naked except for his Brich Clout, Painted all over Black, who run like a Dear to Capt. Crow and took the pole with the Sculps out of his hand and ran as fast back to the Council House."

This was the signal for all the captives to run. But they were exhausted and confused and in spite of the warning Captain Crow had given them they continued to "march coolly." When they came to the top of the grassy rise they could see the council house standing by the small stream in a hollow, the Indian with the scalp-pole almost upon it and "a large body of Indians Rushing down on us with War Whoops."

The prisoners were surrounded in a melee of spirited bucks. "Several of them Slapt me open-handed in the face, head, Back and Sides and one Catched me by the hair and pulled me down to the ground, but had no design of stoping me, as he then forsook me and took after the others. I scampered along as fast as I could and a merry frolick they had. I met with no impediments "amazingly dextrious" use of their brightly colored blankets as they kept "throwing them down about their waists and securing them there I know not how."

Slowly, and around their different fires, Indians "of all ages and ranks mixed in, from women of 70 years of Age down to thirteen." And "after about 20 women had ingaged in the dance, it was begun by men, who made the mose laborous work of it they could, as if the greater extravegenceys they run into in Cutting wild Capers, the Better dancers they was. And some went so far as even to throw their heads into the fires, then jump up with a yell nearly as high as a man's Middle. I believe I may say quite that high and every man at the same time singing his own song. This appeared to me, as a Spectator, as the most fateaging Ruff and Manly exercise which could be invented and, I am apt to conclude, as rational as our dances from the Ittalion musick."

When the dancers grew so warm that they threw off their blankets and the heat from the fires and from their active bodies permeated the long house, Parkerson, Hopkins and some of the other prisoners got up awkwardly and joined the men and women at the nearest council fire. Fitch watched them glumly. In another day they might be dancing not around, but in a fire, their hands tied behind their backs while the heat from the embers scorched their bodies. The prospect of the stake "and tortureing faggot" endowed Fitch with glowering dignity. Although he had been "amazingly Timorous" in the afternoon he now felt as if he were "alloted to die by the hands of savages and did not care how soon and did not wish to gratify them in any one thing."

Finally the deep shouts, the leaping braves, the resounding drum and rattling calabash grew still. The dancers dropped down with crossed legs around their family fires or backed against the dim log walls. From the group nearest the prisoners an old Cherokee chief, with a "countinence" dour as Squire Hart's, the Bucks County tavern keeper, kept looking at Fitch, admiring his striped linen overalls.

Fitch stared back uncompromisingly. He watched the old chief fish in his knapsack and draw out a breech clout, which he handed to one of the Indians with a nod in Fitch's direction.

Fitch guessed what was expected of him. The old chief wanted his striped linen breeches! The messenger came and stood before him, holding out "a Valuable brichclout, decorated with Wampum," which he was offering in exchange.

Shaking his head, Fitch "refused them with uncommon stubberness &c" and waved the handsome breech clout away.

The messenger returned to the old Cherokee chief who was so indignant that "from his manner of speaking" Fitch was persuaded he "wished to take our lives." Snatching the breech clout from the messenger's hands, he angrily sent him to another of the prisoners who had a desirable pair of pants.

"What the consequences would have been had he not" found this time a more complaisant prisoner than Fitch, "I do not know, but probably something serious." However, the other prisoner obediently stripped off his breeches and "quietly gave them up," which satisfied the old Cherokee chief for the evening.

It grew late. The squaws and braves padded silently off to their cabins. As the Indians in their family relationship had advanced no further than the discovery that intercourse among blood relations was deleterious to the race and therefore taboo and as the system of private property had not foisted on them a prudish attitude toward sex, they offered each of the prisoners a squaw for the night. And the monogamous civilization in which Parkerson, Hopkins and the others were brought up was no barrier to their grateful acceptance. But Fitch's sulky fortitude made him reject a squaw just as he had refused to deal with the old Cherokee chief. Lying alone in the faint glow of the row of fires, he could think of nothing but the death sentence which the chiefs were likely to inflict in retaliation for the "Infamous Conduckt of Williamson." He hoped bitterly that Williamson would "be rewarded in this world." If not, then whether he went to Heaven or Hell, he wanted to be in the same place as Williamson; "and I write it now, to be read after my death, that I do not forgive him, but mean to affront him wherever I see him and know him to be the man—not for the injury he did me, but for exercising the quintessence of Wickedness."

Morning came and the chiefs filed back into the council house. They brought two or three white men with them, either British agents or traders, renegades from Fort Pitt or captured Americans who had been adopted into their tribe and preferred the Indian way of life to the competitive society of the states. Letters and other papers had been taken from the prisoners at the time they surrendered and these were given to the interpreters to read. If the papers proved Fitch, Parkerson and the others to be warriors, then they would be burned at the stake; if not, they would be parceled among the Indians or taken to the British garrison at Detroit and turned over to Major De Peyster.

Following an hour's discussion with the interpreters, the chiefs arose from the council. "Altho they might have known it before," Fitch comments with resentful humiliation, "they found we was no warriors." The chiefs withdrew and the captors began to divide up their prisoners, two to Captain Washington, two to Captain Crow and six to Captain Buffalo, who, being a Wyandot or a Miami, with his home near Lake Erie, presented two of his share to the Delawares and made ready to take Fitch, Parkerson, Hopkins and Jared on through the wilderness.

VI

"When I was Taken the Indians took both my Night Caps and Hats, so that I marched all the way Bairheaded and got nothing to cover my head till some time after I got to Prison Island in Canaday, which was a distance of about twelve hundred miles. Before we reached the Indian Towns on the Tuscarawas early in April we had considerable drisling wet weather and two nights of considerable snow mixed with rain which fell near an Inch deep, which made it amazingly uncomfortable to be tied down all night on the wet Ground and nothing to cover my head. By which means I got a Violent Cold which caused a violent pain in my Breast when I stired."

By the time the four prisoners had reached Chief Buffalo's village in the marshy Wyandot country Fitch had become a grotesque example of abject misery. His elbows protruded through his striped linsey coattee, his straight black hair hung like seaweed and he had "got Such sore Eyes" that he could "by no means bear the light and got an old rag and tied over them." Stumbling into Buffalo's camp, he found a dark corner and lay down.

Until the final council in the long house of the Delawares all the prisoners had been bound together by the fear of death. But when they realized they had been saved from the stake they shook themselves free of each other. When the Indians had surprised them on the Ohio they had made no concerted effort to fight off captivity, but now when Chief Buffalo set them to work building a new cabin for him and Fitch remained where he had flung himself they were determined that he should share in the general slavery. Full of rugged individualism in reverse, they exasperatedly pulled Fitch out of his refuge and dragged his lank, protesting figure over the ground to the new building site.

Disgusted, Fitch railed at them "and told them that they had courage enough to take hold of a sick, helpless man, but if they had only that much resolution at the time we were Captured I should not be in this situation. Nay, I told them if I had only half a dozen old women with me at that time that they had only resolution enough to keep their feet and not lay themselves flat down in the Bottom of the Boat I would never have been a prisoner.

"This I spoke much in reference to Hopkins, who was Capt. of the Militia, and who during the whole time that the Indians besieaged us, laid himself flat on the Bottom of the Boat. I further told them that I was not fit to work, neither would I; and if I should die it should be by the tommyhawk, and not by inches." They "might do as they pleased, by their master's orders or risque the tommyhawk, but as to my own part I had made up my mind on that matter." And when he had said this he "turned and walked into the Cabben."

"These sevear reflections was never forgot by Hopkins, Parkerson and Johnson, but was ever afterward my most inveterate enemies," particularly since old Chief Buffalo, "instead of useing severities with me for refuseing to work, went and got some calimus root and ordered me to take it."

For nearly two weeks they remained in Buffalo's village near the Upper Sandusky, with the old chief, his young squaw and two Indian boys of his family. Meanwhile provisions grew scarce. It was April. The winter's supply was nearly exhausted. Since so many tribes had been crowded into the Ohio country it was increasingly hard to get a good supply of game; and though the braves from the camp had gone on a long hunt, there was no telling when they would return. All that was left in the tribal store was a little corn and "some very fat peaces of Venizon dried" which Buffalo eked out to each of them "with the frugality of an Englishman." This amounted to "about half a point of Corn per day per man," which the chief "pounded into homany and boiled for us." Though they "frequently killed a Crain and sometimes a Turkey," Fitch's "hunger for victuals, Salt and Tobacko was exquisite."

While Chief Buffalo shared the scanty stores with prisoners and Indians alike and tried to make them last till summer, Hopkins discovered a quantity of maple sugar in the loft of Buffalo's cabin which had been made by "a good, honest Squaw who had not gone out with the hunters that winter." He promptly stole "a good Cleaver cake of it" which he divided among the prisoners so that "each should be equally guilty with the rest of the Robery."

A few days later Fitch stole "an ear of Corn and secreted it and eat the grains from the Cob." But when the pain in his chest, "which had centered in one place, seemingly in the Boan, and no bigger than the Top of one's fingure," had begun to subside he helped to enlarge the famished diet by gathering "considerable quantities of Wild Onnyions and sometimes Heartychokes." And "one day, with a pinhook," he "Catched five or six small fish."

They stayed in the Sandusky village nearly two weeks. Then, in the middle of April, Buffalo started out with them for Detroit, guarded by the old man, the young squaw and the two little Indian boys. The first night, after marching only six miles, they stopped outside another village where Buffalo had a wife. "She came and sat down without one word passing between them for near one quarter of an hour—Americans may think there was a disgurst between them, but I am sure it was not the case as I always noticed they received their best friends in the same deliberate manner—and when they began to Talk, it was in the mildest way."

That night the prisoners slept on one side of the fire, while

Buffalo lay under a blanket with his wife and "popoose" and the young squaw "withdrew herself eight or ten feet from them and slept by herself." Next morning, "Captain Buffalo killed a Bear and brought it to camp and gave his wife the two hind quarters and she returned with them well pleased and the young Squaw continued her journey with us to Detroit."

After a week's journey through marshy land covered with hazel bushes and clumps of trees, during which time their "hunger increased much" upon them, they came to the eastern shore of the Maumee River and old Buffalo hallooed across the water.

From its junction with the Auglaize forty miles inland, the Maumee River flows northeast through sloping country into Lake Erie. An abundance of streams, forests and wide bottomlands made that northwest section of the Ohio country the headquarters of the Indians. At the upper end of the river stood the Long House of the Miamis, the seat of the western war councils until 1794 when all the tribes of the Northwest Territory were decisively beaten by Federal troops under Major General Anthony Wayne. But now the Indians were in control and the only white men, excepting captives, were British traders who exchanged cheaply manufactured English wares and whisky for valuable furs. Since the Revolution, however, these trading posts had assumed an additional function. They handled the "King's stores"—blankets, guns, ammunition and flour belonging to the British Government—with which they assisted the Indians in their fight against the encroaching Americans.

One of these posts stood where the Auglaize and Maumee meet. There was another about halfway down the river, eighteen miles from Maumee Bay. It was managed by two Britishers, Saunders and Cochran who, the better to do business with the Indians, had become formally adopted into their tribe. They had built a comfortable long house, a barn and outhouses and had a garden surrounded by a neat picket fence.

When Buffalo shouted across the river, Saunders put out in a bark canoe and ferried the bedraggled party back to the trading post. There they were "Hospatibly received" in Saunders' kitchen where the prisoners spent the night while Buffalo, with his young squaw and the Indian boys, retired to a hill overlooking the trading post.

The following night "there came a number of Delawares from Detroit." Pitching their camp on the hill beside Buffalo's, they opened a keg of whisky they had brought from the British garrison and got drunk. By midnight the noise of their frolic had attracted one of Saunders' indentured servants "who loved liquor. He being a ragged, dirty fellow," some of the visiting Delawares mistook him for one of the prisoners Buffalo had brought and "struck their tommyhawks into his head and killed him; at least he died of his wounds the next day, but got down to the House soon after" the Delawares had struck him.

This put Saunders and Cochran in a predicament. To maintain the fiction of white superiority, they must avenge the murder of their white servant. Taking up their tomahawks, they started up the hill. But all the Indians were drunk including Buffalo, and the British traders returned in a "very short time" and when they came in the door Fitch saw "fear impressed in their contineances."

Now all the white men in the village were in danger. From the hill came the sound of the scalp halloo, once for each of the potential victims. Knowing "there was something serious determined against" them, Fitch "took up an ax and slipped thro the Window into the Gardain" where he cut several stout clubs from the beanpoles standing there. Stepping warily back into the kitchen, he told Parkerson, Hopkins, Johnson and Jared that he was "sure the Indians was determined to massicree us and hoped that they would sell their lives as dear as they could."

Parkerson and Hopkins laughed at Fitch for his "phrensy." Knowing he could have no dependence on them and hearing the "Scalp Hallow and War Hoops again," he slipped unnoticed from the kitchen through the garden into the stable. He had "not more than got well into the Stable before I heard them coming down the Hill with Horrable Yells," but "being thus situated," he believed he "could kill three or four before they could take" him.

Meanwhile "the whole Taw Way town was allarmed" and all the braves hurried forth to the trading post to protect their adopted brothers, Saunders and Cochran.

Looking "thro a Crack" in the logs, Fitch "felt much allarmed for the Situation of the Prisoners. The Delawars was next to them, or rather more so than the Taw Ways, and Saunders was standing by with his tommyhawk in his hand. The Delawars appeared to be Very angry and one amongst them who could speak a little English, lifted his Tommyhawk toward the prisoners and stretched out his arm and said 'I have a strong arm!'

"But there being an overmatch of Taw Ways [for them who] would undoubtedly take the part of Saunders, this slackened their hands and they desisted from committing the massicree that evening and went off to their Camp."

Fitch crept back into the stable and lay down with his ax beside him. Night fell. He could still hear the Indians ominously frolicking on the hill and when he slept he could not exclude the scalp halloo from his consciousness, so that it was as if "I was Centery to myself while sleeping. The scalp hallow was given a great number of times that night and each time given equal to our number and I had no expectation of living out the next day unless the Indians should drink so much as to put themselves to sleep." Only for about an hour before dawn did they cease their drunken threats, "but at day Brake was as noisy as ever and gave the scalp hallow again."

"About Sunrize I heard old Buffaloe coming down the Hill and when he was near the bottom he gave the Scalp hallow. I thought then that it was all over, that we must all fall a sacrifice. But when he came into the House I went to it and saw the manner in which he spoke to the other prisoners and was sure there was nothing but Death before us. He pointed to his camp and told them to go." Parkerson, Hopkins and Johnson left as he ordered them to do. "I concluded I might as well submit to my fate as soon as late and resolved to go into the room with him where he sat with an Indian Trader. After he had drove the other prisoners off, I got into the Window and opened the door into his room and went in the most friendly manner up to him and saluted him with a chearful smile.

" 'How do you do, this morning, Captain Buffaloe?' "

With this opening Fitch began to grovel desperately. Captain Buffalo "setting in a chair and a low, three-legged stool standing not far off, I took that and drew it alongside of him and seated myself on it and laid my arm over his Bair thies and sat during his stay in the House lolling upon him; and when he got up he made motion for me to sit there."

When Buffalo, thoroughly mollified toward Fitch, had left, the Indian Trader who had witnessed the affair "told me not to leave the house, for the Indians was all mad." He also said "that Buffalo had requested him to tell me so and that as I always spoke good to him, he wanted me to stay in."

"Affraid by this time that the prisoners was all massicreed," Fitch ran to the door. Hopkins was standing there and in his excitement Fitch blurted out to him to keep away from the camp, for the Indians were determined to kill everybody but himself.

At this, Hopkins became "extravagantly angry," which emotion was not unmixed by bitter scorn. He challenged Fitch, "You are a great friend of the Indians, I suppose?"

Fitch realized he had made a fool of himself by "speaking inadvertently," and turned silently away.

Nevertheless the other prisoners were cautious enough to keep away from the Indian camp. When Buffalo "found them not there he came down much inraged and searched around and found them sculking about and Chaised them with his knife in one hand and tommyhawk in the other, but" being still drunk "he could not get them to the place of exicution," though "he had liked to have killed one William Jarrad, who was a short, Clumsey man and could not run fast."

Fitch, standing in the door of the house, saw the pursuit. "Buffaloe started Jarrad from behind the Corner of the Gardain and out run him. He, having his knife in his right hand, backhanded when he came close to him, made a stroke at him and, reaching a little too far forward and triping at the same time," the knife missed "Jarrad's Body by about six inches" and "Buffaloe came his whole length on the ground."

Whether or not it was this breath-taking contact with the earth that cleared old Buffalo's befuddled head, this was his last attack on the prisoners. When he got up he turned away and went slowly up the hill to his camp again. The prisoners listened for the sound of the warwhoop, but the hill was silent. By the middle of the afternoon Buffalo and his visiting Delaware friends "was all either sober or asleep." Next morning he "seemed ashamed of what he had done" and was ready to take the prisoners on to Detroit.

But after so many threats and such attempts at violence, Saunders "thought it improper for us to go by land with Capt. Buffaloe to detroit for fear something of the sort might happen again before we reached there." Buffalo had a large bundle of pelts and Saunders, suggesting that it "would accomodate the young Squaw so much," proposed that he take the skins and the prisoners in his pirogue and that Buffalo remain in camp until he returned. In no mood for traveling that day, Buffalo consented and the prisoners were so overjoyed that the prisoners began to say "Mister Saunders" and to call him sir.

"It was a happy time," when that great log, which had been hollowed out by fire to make a "noble Cannoe," pushed into the Maumee from the Ottawa town. But when they had paddled through Maumee Bay and started along the western shore of

Lake Erie the prisoners began to reflect that they had been freed of the Indians only to be delivered into the hands of the British. They were five against Saunders and the little Indian boy Chief Buffalo had sent along to guard his interests and when they encamped for the night Hopkins, Parkerson and Johnson began to mutter of insurrection. It would be easy enough, Hopkins said, for them to throw their guard overboard and make their way back to Fort Pitt.

How they would have made their way through two hundred miles of wilderness without falling among Indian hunting parties before they reached the Ohio was not made clear; but Fitch, instead of objecting on that point, rose up on moral grounds and "told them plainly that if they did" he would join Saunders and the Indian boy against them, "for such ingratitude as that should never come from" him.

Parkerson gave him black looks and treasured his resentment for a time when it could be used to better effect and they went on toward the mouth of the Detroit River.

There they saw great numbers of sturgeon and everything else was forgotten but the fact that for once they would have enough to eat. "We stepped out on the rocks and Loaded our Cannoe with them; we struck them with a Tommyhawk and killed six ... and when we came into Detroit River we came to a camp and took out the spawn and boiled them." And though Mr. Saunders had come off in such a hurry that he had forgotten to bring salt and though they had already consumed more than their share of bread, they had "a kettle of fishspawn without Salt or Bread, which was the first time I eat my fill in about 30 days so as any was left remaining. But in an hour's time after I eat I was hungry again and stuck to it that afternoon by turns till I wanted no more."

Next day they paddled up the river till they came to the stockaded bluff from which the British flag was flying. Climbing out on the log wharf, they were led by Saunders up the path to a heavy gate where a redcoat sentry stood.

"Sergeant of the Guard!" the sentry called. Letting Saunders pass on into the garrison, he halted the prisoners and kept them waiting till the sergeant came and sprucely led them through the street to headquarters.

Major Arendt Schuyler de Peyster, the British commandant, was the younger son of a wealthy New York family who had a mansion on Pearl Street. At sixteen he had been sent to London to begin his career in the British army. In 1768 he was a captain in the Eighty King's Regiment of Foot and at the beginning of the Revolution he was sent to Michilimackinac in charge of the British garrison there. He was a loyal officer, who had his Majesty's interests greatly at heart and in his contact with the Indians, first at Michilimackinac and later at Detroit, he had handled many American prisoners.

"Bring them to me," he had instructed the Shawanese warriors in 1779, "I have use for them and you shall be rewarded.... For this war will soon be at an end.... The rebels cannot hold out long. The papers you have sent speak nothing but distress among them." In November, 1781, he was still optimistic of his Majesty's success over the Colonies. "The latest vessels," he wrote, bring news of Lord Cornwallis' rapid success in Virginia and the Carolinas." But in April, 1782, he was made slightly uneasy by the "report spread in this place (which came from Fort Pitt) that Lord Cornwallis surrendered his little army to Washington who besieged him in Yorktown and Gloucester, Virginia." Still, maybe it wasn't true. Perhaps it was only another rumor.

Major De Peyster, the handsome aristocrat, looked up at the prisoners with his bulging eyes and, in a "voice rough and commanding," asked "the News in the Provinces."

"We informed him of the Capture of Cornweallice."

Cornwallis captured? It was preposterous! De Peyster's lips were complacently scornful.

By General Washington and the French, they told him. Hemmed in at Yorktown last October, he gave up his sword and marched out with his drummers sadly beating "The World Turned Upside Down." In short, the prisoners "gave the story so streight he had hardly room to doubt it."

But still they were unable to realize how important was the news they had brought, news five months old when they had left Fort Pitt. And at first, when Major De Peyster dismissed them, they were too full of their private concerns to reflect on the capture of Cornwallis. For De Peyster "ordered the Sergint to take us to the commesarys and draw Cloathing" in place of their dirty rags and from there to the provost "and see we drew our rations according to his orders." And "we drew both Cloathing and Rations that afternoon and had a good Rooff to Shelter us and liberty to go with the Centery to fetch up our Sturgeon" and it was all such a relief after their long journey that Fitch felt "if it was possible for mankind to be happy, I think I was that evening."

Finally the sergeant took them to the guardhouse and gave orders that "all persons was forbid to speak" to them "and none permited to come near the provoe but the Gards." And then they began to realize that the information they had brought of Cornwallis was of importance. "In close Confinement notwithstanding," they began to call out through the window "to the people in the street and tell the news." And for the first time since they had started out together they all had something to shout about in unison:

"Cornweallice is taken! Cornweallice is taken! Cornweallice with his whole army is Taken!"

VII

AFTER Fitch's capture by the Indians he had only an engraving tool to show for his eighteen years' work since his apprenticeship to Benjamin and Timothy Cheney. He had nearly lost this also, but to the Indian who had acquired it when the prisoners were searched, the graver was a strange object and Fitch managed to retrieve it by "at odd times marking his powder horn Very nicely."

At Detroit "the Gards generally had something that they wanted marked and notwithstanding I was so closely confined, I earned with that Graver about 8 Dollars," which enabled him to lay in "a good sea store of Sugar, Tea, Chees, Butter &c" when the captives were taken across Lake Erie and down the St. Lawrence to Prison Island.

Toward the middle of May, Fitch, Parkerson, Hopkins, Johnson, Jared and about fifteen other prisoners who had previously been taken by the Indians were "put on Bord of an Armed Brig commanded by Capt. Burnet, a worthy, good man who treated us with all the humanity he could." After a "long, tedious voiage and one terable storm," they reached Fort Erie and marched overland past Fort Schlosser to Niagara Falls where, to cross Lake Ontario in a ship called the Linebye, they were "put into the hole and made our bead on the Ballass stores with a Horse and a Cow, who had the best part of the Hole, at least the best lodging."

From Carleton Island in the St. Lawrence, where Captain Anchor, the Commandant confined them in a small room "without wood or candle" and ordered the guard to fire if they misbehaved, they were taken to Fort Oswegatchie, thence to Coteau du Lac and ferried from there over to Prison Island.

Prison Island was "a Very Luxuriant Soil" of seventy or eighty acres and "lay in the midst of a Daingerous Rapid" of the St. Lawrence, "which the British thought was a prison sufficient of itself to secure the prisoners." About five hundred Americans captured along the frontier had been sent there from Detroit since the spring of 1780, but many had escaped into New York to make their way home again.

To Fitch, the first day on Prison Island among his fellow captives from the frontier was more miserable than his treatment under Captain Anchor. Parkerson and Hopkins now had a chance to exercise their resentment and Fitch "had not been on the Island two hours before they represented me as the Damdest Tory that remained unhung and told many dismal tales of me and said that they would not be there if it had not been for me." For "they had ment to rise on old Buffaloe one knight and I prevented them, otherwise they would have killed him and made their escape."

It was true, Fitch agreed, that they had suggested rising against old Buffalo. But they had been wandering through the Wyandot country at the time, which was swampy and "sourounded on all hands with Ponds" and he had given it as his opinion "that it was impractical for us to make our escape even if we was sat at liberty and no Indians to hinder our march, but that being penned in behind the Towns, I thought they could not be in earnest." As soon as he had spoken against the scheme they had grown "Very clamorous because I would not join them and said many illnatured things till I got somewhat warmed up and damed them for a set of Couards and told them I would not undertake anything with them but what I thought I could accomplish with my own hands. But if they was so desirious of doing it, I asked them what Prevented? There was but one Indian, a poor little Squaw that a man could lift with one hand and two little Indian poppooses—and I would remain passive and there was four stout, Hearty fellows of them and they certainly did not want my help unless they wanted me to do the whole and told them I was too well acquainted with them to join in such an affair or even to attack one single Poppoose."

"Many other Fourious tales" were reported by Hopkins and Parkerson, which were so generally believed that "I am sure I should have been massicreed by the prisoners if I had not been under the protection of the British gardes." And this resentment was aggravated when he "began to clear a spot of ground for a gardain." For it was the belief among the prisoners that the guards urged them to make gardens for the benefit of the British officers and "of course not more than one fourth of those who were on the island before me had attempted to plant anything." But "believing that lazyness had proppergated that report," Fitch "set about it in two hours after I had got into my Barracks and shifted myself. And having one James McKolloch," who had been sent along on the journey from the Detroit garrison, "who had a considerable dependance on me for a liveing, and he being a Civil, industerous man, the next day I persuaded him out with me, notwithstanding it was exceedingly unpopular among the Prisoners.

"The next day McKolloch and myself had about 20 Poles cleared fit for Planting and Planted a large part of it with Corn, squashes, peas, Cucumbers and some other things of which the British gladly gave us the seeds and I as gladly received them. But the lazy prisoners being so much the most numerous," their jeers "became so invidious that McKolloch would not for some time help me to tend the Gardain.

"As soon as I had got my seeds into the ground I began to think of carrying on my trade, for I could not Indure the thought of being Idle." Though he had only his "old Graver" and though there were no steels on the island from which to make other tools, he went from barrack to barrack, borrowing and trading until he had acquired "an Ax, a handsaw, a chissel, an Iron Wedge for splitting wood, a shoemaker's hammer and also a foreplain." Besides these, he had got his eye on "an augure and grindstone."

"My first thought was to make a Vise, but before I could make that I must have a turning lath[e] to turn the screw." He accomplished this with the "Saw, Ax, Chisel and foreplain." Then he "got a peace of a ramrod of a Gun and made the Centures for my popets. I also got a large Blade of a jack knife and broke it in two, one part of which I made a chisel, the other a Gouge for turning.

"The Iron wedge I fixed in a block and made my anvil. The Shoemaker's hammer I forged with and our common fire, blowed by my mouth or hat, I forged by. I made a punch out of an iron hoop and punched two holes thro each Broken Blade and then took the iron hoop and punched two holes at each end uniform with the first and bent the Hoop and riveted the Broken Blade between the ends of the Hoop. After the chisel and gouge was made I filled the hoop with wood, which made a very good handle. Then I got my lathe compleated and turned an Augure for cutting the Base of the Vise and at the same time turned a peace for the Screw. I then got out the jaws of my vise and cut a peace of paper of an equal width and pasted it onto the peace designed for my augur and laid out my screw, which I sawed round conformable to and in the proper place fixed a peace of iron made out of a hoop to cut the screw. But I had first to make a file to point it properly." Making chisels out of an old razor blade and cutting a file from the steel spring of the jackknife, he obtained the proper tools to complete the vise. And "after it was done I put jaws to it with hoops nearly as nice as could be done in the city of Phila[d] and for some time [they] would punch almost anything which came between them.

"Whilst this was doing, I got some of the Gards, which was

weekly relieved, to get me some Old files over at Cotedelack.[1] He brought a flat file and a handsaw file. The flat file I made a wire plate of, which I think will not disgrace me at this day and I now esteem it more than any of its size and number of holes that I could find in the City. The Handsaw file, I ground and cut a number of times." Next, he needed a blowpipe, which he made by filing the edges of another iron hoop and hammering them so closely together that "it was as clear of leaks as if soddered and an exceedingly good pipe it was, as well as a curious one." There was yet another old hoop, from which he made sliding tongs and thus, within ten days after he had arrived, he had equipped himself with all the necessary implements to make brass buttons.

"One of the soldiers having a small brass kittle wore out, which had been a Camp Kittle," Fitch bought it, cut the sides into narrow strips, "rolled it up and drew it into wire and worked that Brass chiefly up, but could not get any Borax, nor was there any nyer than Montreal, which was 45 miles down the river. I agreed with a British soldier who was going down on command to get me a quarter of a Pound, which he faithfully performed; and in the meantime I got some ashes and boiled them down into salts and calsigned them as well as I could. In short, it was middling good potash which I used for soddering instead of Borax" and though for the making of buttons "I had the greatest difficulty to make my soddering good, I made 30 or 40 pair in that manner before my Borax arrived. These I found a pretty ready sail for, and some, which I cut cyphers upon, a good price, as they was but a little inferior in looks to a good Button."

Not content with making buttons, Fitch branched out into the manufacture of clocks. "There was one John Segar from the Massichusetts, an ingenious, handy lad who lived in my Barrack and was desirous of working with me, which I took as an appren-

[1] In the early maps it is spelled Coteau du Lac.

tice; but he being so worthy a lad and so attentive to business, I gave him generous wages for his work and whilst I was so embarrassed for the want of Borax, him and I got timber sufficient to make 12 wooden timepeaces. We boiled it and took every means to season it quickly and erected a furnace for melting of Silver and hired prisoners with my buttons to bring Wood of the Island into the Barrack yard. There I had got a Cole burner and a German to set it up and in it we burned the wood to Coal and had, I believe, about 80 bushels of good coal which I stored in the loft of my barrack. I then got a peace of sheet iron from Sergiant Moss, who had the principal charge of the prisoners under the officers and also of whatever belonged to the King. This peace of Sheet Iron he sold me as well as a Good, new Brass Kettle, which was of great service to me and none to him. I then made myself an Ingot and Crusables which I melted silver in and" while waiting for the wood to season so as to make clocks, manufactured "silver Buttons as well as Brass ones."

Meanwhile, Parkerson and Hopkins continued to damn Fitch as a most tremendous Tory to all the other prisoners. And in this "they had a Very considerable advantage of me on the Island as they had nothing else to do but go from Barrack to Barrack to inflame the Prisoners against me whilst I was wholly taken up in business. I, finding the prejudice of the Prisoners so much against me, it maid my life exceedingly uncomfortable, as I must daily put up with the greatest insults from them." But "finding the greatest part of the Prisoners to be New England People, and generally more cool and moderate than the southern, I made it my business to visit some of the most leading amongst them and inform them of the true reasons why there was such invetresy against me. And from that and my Tobacko and professing myself to be a yankee, I soon got a partee nearly as strong as theirs, so I dared to speak Boldly on the perade.

"One evening after role call, there being about two or three hundred of us on the Perade, Parkerson got damning Congress at a roun rate for keeping us there a suffering whilst they had prisoners enough to exchange for us and said that they paid no attention to suffering Prisoners but only saught their own emoluments.

"After he had done, I spoke Boldly out in the Croud and said 'Mr. Parkerson, as great a Tory as I am represented to be, you never heard me speak so disrespectful of Congress as you have done. Nay, I am a much greater friend to them than you appear to be. For my own part, I should rather remain a Prisoner for seven years than that Congress should be imposed upon as to exchange British soldiers for us! But if they should have any old women Prisoners in the United States, I think it would bearly justify Congress for exchanging them for us. Therefore I think that above all men our Company ought to be the last to complain!' "

Parkerson remained silent under this heavy sarcasm, but Fitch's "open reflections on Perade had no tendancy of healing the breach between us."

Fitch's craftsmanship helped to widen the gap still farther. "My geting to work in the manner I did pleased all the officers and many of them rather than to set alone would frequently come and set with me and see me work and sometimes for a considerable length of time." Also "they would frequently invite me to go into the Officers' House and take a Glass of Toddy with them. This did me no good. It raised an envy in the more leading prisoners and beliefs in the more Ignorant that what was reported of me was true, as not another on the whole Island met with the same indulgence, unless it was Sergiant Morss; and I believe him not in the drinking way."

But while his industriousness deepened the prisoners' resentment, it also gave Fitch opportunity partly to allay their anger. "Soon after my arrival on the Island, the prisoners began to make their Escape and continued to do it all summer. They generally made a raft at the upper end of the Island and went over the

Rapids on that. Great numbers escaped, but many were brought back and Confined in Irons. About midsummer we had all our Barracks picqueted in." But instead of decreasing the number who attempted to escape, the picketing provided another "stimulus to make the Prisoners desert." About thirty of them "left the Island one night and ten or fifteen more were taken on the Island whilst attempting to escape." In fact "as soon as these picquets was put up and the Prisoners confined to a Squair of about 40 Poles by ten, the principal part of the day and night they was continually a ploting for making their escape and began to Burrow under the floor of the next Barrack to me. I was dayly informed of their progress and they had got it beyond the Picquet, which was about 10 feet from the Barrack, and they were ready to break the ground up thro the outside when there came a heavy rain and the Picquet which stood over the hole settled down into it and stopped the passage.

"I had at that time got into a considerable business at my Trade and had a considerable number of tools and had the name of an ingenious man, when several of them came in to ask my advice how they should overcome their imbarrassments. I told them it needed not one minute's Consideration. I had cut a day or two before an exceedingly good handsaw file and there was a great plenty of old iron hoops about the Island. I told them I had a very good Vise that would hold one of the Hoops till they could file 20 notches in it and that I was going out to work in my gardain that forenoon. They took the hint and made a saw in my absence and cleared the way for 40 or 50 to escape on the outside of the Picquets and there were between twenty and thirty who escaped from the Island."

Besides, from his garden and from the money he made selling buttons, Fitch always had an extra supply of provisions and "six or eight lb of Pork" from the week's rations. "This Pork we generally gave way to the Prisoners who were intending to make their escape. I believe I gave away all except one Peace, which the man gave me a Fur Cap for, as he could not take it with him. This was the first time I had anything to cover my head since my capture. My industry enabled me not only to be of service to myself, but of great good to others, in particular some of the Sick, whome I furnished with every necessary that could be procured on the Island from Sergiant Morss who kept a sort of Huxter's Shop. . . . My Tobacko was generally about one dollar a week, for a great number of them depended almost altogether on me. I was also enabled to furnish them with most kinds of Garden Truck, as I had a great abundance, even more than I could destroy, but I gave none to those who came on the Island with or before me.

"After I had got pretty well to work, I took one John Raynolds from Vermont as my apprentice and, toward the last, one Clark from Virginia. Dureing my stay there, which was between four and five months, with their help I made 9 wooden timepeaces which I sold at four Dollars apeace, about 300 pr of Brass sleave Buttons and about 80 pr of Silver ones and had made myself tools to repair Watches and had repaired three or four before I left the Island.

"I also had cloathed myself in a Superfine suit with a great pleanty of Cours working Cloaths for the winter and had got a good Russia Sheating Hammock hung in the Middle of my Barracks to keep me from the lice and had provided myself with five Blankets for the Winter and had got between two and three Cord of wood and my Barrack fitted up in the warmest manner. In short, in about four months I had got to be as rich as Roberson Cruso. But early in October there came news of our being exchanged and orders for our departure. It came in the evening, just before rolecall. I heard such a shouting in the Yard that I left my work to see what was the matter.

"It was a long time before I could get the news, as all was too overjoyed to hear any questions asked and thought of nothing but hooping and see who could make the loudest nois." But

Fitch finally discovered "our orders was for us to be ready to depart the next day." And a little later "the Officers came into my Barrack and congratulated me on my releas."

Fitch was not overjoyed. He had made himself comfortable for the winter and was doing very well on Prison Island. Without money to set up his trade in Massachusetts, Pennsylvania or Connecticut, he might have to become a journeyman when he returned. He realized this and informed the officers "I could not get ready on so short a notice."

The officers "made themselves Very merry" at this objection, but when Fitch persisted, they became stern. He was to be taken to Montreal with the rest of the prisoners, put on board a vessel bound down the St. Lawrence and along the New England shore line to the United States where the authorities would dispose of him as they pleased.

"Born a Natural Couard to the Water, I much dreaded the going Round by Sea and solicited earnestly that I might be sent across with the Vermont people by way of Crown Point." But again the officers refused. Fitch was an entertaining character with a curious mind and could be made useful to divert them from their boring hours or even to share a convivial glass of rum. But he did not belong to the class which can command special favors even in captivity. Next day he was taken down to Montreal where the prison ship lay waiting. In spite of his four hundred pairs of useful buttons and nine clocks, he left the island nearly as poor as he had come.

And now the American officers began to order him about.

"The first night after I left Montreall, while the Vessel lay at Anchor and the boat by her side, I had a great mind to desert, but could not get anyone to accompany me, therefore I continued with the Vessel down to Quebec where we was put on Board the Ship John, bound for Boston.

"When we had got on Bord that Ship there seemed to be as many impediments in our way for sailing as there is in the building of Steam Boats and we lay in the stream before Quebeck more than one month before we sailed. Several pretty heavy snows came on, with a great deal of pretty wet, cold weather and no fire to go to but the caboos upon deck," which the officers had appropriated. This "damped my spirits in a pretty great degree. And as we went on Bord Lousey the chief of my time was imployed in hunting and killing lice, till such time as I got tired of that imploy."

Meanwhile another ship arrived. It was the *Baker & Atlee*, sailing out of Philadelphia and had been sent to bring back part of the prisoners. The men were to be divided into two shiploads and Colonel Campbell, who was one of the American captives, was appointed to sort the prisoners for the two ships. Fitch was anxious to stay on the *John*, so as to make the journey with the friendly yankees to Boston. When Colonel Campbell assigned him to the *Baker & Atlee* Fitch appealed to him in "the most earnest manner" and was "refused in the most indilicate language by the Gentleman."

Colonel Campbell "consulted his own humer only and treated me in the most tyranical manner. Perhaps the reason might be that it was the first time for a great while that he had a right to show his authority and wished to exercise it on me and thought he knew my business better than I did myself. However disagreeable it was to me to gratify his humer, I was obliged to go in the Baker & Atly, which determined me to ask no more favors from him."

November came and the two ships still lay at anchor in front of Quebec. Provisions were poor and Fitch, thinking of the long voyage to be made, looked wistfully ashore and jingled the few coins he had in his pocket. He could think of nothing but the butter, tea and cheese which were to be had for the purchase in the Quebec stores. There was no use asking Colonel Campbell for permission, so he waited till Captain Tung, the King's officer who was to command the voyage, came aboard; then "I went to my birth and Wrote a Very humble petition to him, praying leave to go on shore to lay in some seastores for myself." But here again "I was in a Very imperious manner refused—I think Very probably thro Conl Campbell."

Every day grew colder. In the middle of November, with its ropes stiff and ice glistening on its sides, the *Baker & Atlee* weighed anchor. Down in the hold Fitch and the common prisoners shivered under thin blankets, but up in the caboose Colonel Campbell sat comfortably beside the stove with Captain Tung and there were servants to bring them food and whisky.

"But we had not sailed more than a day or two before Conl Campbell sent his Weighter to me, requesting me to come and alter the Pipe of the Cabben Stove. He said that the Cabben smoked so that they could not stay in it. I sent word back by the weighter that I would not do it and that if he could not stay there he might come and Share of my Birth. He soon returned with a message from Capt. Tung who told me if I would do it he would give me a good drink. I returned answer that if he had been a man of fealing and had allowed me to go on Shore at Quebec I should not have wanted any of his grog and as it was I would not accept it."

Like an engine of vengeance, the stovepipe smoked till Captain Tung, Colonel Campbell and the other officers were forced out on the freezing deck, "when they sent their servant again with a particular request from Capt. Tung that I would lend them my tools. I returned them word back that I would sooner throw them overboard.

"They worried out the Smoke that day as well as they could— I believe, by quinching out the fire—but the next day it seemed to be worse, when they sent one of the officers in a Very Friendly manner who was known to be respected by me. I think, if I am not Mistaken, it was Capt. Stokely, who requested me for his sake to lend my tools." Yielding to this particular flattery, Fitch "told Capt. Stokely I did not wish to punish him for the sake of punishing wicked, unfealing men and that for his sake alone I would lend them the tools if he could get anybody to do the business. Accordingly, he did and the Pipes was altered and a Point tumbler of Spirits sent to him and me for the service, of which I drank in complyance to Capt. Stokely.

"We had a most violent gale from the N. W. till we passed Capretoon [Cape Breton] and got to sea, so Violent that we could not put our Pilot ashore, but brought him all the way with us." When the *Baker & Atlee* reached the ocean there were "storms every two or three days, till I looked for nothing else." But Captain Tung, "altho a moross, illnatured fellow, was perhaps the best and most cairful Navigator that was to be found" and the *Baker & Atlee* even weathered the storm which "cast away the Jamaica fleet with the Vale [Ville] de Parris &c altho we was not far from them. After which we had nothing but Storms, Calms and head winds till I had got such a disgurst to the Sea that I told the Capt. if he would once set me safe on Shore again I would sign any article that he should produce if he ever Catched me on the Atlantick any more.

"By the Culling the Prisoners in the manner they did, I had not many friends amongst them and from my forwardness from the Capt., Mate & Sailors I could not set much store on their friendship and I am sure I had not many in the Great Cabben," therefore his cantankerous behavior was a risky business which he "never could account for, unless it was that I was sick the whole passage and had got conquered by the Lice so that I would not even kill one had he come between my two thumb nails."

One day "it happened by chance that we had a fair, gentle Breeze and I, being so tired of the Sea, wanted to know where we was and how far from Port." Though Fitch had been to sea only once before and had no experience in taking directions he felt as confident of finding a way to do it as he had been when Governor Wolcott had let him survey the Podunk bottomlands. "I got a book from Capt. Stokely which informed me the latitude of Cape May and New York and the latitude of the place I was informed; and knowing we could lay any course we pleased, I concluded we was stearing streight for our Port. I borrowed a scale and dividers from one of the Seamen, went to the Bow and on the Deck made my drafts and laid down the Latitude of the two places and where we was and then drew the diagonal line of the course we steared and found the distance. I then told the prisoners if we was going to New York we had such a distance to go, if to Phila^d, such a distance; which much offended the Capt and mate. And from my experience at that and other times I am sure the greatest recomadation that a man can take to sea with him is profound Ignorance."

A few days later "we came inland and I knew that we must be on the Jersey shore. About dusk we sounded and found only 15 fathom of water. The ship was immediately ordered to put about." In this worst possible time, when the *Baker & Atlee* could easily be driven aground, the wind "Blew a gale which in a short time increased to a near hurrycane, the Wind Blowing right on Shore. I calculated our leaway to strike the shore about one oClock, which allarmed me considerably and I expected nothing but that we should be cast away before morning."

Preparing to be driven on the breakers, Fitch "went under Deck and eat as hearty a Supper as I could. After I had eaten all I could I stripped myself of my long blanket matchcoat, which would have entangled my legs in the water, and put on a Streight bordered coattee. I also took off my overhalls and put on Breeches, stockins and shoes and then put on my Fur Cap. But finding the ears would fall down over my mouth and hinder my breathing when wet, I got a needle and thread and sewed them up strong so that the Surf would not readily Break them. After which, I took out a large pair of Shoemaker's Nippers out of my box of Tools and put them in my pocket, thinking that if I should want to get through the Surf that I could take hold of one handle and grab with the other in the Sand to prevent it washing me off. And knowing the Jersey shore to be Very dessolate and filled with Ceedar swamps and thinking that if I could get on shore as I was I could do with a few bisket in my pocket, accordingly I put in my pocket about half a Doz.

"All this I compleated and sat patiently waiting for the fatal hour to arrive when we should strike the ground. But heaven had ordered it otherwise, for about 10 oClock the wind ceased about one minute and altho it blew as hard as it could from the S. E. before, it tacked about into a Nwester and blew a little harder, if possible.

"The news of this I did not get till between 11 and 12 oClock as the Saylors was so ingaged.... And the next day I was insulted for my precautions by Capt. Tung on Deck in the presence of the Saylors and Prisoners, which gave them great liberties. They, finding themselves safe, probably spoke more freely than what they would have done in the time of the storm and had they not been afraid of being thought Couardly would probably have done as I did. Which fear I esteam the worst and most daingerous sort of Courdice and their insults would not have deterred me from doing the like again on the like occation. And to this day I believe it was no imprudent act of mine, however ridiculous it may appear, as long as I met with no inconveanancy from it, but only insults from men I despized.

"The day following we had a fine day and a gentle breeze from the S. W. Standing about N. W. [we] heared the Fireing of Cannon right over our bows about nine or 10 o'Clock in the morning. A saylor was ordered to masthead to look out and in about an hour discovered a Sail and, shortly after, several more. And in about one quarter of an hour I discovered it on Deck, which appeared about as big as a hat, they stearing directly towards us and we directly towards them.

"We met them about one oClock, being the first shiping we had seen since we left Quebeck. The South Carolina passed us to windward with Top Gallant Royals and every Sail Spread. We were standing about S. E. and a British Fregit passed us to leeward and when we came nearer between the British fregit and the South Carolina the British fregit fired more than she had done for the whole forenoon, which not only frightened but confused Capt Tung prodigiously.

"Notwithstanding Capt Tung carried a flag at masthead and had lowered all his sails, the fireing continued till he could not tell what the Devil they wanted. At last he ordered the British flag be hoisted. But as it had not been done the voiage before, the lines had got tangled and they could not get it above half up." By that time "the South Carolina was almost in Pistol shot of us and right to windward, and the wind blowing their Colours round, Capt. Tung discovered them to be Americans and cried out:

" 'For God's sake, don't Hoist!'

"He ordered the British Colours out of sight immediately or we should have been blown out of the water."

The two fighting vessels passed and the prison ship stood by. In his excitement over the engagement of the *South Carolina* with the British frigates, Fitch turned critic and patriot and "got so inraged at the South Carolina for not tacking about and giving the British fregit a broadside that I could not keep from stomping with Both feet and expressed many improper things in my Station, till checked by one of the British sailors."

About sunset the *South Carolina* was forced to strike her colors after being overpowered by the British fleet. "The night following and the day after that we was all locked close under Deck with the hatchways spiked down. Not more than two of us prisoners were allowed to be on deck together. Some of us in the night had to ease nature by our Births. There being so many of us and so closely confined and with not even the Hatchway allowed to be open, the air became very offensive.

"This meanace on the part of Capt Tung for ordering the hatchways kept shut exasperated me beyond measure and I frequently urged to some of the leading prisoners the necessity of riseing and confining those who had confined us. And notwithstanding we was in company of four British fregits, we could have effected it, for they might depend we was on the Jersey Shore and two or three hours' sail would set the ship aground. All this could be effected by only cutting the Ceedar bord pattision between us and the Stearage, which I would do in less than an hour with my knife, unknown to the Saylors. Then in the evening we could stear off from the fleet unnoticed and I would be the last man who would leave the ship and if any was taken I would be the man. But I could not bring my fellow prisoners into my opinion, therefore it was not exicuted, but had I had more friends and less enemies I could have effected it."

Instead of sailing to Philadelphia, the *Baker & Atlee* sailed to New York. When the ship sighted Sandy Hook the prisoners were allowed to come up on deck. They landed "on Christmas Day, it having been 40 days passage and more than Ten weeks I was on the water." As a result of lice and scurvy Fitch was "in a very bad state of health and had I not bribed Conl Campbell's weighter—and that at a pretty dear rate—to steal me two heads of Cabbage, which I eat leaf by leaf off the stork, and the Stork besides, I believe I should have little more than reached New York.

"Not doubting but I should get a great plenty of supplyes as soon as I came to New York, I wrote to my old Friends, Richard Souse, Cutler and William White, Braasfounder, informing them what things I wanted and requesting them to come on bord. I wrote two notes, thinking the first had miscarried. To the 2nd note I got an answer from Richard Souse that he had received the first and had spoken to the Comesary to come on bord and inquire into our wants, but offered to do no more." From which, Fitch "concluded they thought I had asked for Charity and that they had best stay away. They had made great fortunes in that Citty and was two principal, leading men in the Methodist congregation, of which I at that time was a member. It gave me such a disgurst to Christianity that I thought if ever I could see their master I would tell him plainly that I was both hungry and thirsty, sick and in Prison, and two of his cussed Scounderals would administer nothing for my necessities."

And now Colonel Campbell, who had enjoyed the voyage in the Warm cabin of Captain Tung, who had a servant to wait on him and plenty of food, came down among the passengers to solicit the prisoners "to return Captain Tung their thanks for his good usage of them."

Fitch spoke up boldly and "told Campbell that I thought it improper to return thanks until he should assign some reason why Capt Tung had confined us under deck so closely and that after he had four British fregits to protect him. I also said that I could see no reason for my part why he did it, for if he had any suspicions of our Rising it would have been an easy matter for him to have got one of the Fregits to have kept close company with us. Which, if I had been in his place with such suspicions, I should sooner have done than to have punished a sett of innocent men on suspicions only. It rather appeared to me that there was some personal pike [pique] which he wanted to resent, and I said that I looked upon it as an unmanly way of doing it, for I could not suppose him base enough to punish us out of mear wantonness. For my own part, I told Colonel Campbell, I should protest against returning him my thanks till he gave sufficient reason for that Conduckt.

"This Chagrianed Conl Campbell Considerably. But I being very unpopular, there was not the same attention paid to what I said as otherwise might have been, but some of my Great Enemies joined me in sentiment and the Mob was much divided and I believe more against than for it, notwithstanding Conl Campbell's smooth tong."

But Campbell solved the difficult point of etiquette by ignoring the objections raised against the testimonial to Captain Tung and when he left "he said he would return him our thanks" anyway, "which was an ill way of Getting honor, which none but a mean-spirited wretch would accept after what had been said."

From New York the prisoners were marched up to Dobbs Ferry to sign a parole and be released, which occasioned more bickering. For Fitch refused to sign the parole unless he was furnished with a copy of it. Seeing the crowd behind Fitch, the officer agreed to this, but broke his promise and sent the prisoners on without a copy.

Fitch was insistent. "When we arrived to the American Post I went to the house where the officers were all assembled and Conl Campbell was walking in the entry. As soon as I entered the door he says to me, 'Damn you, what do you want hear?'

"My answer was short and I said, 'I want to see Capt Tung.'

"He said, 'He is ingaged and not to be spoken with.'

"I told him I ment both to see him and speak with him and went to the door and Campbell did not lay hands on me to stop me, but followed me into the room as if he was afraid that I had a mind to rise as a Piret against him.

"The officers seeing me come into the room in the manner I did, seemed to cause a Silence. I made a deacent obeasance to them and addressed myself to Capt Tung and begged of him to furnish me with a Copy of my Parole, when he told me he had not got it in print as was expected.

"I informed him that I was going to the United States and that I had no protection from the militia duty unless I had it; not only that, but unless I had a Coppy I could not be accountable for one thing it contained, for my memory might deceive me and unless he furnished me with a Coppy I renounced the parole altogether before all those Gentlemen present and would hold myself a prisoner and liable to return back with him to new York.

"At this Capt Tung seemed to turn from me with a snear and

Significant looks to the other officers; when I spoke out boldly and positively to him in the following words, Viz:—

" 'Capt Tung, I do not hold myself bound by that parole unless you furnish me with a Coppy, but hold myself your Prisoner and give you one minute's time to say whether I shall return with you to New York or no!' "

"I stayed in the room till I thought that the minute had expired, in which time I saw many Significant looks and smiles by our own officers as well as by him and then retired, leaving them to themselves."

By this naïve trickery Fitch evidently felt that he had changed his status from that of a paroled prisoner to that of a man who had escaped by himself and was therefore no longer bound by the British in any way. And with one "John Burnet of Kentuckey" who had become his friend during the voyage from Prison Island, he left Dobbs Ferry and headed south immediately.

Burnet was going back to Kentucky, but he would accompany Fitch as far as Bucks County. Perhaps Fitch could do something for him among his friends in Warminster, for it was hard for a man to tramp hundreds of miles without a penny in his pocket. Burnet was a Baptist and there were a number of Baptists in that country. Maybe the Baptists were more generous with their brethren than the "Cussed Methodists" and would take up a collection.

Three miles from Dobbs Ferry Fitch and Burnet came to a "deacent, well looking House, where we went in and made our wants known. When they asked us our names I told them my name was Leg[i]ons, but that I wanted them to alter it to John Fitch only. They Curtiously received us" and thus encouraged and freed at last from nine months of captivity "we killed the principal part of our Lice that night."

Next day they went on toward the Delaware. Fitch "traviled with this John Burnet to Warminster and arrived there on a Saturday night." It was rainy and they were both hungry and forlorn. Fitch led the way to Cobe Scout's old log shop and pushed in the door. When Cobe recognized him through the candlelight he started toward him and they met in the middle of the room, where Fitch, from sheer relief, began to weep like an old woman.

After spending the night at Scout's and Burnet "being a Baptis, the next day we both went to Southampton meeting where we had public thanks returned for our safe deliverance from Captivity to God almighty and to Jesus Christ Both. At any rate, it was as good as an advertisement in the newspaper and the whole story was told them as far as the person knew it and he did a real good, for he collected that day for Burnet about 12 Dollars to take him to Kentucky, which was much better than the methodists did by me at New York."

VIII

NAÏVE and enterprising Fitch still looked toward the west to make his fortune. In spite of his experience with the Indians, he determined to recross the Ohio and survey the best bottomlands along the Muskingum and Hockhocking so that when Congress opened a land office in the Northwest Territory he would be enabled to claim the choicest section. Congress, he reasoned, would have to sell that land in order to pay its debts and he assumed that its agents "would open their Land Office the same as all Land Offices had been opened before and to let everyone pick his own Boundarys conformable to certain Rules which they might Prescribe."

In "Narrow Circumstances," his first task was to raise money for the journey, or rather to find a respectable man to accompany him so that the people he had in mind as backers would more willingly risk paying for the venture. He found Colonel Joshua Anderson of Bucks County who agreed to join him when he had raised the necessary funds and with this assurance he collected twenty pounds apiece from Rev. Irwin of Neshaminy, Stacy Potts, the Trenton Quaker, Dr. John Ewing, Provost of the University of Philadelphia, Jonathan Sergeant and William Houston.

Late that summer of 1783 Fitch, Colonel Anderson and several of Anderson's friends set out for Fort Pitt to survey a hundred thousand acres beyond the Ohio. They were all very respectable, so much so that it "made them Very unsuitable for that Expedition" in the wilderness. "Men of repute, good livers and of Course Very unbidibble, they was more accustomed to command than be commanded," the party "never could get to work till eight or 9 oClock in the Morning and then could not work above an hour before they would complain of being Tired and set down on every log they came across and there was no other way to start them but by gieving them a drink of Grog."

Colonel Anderson, "a sociable, well meaning old woman," blandly ousted Fitch from his position as leader of the expedition and made him a general servant for himself and his friends. "Notwithstanding I had all the business on myself of keeping minutes, making drafts and correcting all our work, when we came to Camp at night I was obliged instead of attending to my own business, to help pitch the tent, gett wood, kindle fires and do the slavery of the Camp more than anyone. And if I was to get up in the morning and get breakfast ready by Sunrize I could not get them to eat it and ready to work before 8 oClock, which kept me constantly fretting; when probably at last I said more than became me and Nathaniel Mashon, Conl Anderson's Cousen, tried to whip me for it and made an attempt as if he was coming at me, when I catched up a Tommyhawk which lay by me and spoke to him as followeth:

" 'You damd, Lazy, Scounderal! If you attempt to strike me, depend on it, I will disable you that your strength shall be reduced equal to mine and when I am on equal terms with you as to strength I will Box it out with you fairly!' "

"This resolute speech checked Nathaniel Mashon and he drew off to the fire again. Yet he was counteananced by Conl Anderson, whose business it was to forward the work. But ease and moderation best suited his Turn."

They had gone into the woods from Decker's Fort on the Ohio and had begun to survey at the mouth of the Hochhocking, up that river until they had located about thirty-six thousand acres. As the stream was dwindling and the land looked poor, Fitch suggested that they portage over to Measle Creek and go down the Muskingum where there were large, level bottoms, groves of black walnut trees twenty-two feet in circumference five feet from the ground, sycamores twice as big and sugar maples with pure, white sap. But there were also Indians along the upper Muskingum and the first night they spent there the camp was "allarmed. Our allarm was occationed by Maj. Brearly seeing considerable fresh signs the day before and Nat Mershon being on Centery heared the walking like a man across the river, the dog Barking as if it was at a Human person."

Everybody was frightened by these "Corroberating circumstances," including Fitch who gave it as his opinion "that there was an Enemy a spying us out and that the most likely to Effect our Business was to decamp and cross the country from Deckers." But even in the midst of the night alarm Fitch thought anxiously of the surveying that had yet to be done and made it a condition that they all come back to the Muskingum, "otherwise, I would not consent to leave the place upon uncertaintys but would wait until day and know for certain" whether Indians were prowling around their camp or not.

Anderson and the rest consented and they broke camp that night. But once they got back to the "Christian shore"—the east bank of the Ohio—they showed they had no inclination to return. When Fitch protested that they had done less than half the work they had come to do, Anderson made the excuse that they could complete their surveying along the Ohio. To this Fitch snorted that those lands were not worth taking, that when they were deeded they would not sell for as much as the warrants would cost.

Well, Anderson said, he would go on the Muskingum another time, "when matters was settled and he could come safely."

Fitch reminded him this would "equally frusterate" them, for then "we could only have a chance with the many millions of the United States. We could not pitch upon a good tract of land but we should have someone before us or someone to contend with for it." Moreover, "the surveys would be interlocking and lawsuits so frequant that it would cost more to defend the land" than their share in it. No, Fitch said, he had "set out with an intent to perform what I undertook and they should ever find me as faithful as a spannel."

Now they began to sneer at him, charging him with lying when he said he meant to go back into the woods. But he wasn't lying, he persisted; if Anderson would leave him enough money to hire hands he would go back into the wilderness and finish surveying the hundred thousand acres. Sixty dollars, he estimated, would be enough. Anderson had more than that left of the money Fitch had raised for the expedition.

Traveling expenses, Anderson said. The money was needed to take himself and his friends back to Bucks County. Fitch doubled up over Decker's rough table and wrote out his demands, with which he began to talk Anderson into compliance.

"For Conl. Anderson to advance to John Fitch sixty Dollars with all the camp Equipage and to lend his compasses, also to Relinquish his right to what the sd John Fitch shall do; that the sd John Fitch does ingage to use his utmost indeavours, not withstanding the aspersions that have been flung out of his courdice and insincerity, to get hands and fulfill the obligation entered into with Doct. Ewing and others to the Extream Bounds of possibilities. That the said John Fitch does solemly declair it his sincear intention and it appears to him reasonable for these Reasons;—first, because the money was advanced for that use, second, we should not keep cash out of the stock to take us home, but should advance of our own as far as we can. For these reasons I am desirous of making one effort more, but do not ask the money unless I get the hands."

Still, Anderson continued to refuse. "Finely," Fitch "Virbally offered to take 12 Dollars."

"I cannot say that I am not afraid of an Indian. I think that no man ought to be more affraid than I am, yet my overanxiety to live up to them articles carried me to greater lengths than it did them." Fitch came to an agreement with Anderson about the money and while the Colonel and his friends remained at Decker's fort, Fitch began to bargain with outlying frontiersmen to accompany him across the Ohio to "the savage shore."

A prodigious walker, he set off at dawn, October 28, "for Vincent Calvin's to Hire hands" and though the distance was forty miles over a footpath he arrived there that night. Next day, with "Vincen and one other in his imploy," he pushed back toward Decker's and lodged at Mr. Foreman's where he "Bargoned with one Richard West to go with me for 5 Shillings per Day, to pay him 4 Pounds Six shillings in cash and the remainder in skins." Going on, he rounded up "Mr. Hartley Sapington and Mr. William Winchester" and on the morning of November 4 they crossed the Ohio and set to work.

All these men were used to the hardships of frontier life and "no more afraid of an Indian than a Bullack is of a Slaughter House. With them, I might truly be called a Couard, but as I never heard that stigma from them, therefore I am persuaded that the Appelation of Bravery and Couardice is more from people's address than from real Bravery or timidity. The Couard who is beloved can never have that stigma; the Brave who is not, can never be without it."

They surveyed till November 12, when they came to the Mingo Path which led up to the Delaware towns where Williamson's Massacre had occurred. It was a "very snowy, stormy day." Realizing that winter would soon drive him off, Fitch sent Foreman and Sapington back to "our Sunday's camp with the Horses and Baggage to prepair for us on our return," while he pushed on with Winchester, West and Vincent Calvin. But the next day Winchester "was suddenly taken with a pain in his knee and unable to walk." Fitch "sent Dicky West to camp for a horse and cut a pair of Crutches for Winchester." They "got him in safe," and went on the next day, which was "could and cloudy and the rain froze over." But on November 15 the weather was worse. "Joseph Foreman scalded one of his feet," probably trying to get warm, and now, with two of the five men crippled, Fitch was finally driven back toward Decker's, where Colonel Anderson and his friends still loitered.

On November 19, only two days after Colonel Anderson and his friends had finally started home on horseback, Fitch returned to Decker's Fort. He had "2 English guineas & 2 French D, one Pistole, one fifteen-shilling piece, 6 Dollars and a quarter" to settle with his frontier companions. He sold Richard West his tomahawk for two shillings, sixpence, three spoons for sixpence. Decker bought four porringers at one and six and Mr. Ross sold him three quarts of whisky for the price of the three spoons. Next day, with five pounds of butter in his knapsack, he started on his long journey over the snowy Alleghenies on foot.

The first night he reached Calvin's cabin in the woods where the next day he "lay by on account of a Bitear Cold and Sunday." In return for a pair of silver buttons Vincent's daughter did his washing while he "exicuted some Writings" and sat talking with Calvin about another expedition early in the spring. He had surveyed about eighty thousand acres and he knew he could have done a good deal better if Colonel Anderson hadn't been such a continual hindrance. Before he set out in the morning he left with Calvin to take care of during the winter his portfolio, compass, magnet, chain, two canteens, a pair of breeches, leggings, stockings, a razor and "one pr. striped linnen trousers."

His Sunday at Vincent Calvin's had given Colonel Anderson another day's start on the way back to Bucks County. Now Fitch decided to show the Colonel how an energetic man on foot could outdistance a lazy man on horseback. On November 25 he came to Colonel Cook's where he "bargoned with James Starret for my compass and surveying instruments" and "payed to Mr. Spear's Negro four pence for setting me across the Monongahela." Next day he walked twenty miles to Cherry's, where he lodged for the night. The day following he reached Laurel Hill through eighteen miles of rain and sleet, then went twelve miles farther through ankle-deep snow to Mr. Duncan's, with whom he drank half a pint of whisky and spent the night.

When Fitch woke in the morning the snow was knee-deep, so he "agreed with some packhorse men to take me on the road" and treated them to two gills of whisky. But after traveling with them about eight miles and finding "the road tollerably well Beat and the weather too cold for more snow" he "grew sick of" his "company and quit them" and fortified by "one point cyder and one point milk," he tramped seventeen miles to Mr. Speaker's. Starting before daybreak the next morning, he walked twenty-nine miles to the foot of Allegheny and the following day reached Bedford. There it was snowing "pretty hard and somewhat cold" and "riding on a packsaddle was too uncomfortable" so he concluded to stop at Bedford till the storm abated.

Colonel Anderson and his party were also there, waiting for clear weather to ride on. Though it was "very wet, slippery and bad walking," Fitch passed them contemptuously and "Traiviled about 7 mi to Bloody Run," seven more to the Juniata and then, not having lodgings for the night, he undertook to keep himself warm by drinking a toddy made of cider, butter and whisky.

On December 5 he reached Abbotstown and went five miles on to Yorktown where he "agreed with a man with a led horse to carry" him "to Lancaster for half a dollar and sixpence for ferriage" over the Susquehanna, which he reached at nine o'clock that night, having "traviled this day 24 miles on foot and 19 miles on horseback." But it was a triumph, for Anderson and his party reached Wright's Ferry on the Susquehanna just behind him. Averaging twenty-five miles a day, he arrived in Warminster three days later and marched to the log shop, where Cobe Scout welcomed him.

"Far from being satisfied with this year's campaign," Fitch

"prepaired to make an Early expedition in the Spring." With the financial support of Dr. Ewing, Stacy Potts, Nathaniel Irwin, William Houston and Jonathan Sergeant, he bought a pack team and left Bucks County late in February. Before the end of the month he "crossed the Sisquehannah on the ice" and drove on through Downington to Abbotstown where he bought fishhooks, needles, whisky, bacon, oats, rum, hay, bread and cider. It was snowy weather most of the way, but the Monongahela broke up on March 10 and the Youghiogheny on the 14th. Though there was "a great fresh" the following day, with driftwood swirling on the swollen streams, they lost none of their supplies and by St. Patrick's Day the weather had become "cold, clear and dry with a steady west wind."

Fitch hired thirteen hands, including John Starret and Robert Cowell. They made a canoe by felling a tree at the mouth of a run and hollowing it out. In this they floated down to the mouth of the little Muskingum, where they encamped on April 7, ready to carry their chains and compasses up into the Indian country.

It was the most favorable season for surveying. The weeds were dead, there was little undergrowth and most of the Indians had "returned from their Huntings to their Towns." But after they had passed Licking Creek, which was more than halfway up the Muskingum to the old Indian village of Wapatomica, they were in constant danger of being captured. They began to see "fresh sines of Indians for two or three days and two or three times where they had not been many hours before us."

Fitch divided the party so that there would be five men under Starret on one bank of the Muskingum and six under himself on the other side, but "took the precaution to camp together every night." Before their prudence drove them back down the Muskingum to the Ohio they surveyed within a quarter of a mile of a large Indian camp and on the day they began to withdraw they "saw a new raft come floating down the stream, which gave reason to believe" there were more Indians "not far about."

From the mouth of the Muskingum they floated down the Ohio to the Hockhocking and paddled up that stream about forty-six miles over freestone beds of iron ore and past white and blue clay banks till they came to an island whose channels on either side were "Choked up with Logs." The Hockhocking, though more to the southwest, flows down from the same country as the Muskingum and here as there they had seen Indian tracks on the banks after every shower. "We had also seen their Camps, where they had lain the night before, two or three days" earlier and that very morning Fitch "had seen where they had crossed water and muddy water stood in their tracks.

"Considering our impediments, I thought it the most advisable to return, when Starret urged our going forward, when he said that he and the five men with him would Travers the Hockhocking to its head, from thence cross the Country to White Woman's Creek and from there return by land."

This meant crossing the Muskingum in the heart of the Indian country, marching northeast of Wapatomica. "I must confess that it was contrary to my opinion, but I consented that he should make the attempt. This conclusion we entered into in the forepart of the day, when Starret and his men loaded themselves with about 20 lb of flower each besides other Provisions and Baggage," and went on up the trail beside the Hockhocking.

Fitch turned back with his chain carriers in the canoe. About an hour before sundown they saw three Indians walking among the trees about forty poles from the river. At that point the Hockhocking swung in a great bend of seven or eight miles, which meant that by walking half a mile the Indians could lie in ambush until the canoe came past on its way downstream. "We paddled on for about one mile, when I ordered my people to see their arms was all in good order and well Loaded, which was done. And when we came to the lower end [of the bend] we heared them steping in the willows, Breaking off sticks as they walked &c.; but it being dusk, they did not fire upon us.

"We went down the River about one mile and came to Camp, as we could not see to travil any longer. To conceal ourselves that night we slept without kindling a fire and about an hour before day I ordered all the bagage on Bord and all hands in the Cannoe and weighted for light to travil by. We took the day by the foretop and met with no impediments and went down the Ohio below the Great Kanawha and surveyed up the Mouth of the Hockhocking with considerable inland surveys wherever we found the good land to extend any considerable distance.

"Meanwhile, Starret went on up the Hockhocking about 8 or 10 miles beyond the Island and fell in with a party of six Indians, when his hunter and one hand was separated from him and made prisoners by them. The Indians kept them prisoner two nights and a day and then, after reserving what effects they stood in need of themselves, set them at liberty. In Short, the Indians gave the prisoners Very generous preasants for some things which they took." And several days later they were all reunited on "the Christian shore."

Fitch and his crew had surveyed nearly "250 Thousand Acres of most Valuable Lands" since March and it was now near the end of May. Boatmen from Kentucky who passed them on the Ohio gave them "Very unfavorable accounts of the Indians down river." They also said that the "Indians had done mischief near Wheeling." On May 31 Fitch "got a touch of snake bite, but having thick leggins and Stockins it scarse pierced the skin and putting salt and powder to it, found very little inconveanancy from it." A day or so later he "killed a large bear and encamped early to take care of it." And soon afterward he discharged his hands and then, after surveying for Vincent Calvin in Mingo Bottom, he left his tools, tent, greatcoat, blankets and surveying instruments with friends along the frontier and started back to Bucks County.

Judged as a surveying venture under adverse conditions, Fitch's expeditions were successful and he returned "well satisfied," and "morrally certain" that he "should one day or other become a man of fortune." His reasoning that Congress would parcel out the Northwest Territory to pay its debts was sensible enough. And it was a reasonable supposition that the national government would use the same method in disposing of the land as Virginia. The system of Virginia was to lay land warrants on such acres of the new territory as would provide a good plantation. Warrants were cheap and the man who settled or surveyed the best land got it. While this enabled wealthy men like Washington to acquire large tracts through their agents, it did not prevent the comparatively poor man from choosing his home and hewing it out of the wilderness. By the end of the war thousands of poor Easterners had settled in Kentucky, so many thousands that this was the chief reason Fitch, instead of returning to Kentucky, had begun to survey in the Northwest.

The Northwest had become a part of the national domain and thus New England had a voice in its disposal. Massachusetts, Connecticut, New Hampshire and Rhode Island had been settled on the township system, which was directly opposed to the method of Virginia. According to the New England plan the new land was not only to be settled in townships, but the townships were to be under the control of the proprietors—the men who had received the grant or bought the land from the government—and, excepting lots for the preacher, the meeting house and school, the proprietors could dispose of land within the township to newcomers as prices rose and the town grew.

These two systems, the Virginia plan of large scattered tracts, which was most favorable to the owners of slave-worked plantations, and the New England plan, which enriched the proprietors, had been argued since 1750 and doubtless before, but the first test between the two kinds of economy was made in Congress in 1784, while Fitch was still on his second surveying expedition. After a long debate the New England officials won and when Fitch returned he discovered that by the Northwest Ordinance of 1784 Congress had resolved that all lands in the territory northwest of the Ohio River "should be laid out at Right angles in lotts of one mile Squair and located by lotts."

"Altho this made much against me, it did not allarm me much, as I knew that I could Locate the principal part of the Lands which I had surveyed upon them principles, but stood a Chance to take in a good deal of Bad Land with the good. But concluding within myself that I would take them in their own way and make more expeditious work than making actual Surveys, ... I went to the frontiers and hired three men to ride thro the Country with me and when I came to a good peace of land I made such landmarks and such notes that my designations could not be misunderstood. This was an expeditious way of surveying and in a Short time enabled myself to make Locations of near 200 Thousand Acres more on lands that would probably be of the first quality."

But this brisk journey, which necessitated traveling several hundred more miles and involved him in another engagement with the Indians, was no more effective than if he had stayed at home. The way to acquire land in the Northwest Territory was not to journey through the forest with chain and compass; it was much more complicated than that. The first step was the formation of a company with influential people either at the head or in close connection, as the Rev. Manasseh Cutler and General Rufus Putnam did in 1786 when they organized the Ohio Company, which included all the territory Fitch had been surveying. The next step was to visit Congress and meet William Duer, a famous land speculator who was at that time secretary of the Board of the Treasury. Modestly petitioning for a million acres, Cutler was advised by Duer to increase his application to four million acres, and that the odd three million should be assigned to a company "composed of a number of the principal characters of the City," of which he, Duer, would, in "profound secret," be the head. In return for which, Duer used his influence with Samuel Osgood and Walter Livingston, his two colleagues on the Treasury Board and they theirs with members of Congress until the business was completed on such favorable terms for Cutler and Duer and their associates that it called for "an elegant oyster dinner" by way of celebration.

Meanwhile Congress fixed the method by which the Northwest Territory was to be marked out. Surveys were to be made in government ranges, towns and sections, with townships six miles square, divided into 36 sections of 640 acres each. Titles were to be obtained by entering them in a government recording office. As this would require the work of several surveyors, Fitch "petitioned Congress for an appointment as a Surveyor in that Country." Going to Philadelphia, he called on Dr. Ewing, Thomas Hutchins, who was Geographer General of the United States, Cadwallader Morris and Jonathan Sergeant, all of whom recommended him for the position. And feeling that "with so warm recomadations from a number of the first characters," he "could hardly doubt of the appointment," he "then returned to Bucks County to weite the Event of Congress" and notification that he had been made surveyor for the Northwest.

"Haveing nothing to do" that winter of 1785, Fitch remained idle in Bucks County while his thoughts continued to develop on the subject of the Northwest. If he became surveyor for that country it would be like a vocation—a way of earning a living and of developing his capacities at the same time. He had never been as far west as the Mississippi or as far north as Lake Michigan, but he had been down the Ohio as far as the Great Falls and he knew all the wilderness that lay northwest between the Scioto and Lake Erie. He knew Licking Creek, White Woman's Creek, Measle Creek and the bends in the Hockhocking. He knew the Sandusky and the Maumee. And from his earliest journey west he remembered all the stations in Kentucky from the Big Sandy to Salt River.

He bought a copy of Hutchins' and McMurray's map of the northwest. Much of the country he knew so well was not even indicated on the Hutchins and McMurray map. And for his "own amusement" he "sat to and made a draft of that Country ... with the additions of" his "knollege." This was "more to keep the Ideas of the country in" his "mind than for any other purpose." But when he had finished the draft he realized "that a map of such sort would be useful to the World," for he knew he could engrave one that would be more accurate than any of its predecessors. Also, though Hutchins' and McMurray's map was good "It was too large and expensive for men to carry into the Woods; and thinking that a great part of the Continent at that time turned their attention to the Western Country and wished every information of it," he bought a sheet of copper, got out his old Graver and sat down to work in Cobe Scout's log shop.

Of the many tools considered necessary for the work of engraving and printing, Fitch had only the Graver, with which he had marked powder horns for the Indians and ciphered buttons for the British guards on Prison Island. When he bought the sheet of copper it was rough, so that he spent much time before he had "hammered and pollished" it into proper shape. He had no printing press, nor was he in need of one so long as Charles Garrison had a cider press he would let him use.

Fitch's "Map of the Northwest Parts of the United States of America" was a unique achievement, if for no other reason than that it is the only map known which was made, engraved and printed by the same man. If not unique, it is at least singular in that when Fitch came to a description of Niagara Falls this natural wonder failed to shake his candor and his graver cut the letters deep:

"The falls of NIAGARA are at present in the middle of a

plane about five miles back from the summit of the mountain, over which the waters once tumbled, we may suppose. The action of the water in a long course of time, has worn away the solid rock and formed an immense ditch which none may approach without horror. After falling perpendicular 150 feet (as some have computed) it continued to descend in a rapid seven miles further to the Landing place."

The map was dedicated to Thomas Hutchins as "a very humble attempt to promote a Science of which you are so bright an ornament. I wish it were more worthy your patronage. Unaccustomed to the business of engraving, I could not render it as pleasing to the eye as I could have wished. But this, I flatter myself, will be easily forgiven by a Gentleman who knows how to distinguish between form and Substance in all things." That was also Fitch's private opinion of his work, for though the job was "cours done," it served his purpose, being "very Cheap, portable to anyone who wanted to go into the Woods and more to be relyed upon than any published."

The map was finished in the spring of 1785, about the time that Congress appointed "one Mr. Hoops" as surveyor to the Northwest instead of Fitch. The same season Congress revised the Northwest Ordinance of 1784 and ordered that all lots in the Northwest Territory "should be sold at public Vendue." This "wholly disconcerted" Fitch, "for by said Resolve, from an immense fortune [I] was reduced to nothing at one Blow. For I could have located about 200 Thousand acres besides what the Co. was entitled to and this I could have located on the halves and found Plenty of Certificates to purchase warrants at that day."

But he could not be defrauded of his knowledge of the Northwest; it was already incorporated in his map. The map itself was soon to become unique for still another reason: as a means of keeping him in funds when he commenced to build the steamboat.

Steamboat Inventor

IX

ONE bright, dry April Sunday in 1785 while he was still printing copies of his map of the Northwest, Fitch and James Ogleby, an old crony of his, were returning to Warminster from Neshaminy congregation where they had gone to hear the Rev. Nathaniel Irwin preach. Even when the sermon was on the "most absurd text that could be picked out of a jargen of absurdities," Irwin had a way of making it "rather of an entertainment than a Burthen." And though Fitch "never troubled churches much," he enjoyed listening to Irwin, whose "discourses were the most candid and ingenious" he "had ever heard from a pulpit."

Always agitated by questions of immortality, conduct, virtue and natural phenomena, Fitch quarreled with Presbyterians, Methodists and Baptists. He had recently joined the Masonic Bristol Lodge, No. 25 A.Y.M. of Pennsylvania, but he valued that order more for its secret signs of brotherliness than for its faint illumination of the unmarked stretches of the mind. He was as "crazey after learning" as he had been as a child and he would hold forth for hours on whether conscience existed of itself or arose "altogether from Education"; on whether any religion could be useful to society. And while he and Ogleby walked back toward the Billet, which was his name for the log shop where he lived with Cobe Scout, they dealt dexterously with the sermon the Rev. Irwin had preached from the pulpit, till a stab of rheumatism struck Fitch "pretty severely" in the knee.

Fitch bent forward and clutched his suddenly knotted tendons. He had "let" his "horse out to work for its living," which he regretted now as he stood wincing and glowering over the painful difficulty of getting home. He started to hobble forward, when Mr. Sinton, one of the first characters of Hatborough, drove smartly past "in a Chair with a Noble Horse." Fitch stopped and stared as the big, spindly wheels flashed by through the dust. A moment later he went on thoughtfully.

James Ogleby was for continuing their discussion of the Rev. Irwin's sermon. But Fitch had become curiously silent and when Ogleby tried to talk to him he hunched his head and twitched his lean shoulders irritably. His mind, which had been formed and strengthened by all the forces of his environment, had begun to work to change that environment, to improve it, to create something useful for the world. He had let his horse out for the day to help pay for its upkeep, because he could not afford to ride it to church when he had a chance of earning a shilling or so from its labors. But "what a noble thing it would be," he thought, "if I could have such a carriage without the expense of keeping a horse!" And that thought, born of desire, bred another that was full of challenge. "What cannot you do," he demanded of himself, "if only you will get yourself about it!"

Steam!

Beside him, Ogleby went on at a great rate about the Rev. Irwin's sermon, but Fitch was so preoccupied he "could not reply to his discourse." You could get a force by steam if you set yourself about it, a force that would move a carriage straight along the road!

Fitch had never heard of a steam engine. Descriptions of early types such as Savary's, Cowley's and Newcomen's had been in print for fifty years, but he was unaware of it. At that time there were only three engines in the United States, two of them in New England while the third was at Passaic, New Jersey, where a British mechanic named Hornblower operated it in General Philip Schuyler's copper mine. These engines had been made in England and were of the old-fashioned, atmospheric type. It was also in England that the only contemporary experiments in actual steam power were being made, in Soho, London, where Watt and Bolton were secretly working on a new, double-acting type.

Parting from Ogleby as soon as he could, Fitch went back to the Billet where he plunged bare-handed into the overpowering task of designing an engine, harnessing its power to a vehicle and indicating some kind of road on which the carriage could run. But the problem of traction soon discouraged him. On an ordinary road a carriage often mired to the hubs and even on the main highways travel was slow and lurching. The conception of metal tracks spiked down to crossties was even beyond speculation. With the greatest steel furnace in Pennsylvania capable of producing, at most, two hundred and thirty tons of steel in a year, the manufacture of rails would have been impossible. The steel industry had first to advance through many stages.

But transportation by water was not compelled to wait upon a series of major inventions. Barges and keelboats were already afloat. After a week's struggle with the baffling task of improving overland travel, Fitch transferred his hopes to the rivers. For there were no large boats that could be propelled upstream except by sail or many oars. Most of the ships which carried goods down the Ohio and Mississippi were broken up for lumber when the cargo was unloaded and the boatmen had to make the long journey home by land.

Fitch finished his drawings within a couple of weeks and carried them to Neshaminy for the approval of Nathaniel Irwin, who had a lively interest in natural and mechanical science. He had not got much further than the draft of an engine, but he had formed the conception entirely by himself and he believed it was a contribution to the world's knowledge.

Nathaniel Irwin examined the sketch and turned to his bookcase. He took down a copy of Benjamin Martin's Philosophia Brittanica and began turning the pages while Fitch waited anxiously. When Irwin opened the volume to a description of

Thomas Newcomen's atmospheric steam engine with piston and cylinders, Fitch was "considerably chagrianed."

There was a model of the engine at Glasgow University, but Newcomen had been dead since 1729. The engine had been used chiefly to pump water out of mines. Reflecting on this, Fitch's composure returned. He had been right, at any rate: power *could* be generated by steam. The existence of such a machine "strengthened" his "opinion of the scheme" to build a steamboat. "Knowing that the machinery could not fail of Propeling" the craft, his only "doubts lay in gaining the force itself."

Fitch went back to the Billet and set to work. His first object was to make a propeller which would drive a boat through the water and he began to construct a revolving chain on a pair of sprockets, with flat wooden paddles attached to the chain like perpendicular fins. This contraption he fitted in the side of a model skiff about two feet long. He tried it out by hand in a small stream that ran through the meadow of his friend, Joseph Longstreth. According to Nathaniel Boileau, who was then a student at Princeton home for vacation, he also designed a circular paddle-wheel, for which Boileau whittled the small waterwheels out of wood. Both these were tried and "realized every expectation."

This was merely the beginning. Fitch was now confronted with the task of manufacturing a steam engine and of devising some means of transferring the power to the propeller by rotary motion. A great deal of money would be needed for experiments, but though he was poor he had several well-to-do acquaintances among the scientific men of Philadelphia; he had a wild hope of assistance from Congress and he had also printed several hundred copies of saleable maps. That summer he went down to Philadelphia.

In Philadelphia a man could find almost anything he wanted.

Miss Peggy Patterson, perhaps the daughter of Robert Patterson, the teacher of mathematics, agreed to color Fitch's map for him and was in no hurry for her money. William Prichard, who had a bookshop on the north side of Market Street opposite Laetitia Court, was willing to sell the maps on commission and the weekly *Pennsylvania Packet* was a profitable advertising medium. A few blocks farther along Market, and around the corner on Seventh toward Chestnut, Whitehead Humphreys had his steel furnace where he was manufacturing small quantities of bar iron. And two blocks beyond, at the corner of Ninth Street, was housed the joint-stock "United Company of Philadelphia for the Promotion of American Manufactures," which had looms, jennies and machinery for making linen, cotton and wool.

A tight, hardheaded city, with close-flanking red brick houses facing each other across narrow streets, Philadelphia drove its theater beyond the city limits, but generously welcomed all manner of scientific learning. By its geographical position, on two navigable rivers with an outlet to the Atlantic and accessible from thousands of rich, rolling farms, it had become the wealthiest city in America and it was therefore the most culturally advanced. It had a university, a library company and a philosophical society. It supported a hospital, fostered printing presses for books and magazines and possessed a "celebrated Orrery," invented by Dr. David Rittenhouse, to calculate the stars.

The wealth of the city, made from profits on apprentices, indentured servants, journeymen, farmers and, in general, "the industrious poor," drew craftsmen to Philadelphia and increased their opportunities. There were skilled shipwrights in the shipyards on the Delaware, expert carpenters, joiners, master masons, watchmakers, clockmakers, weavers, ironmongers and silversmiths living in wooden houses, in two or three rooms of the brick houses that lined the well-kept streets, while many of the submerged poor were crowded into the "narrow and very often filthy alleys."

But when Fitch first came to Philadelphia with his bundle of maps, his cantankerous ways, his drafts, his "moddle" for the steamboat and his fiercely determined hopes, he went to the primly dignified houses where his patrons of the surveying expedition lived, down on South Third Street, along a brick sidewalk with a gutter to drain the water and posts to protect pedestrians from passing carriages, to the home of Dr. John Ewing, Provost of the University. For he knew that no matter how useful his invention might be, it would never become of practical worth without the support of men with money and influence.

His first plan was to gain the moral support of these men, who would introduce him to Congress which was then sitting in New York, making the laws of the land. It was impossible for him to think of a more fitting place to take his invention and ask for assistance. Congress was the supreme body of the United States and a steamboat was of the greatest advantage to America as a whole. Once the principle had been achieved and demonstrated, it could be applied to the United States Navy, which would become second to none. And all the back country at the foot of the Alleghenies and all the land west of the mountains, which was so poor because it was so far from the big markets, would be brought into contact with the cities wherever there were rivers that flowed toward the sea.

Dr. Ewing was a scientifically inclined, liberal-minded man. He gave Fitch a letter to their mutual acquaintance, William C. Houston of Trenton, saying he had examined "Mr. Fitche's machine for rowing a Boat, by the alternate operation of steam and the atmosphere," and had "no doubt of the success of the scheme if executed by a skillful workman." And as Fitch proposed to lay his invention before Congress, he hoped the inventor would "meet with the incouragement which his mechanical genius deserves."

With his model in a horse cart and a large supply of maps in his portfolio, Fitch crossed over to Trenton and called on Mr. Houston who, after examining "the Principles and construction of Mr. Fitche's steamboat, and though not troubled with a Penchant for projects," could not "help approving the simplicity of the plan." Giving Fitch a letter of recommendation, he sent him on to the Honorable Lambert Cadwallader, one of the delegates in Congress from New Jersey.

Fitch traveled on up the Delaware, selling each day two or three copies of his map at five shillings and stopping for the night at some tavern whose owner would give him supper, rum, bed and a few shillings besides in return for a copy. At Freehold, New Jersey John Paine and Cornelius Hagerman each took four and Dereck Sutphen bought one. At Maidenhead, Briston, Holly, Springfield and Newtown he found purchasers. At Princeton Enos Kelsey ordered six copies and Jonathan Baldwin, former steward of Princeton College and a commissary officer in the Revolutionary Army, requested a dozen to be delivered to him at New York.

In high spirits, with testimonials from Dr. Ewing, Houston, Dr. Samuel Smith, the Provost of Princeton and letters to several Congressmen, Fitch reached New York and addressed the following petition to "His Excellency, the President of Congress:

"Sir:—The Subscriber begs leave to lay at the feet of Congress, an attempt he has made to facilitate the internal Navigation of the United States, adapted especially to the Waters of the Mississippi.

"The Machine he has invented for the purpose has been examined by several Gentlemen of Learning and Ingenuity, who have given it their approbation.

"Being thus encouraged, he is desirous to solicit the attention of Congress to a rough model of it now with him, that, after examination into the principles upon which it operates, they may be enabled to judge whether it deserves encouragement. And he, as in duty bound, shall ever pray."

Now, whatever action Congress might otherwise have taken on Fitch's application, that phrase in the first paragraph, *"especially to the waters of the Mississippi,"* damned the project in the eyes of the delegates. Their economic interest, like that of all the wealthy Easterners, was violently opposed to the development of the West.

To the frontiersmen in Western Pennsylvania and Kentucky, free navigation of the Mississippi was of first importance. But to the employers, merchants and shipowners in the East this meant increasing the growth of the western country and they had begun to look on expansion beyond the mountains with a resentful, bitter eye. Employers were opposed to it because every man who left the settled towns and crossed the Alleghenies to become a farmer reduced the supply of surplus labor in the east and thus automatically increased the wages of those who remained. Merchants and shippers were against a free port at New Orleans and the consequent growth of the West because that would mean the establishment of a rival port which would interfere with their handling all the country's raw materials.

Besides the merchants, the struggling manufacturers and the shippers—all the people who were to form themselves into the Federal party—this attitude of opposition to the West was supported by the large landholders along the rivers which flowed into the Atlantic. For it was their avowed object to enrich their holdings and bind the West to the East by extending canals from the rivers to the Blue Ridge and Allegheny Mountains.

As Fitch had planned, the kind of boat he hoped to build would operate best on the Ohio and Mississippi Rivers. From Pittsburgh to the Spanish port of New Orleans those waters flowed past hundreds of miles of growing settlements and productive farms. Shut off from the eastern markets by the mountains, the almost impassable roads and high cost of transportation, these producers of corn, wheat, tobacco and hogs had nowhere else to sell their goods but New Orleans. Because of the rivers it was cheaper to send a cargo from Fort Pitt clear to the mouth of the Mississippi than to transport it over the Alleghenies to Lancaster or Philadelphia.

But nearly all of these shipments were made by flatboat. And the flatboat had no means of getting back upstream. At New Orleans they were broken up and sold for lumber, which left the boatmen facing a journey of weeks through the wilderness before they got home again. From 1782, when the first flatboat made the long voyage from Fort Pitt, downriver trade grew so rapidly that the town of Algiers, opposite New Orleans, was being built almost entirely of flatboat lumber.

America's treaty with Spain that year gave Congress its first chance to cripple the West for the benefit of the eastern mercantile interests which were in search of foreign markets and had determined on Valencia and Cadiz. Don Diego de Gardoqui, the Spanish Minister, was in New York when Fitch arrived and Congress was already quarreling over whether to bargain for free navigation of the Mississippi or for a commercial treaty. "The eastern states," Light-horse Harry Lee, a large landholding Congressman from the Potomac, wrote to General Washington, an even larger landholder on the Potomac, "consider a commercial connexion with Spain as the only remedy for their distresses which oppress their citizens, most of which they say flow from a decay of their commerce. Their delegates have consequently zealously pressed the formation of this connexion... In this opinion they have been joined by 2 of the middle states. On the other hand Virginia has with equal zeal opposed the connexion, because the project involves expressly the disuse of the navigation of the Mississippi for a given time & eventually they think will sacrifice our right to it."

As a whole, the farmers of Virginia were looking toward the

West, and their delegates in Congress, including Lee, had been expressly instructed to vote for free navigation of the Mississippi. But Lee, with the Potomac running in front of his Stratford estate and on to the Atlantic, disobeyed his instructions and General Washington, his neighbor, approved his attitude:

"If I stopped short of your ideas respecting the navigation of the Miss." he answered Lee, "or of what may be the opinion of Congress on the subject, it was not from want of coincidence of sentiments, but because I was ignorant, at the time, of the rubs which are in the way of your commercial treaty with Spain, and because I thought some address might be necessary to temporize with Kentucky and keep that settlement in a state of quietness. At this moment it is formidable and the population is rapidly increasing. There are many ambitious and turbulent spirits among its inhabitants who, from their present difficulties in their intercourse with the Atlantic states, have turned their eyes to New Orleans and may become riotous and ungovernable if the hope of traffic with it is cut off by treaty. Notwithstanding, if the cession is counterpoised, it may be a more favorable time for Congress to speak decisively to them than when they have become stronger, but not sufficiently matured to force the passage of the Mississippi themselves; whilst these plans, which are in agitation for openly communicating with that territory may, if successful, unfold to them new prospects mutually beneficial to the old and the new states."

Ignorant of these forces which were shaping the future of America for their own ends, Fitch waited day after day to show his model to the wise men of Congress. He finally learned that his petition had been referred to a committee of three, Reed and King of Massachusetts, and James McHenry of Maryland. There it remained, so successfully hidden that not even a report was made upon it.

Exasperated by the committee's silence, Fitch railed that Congress was "a set of ignorant boys" and went to see the Spanish Minister.

Don Diego's ruffled hands examined the little model with its blade-like paddle-wheels spaced along the revolving chain. He also studied the drawings. Steam? Yes, he knew about steam. Very powerful. And a very ingenious invention. But would Mr. Fitch, if Gardoqui helped him with Spanish milled dollars, grant the exclusive right of manufacture to his most Christian Majesty, the King of Spain?

This was contrary to Fitch's simple idea of patriotism. Later he was to write bitterly "God forbid that I should ever be in like error again, if ever in my power to prevent it. The strange ideas I had at that time of serving my Country, without the least suspicion that my only reward would be nothing but contempt and opprobrious names, has taught me a mighty lesson in mankind—to do it at the displeasure of the whole Spanish nation, is one of the most impolite strokes that a Blockhead could be guilty of." But now, when Don Diego made a tentative offer to help him if he would grant the patent to Spain, Fitch determinedly shook his head and walked out into the street.

With "Grand Views to render service to" his "Country, and Chastize the Ignorant Boys of Congress," Fitch drove his horse cart and the model back to Philadelphia and sought out Benjamin Franklin.

That learned octogenarian was one of the shrewdest, blandest men of his time. By his pacific manner and unhurried persistence he had spent a long, active life in getting what he wanted, riches, recognition, a loan of millions from the French Government to the United States, and electricity from the skies. He was a corresponding member of various scientific societies in Europe and he had done more to raise the level of philosophical inquiry than any other American. When he was a younger man he had actively supported the inventions of others as well as his own and had been a vigorous champion of bourgeois democracy. But now in his old age, when he found democracy less liberal than he had hoped, when he found his counsel rejected by the more acquisitive leaders of America he drew into himself and was so preoccupied with his own numerous conceits that he had little interest in another's projects unless the germ of the project already lay in his own mind.

A lightning rod outside his house advertised the Doctor's ingenuity. It was not only the first lightning rod Fitch had ever seen, it was unique in the history of lightning rods. Rising from the ground toward the second story, the rod was broken between the top of the first floor and the bottom of the upper floor windows and joined by a chime of bells which, "whenever an electric cloud passed over the city, were set to ringing and throwing out sparks of electricity." Inside the large, comfortable house the Doctor sat in his private study, a plump, wide-bottomed old man with a vastly wrinkled face and thin, gray hair.

The Doctor sat among his boxes of musical glasses, curious electrical instruments, large chests heavy with valuable papers. There was an harmonica made like a desk and a mechanical arm to reach down books from the rows of shelves. Welcoming Fitch with his customary benevolent expression, which concealed "a rare talent of himself profiting by the conversation of others, and turning their hints to such purposes as he desired," Franklin spoke "very flatteringly" of the plans Fitch had brought to show him.

But when Fitch asked him for a letter of recommendation, the Doctor became cautious. Oh, he approved of the invention. A steamboat would be very fine and of great benefit to the world. In short, though Fitch "could obtain nothing from him writing," his manner was so agreeable that when Fitch left, he "doubted not of his patronage in" his invention.

Taking it for granted that Dr. Franklin would help him, Fitch went to the American Philosophical Society, of which Franklin was the most celebrated member, and presented that body with his model. Sam Magaw, the secretary, noted that "the model, with a Drawing and Description, of a Machine for working a boat against the stream by means of a steam engine, was laid before the Society by Mr. John Fitch." And Fitch sat back to await the developments which were sure to result from such a powerful combination as Dr. Franklin's support and the exhibit of the model and drawings before all the learned members of the American Philosophical Society.

Two weeks passed and Fitch heard nothing. He had gone back to Bucks County and the third week after he had seen Franklin he tried to spur the Doctor out of his silence by a letter in which he advised him that the steamboat was "a matter of the first Magnitude, not only to the United States, but to every Maratime power in the World," for the steamboat would "answer for sea voiages, as well as for inland Navigation, in particular for Packets where there should be a great number of passengers." What emboldened him "to be thus presuming in the good effects of the machine, is the almost Omnipotent force by which it is actuated, and the very Simple, easy and natural way by which the Screw or Paddles are turned to answer the purpose of Oars."

After waiting another week for a reply from Franklin, and being disappointed in even so much as a note, Fitch packed up his budget and set out for Kentucky. For he had begun to realize —though he never quite gave up hoping that the Federal government would assist him—that if he was to gain official support for his invention it was most likely to come from the Kentuckians themselves, whose means of transportation the steamboat was so greatly to improve. Also, there was one "man by the name of Wilson that had laid a preemption on Fitch's Thousand Acre tract on Cox's Creek;" and while Fitch had written his friend Evan Williams to "throw a Caveat against said claim," there was still a question of whether he had lost the tract or not.

Dispute over these warrants made it necessary for Fitch to go to Kentucky by way of Richmond, where the land office was located. His first stop was at Lancaster. There he learned in conversation with William Henry that the use of steam to propel a boat was a thought that had occupied more than one ingenious mind. He, himself, William Henry said dryly, had considered the possibility of steam as early as 1776, but he wasn't going to lay any claims of priority because Tom Paine had actually spoken of just such a means of locomotion in 1778 and there was no telling how long it had been in his mind. For that matter, Henry and Andrew Ellicott, the surveyor who taught mathematics at the University of Philadelphia, had held long conversations on the subject from time to time. But as none of them, neither himself, Ellicott nor Paine, had ever tried to work the idea out on paper, as Fitch had done, the credit must belong to Fitch. Here Henry began to mutter vaguely about a "steam wheel" project he had long had in mind and as Fitch could not follow his rambling description he promised half-heartedly to make a model of it and send it to Fitch for inspection.

Undisturbed by the fact that others had thought of making a steamboat before him, Fitch crossed the Susquehanna into Maryland on his way into Virginia. A thousand people could have conceived such a possibility as he was now trying to reduce to concrete form, but so long as he was the only person engaged in the invention he had no reason to believe his right would be challenged.

But at Fredericktown Fitch heard more disconcerting news. James Rumsey, of Bath, who kept the tavern "At the Sign of the Liberty Pole and Flag" had made a boat in the previous year which was said to be able to go against the current. Fitch learned of this when he visited Thomas Johnson, a former governor of Maryland, whom he had hoped to interest in his own behalf. Johnson was one of the owners of the Catoctin Iron Works on the Susquehanna and would be a valuable patron.

This Rumsey boat, Fitch asked anxiously: how had it gone? Had it gone by steam?

No, Johnson answered, the boat hadn't been propelled by force of steam. It was more of a contraption, with a wheel that was turned by the current and setting poles attached to the boat so that it went stalking forward against the drift of the river.

Fitch's apprehension was relieved. Since the Rumsey boat was not driven by steam there could be no question of prior rights. From what he could learn through his talk with Johnson he discovered that the Rumsey boat, depending on the river current to turn the wheel, was impotent in still water. Not only that, a boat which worked on the principle of a mill-wheel could never carry much of a cargo. Also, men were required to work the machinery.

At that first meeting Johnson's answers were candid. And as Fitch was about to leave he advised him to stop at Mount Vernon on his way to Richmond. For General Washington, he said, had seen the Rumsey boat in operation while he had been spending a few days at Bath in Rumsey's "commodious boarding house."

Fitch nodded eagerly at the suggestion. He was not concerned particularly over what Washington might say with regard to the Rumsey boat, but here was a chance to enlist the support of the best known man in America in behalf of his steamboat.

Next day he ferried across the Potomac and went up the long, red clay road to Mount Vernon, through its hundreds of acres of harvested fields, past the neat stock fences, the huddle of slave quarters and on to the large, white clapboard house with its connecting colonnades, its cramped little rooms, its narrow staircase and its slim-columned portico overlooking the broad river beyond the trees.

People were always coming to Mount Vernon from all over the United States and the General welcomed Fitch with his customary manner of stiff but not forbidding dignity. He had been poor as a young man, but he had a rich half-brother from whom he had inherited the Mount Vernon estate. Then he had married a wealthy widow and now, since the war, he spent most of his days riding about his slave-tilled fields or overseeing the various shopwork which was a necessary part of so large a plantation. As the whole estate was operated on a slave economy, he was without experience in machinery and had little use for it. Labor was cheaper. And the few attempts he had made to use mechanical means had discouraged him, for his machinery had been cared for and operated by slaves and the cultural leap through centuries of history of the human race was too much for two or three generations kidnaped from Africa. Lacking experience of his own in machinery, he could hardly be expected to teach his slaves. And when they broke a part or were negligent in caring for farm implements, the General grumblingly blamed the accident on "the imperfectibility of human nature."

But Rumsey's experiment—it had not been with a boat, but with a small model—had entertained him that day he spent at "The Sign of the Liberty Pole and Flag." It had made him believe that "with small manual assistance" and, "the counteraction being proportioned to the action, it must ascend a swift current faster than a gentle stream," that there was "a point beyond which it cannot go, without involving difficulties which may be found insurmountable," but that "if a model, or thing in miniature, is a just representation of a thing in practice," there was "no doubt of the utility of the invention." And he had given Rumsey a certificate stating that, to his knowledge, the innkeeper had "discovered the art of working boats by mechanism and small manual assistance against rapid currents."

Now, when Fitch began to describe his plan to build a steamboat, the General listened with growing "signs of agitation" on his broad, bony "countineance." Apparently he had no conception of the powers of steam as applied to motion and, unable to imagine that here was an idea that would revolutionize transportation, he considered Fitch's scheme as competing with Rumsey's stilted contraption.

As the General remained silent, Fitch asked point-blank if his invention was similar to Rumsey's; had Rumsey employed the use of steam?

Washington answered out of his cold reserve that he "could not give Mr. Rumsey's plan by negatives." After this statement he abruptly left the room.

Fitch sat waiting till the General returned. He was gone for some time, but when he reappeared he admitted that Fitch's plan "was not the same as Rumsey had presented to him at Bath. But," he added, "some time after that, at Richmond, Rumsey had mentioned something of the sort to him, but he had been so engaged in company that he did not attend to it" sufficiently to recollect what Rumsey had actually said.

Fitch left. He had not got the General's endorsement, but it was at least certain from the interview that Rumsey had not relied on steam for his experiment at Bath, even though he might have thought of it later. "Knowing that the thought of applying steam to boats had been suggested by other gentlemen long before," Fitch "left his Excellency with all the elated prospects that an aspiring projector could entertain, not doubting" that he "should reap the full benefit of the project." For, "altho some others had conceived the thought before, yet" he knew he was "the first to exhibit a plan to the public." He was "fully convinced" that his invention did not infringe on Rumsey's, "otherwise the well known candour of General Washington would have pointed out such interference."

From Mount Vernon Fitch went on down through Fredericksburg to Richmond. The Virginia Assembly was in session when he arrived and old Patrick Henry was occupying the plain, two-story frame house known as the Governor's Mansion. Henry and many of the delegates were from the mountains or beyond. John Edwards was there as a representative of the county of Kentucky. All the long streets stretched toward the west and the stores were stocked with the kind of goods people needed when they set out for the frontier. Here the whole atmosphere was different from what it had been in Philadelphia and New York. In the legislature there was a restless feeling against the great landowners of the Northern Neck and the Lower James, a sense of turbulence and expansion brought from the West by the wearers of coonskin caps.

When Fitch met John Edwards and showed him the drawings for a steamboat Edwards at once urged him to petition the Virginia Assembly for help. Kentucky was a land of plenty, but the Kentuckians needed money to pay for things they could only buy in the East, so that their greatest problem was one of transportation. With an invention like Fitch's, there was no need for him to bother about introductions and recommendations as they did in the East. James Madison of Orange, for all his manners of pale discretion, would present a lively, well-reasoned memorial before the Assembly and there was no doubt that Governor Henry would support it as far as possible.

This came about as Edwards had predicted, except that the Assembly was unwilling to vote money to finance Fitch's invention. However, Fitch recollected his map as a means of raising funds. In this enthusiastic atmosphere it seemed extremely feasible that with the help of the delegates he would be enabled to raise money enough from the sale of his maps to build a steamboat. Henry approved the scheme. Fitch signed a bond for three hundred and fifty Pounds, on the condition that if he sold a thousand copies of his map of the Northwest at six shillings, eightpence each he would, within nine months, exhibit a steamboat on Virginia waters or forfeit the bond. The delegates were all given subscription papers to circulate in their various counties and Fitch, abandoning his journey to Kentucky, started back to Bucks County and his cider press.

X

THE Virginia delegates' encouragement of Fitch and his steamboat remained merely verbal. Dunscomb of Richmond sold twenty maps and Fitch received eight crowns, but the other representatives returned their subscription lists as empty of names as they had come from the printer. To Fitch this was no more than a petty annoyance. Heated by incessant thoughts of his invention, his mind was like a crucible which burned away every disheartening fact. He reappeared in Maryland, where Thomas Johnson accepted some subscription papers for his map and gave him a letter to Governor Smallwood. His gaunt body and determined face besieged the legislators at Annapolis, at Dover, where the Delaware assembly met, at Philadelphia and at Trenton.

At Trenton he made progress. Supported by a petition signed by the friends of his silversmithing days, Stacy Potts, Samuel Stockton, William Houston, the Clunns, Thomas Yard, Abraham Hunt and several others, Fitch was granted by the New Jersey Legislature "the sole and exclusive right of constructing, making, using and employing, or navigating, all and every species or kind of boats, or water craft, which might be urged or impelled by the force of fire or steam, on all the creeks, rivers &c within the territory or jurisdiction of this State" from March 18, 1786 for a period of fourteen years.

At Bordentown Fitch called on Thomas Paine, who helped him along by buying a copy of his map. Paine was living in a little house on Colonel Kirkbride's estate with a few hundred feet of garden plot. He and John Hall, a mechanic who had recently come from England, were making a model of an iron suspension bridge and could do nothing for Fitch but wish him well and recognize him as a fellow "Saint-Maker," which was John Hall's name for all inventors.

With his New Jersey monopoly assured, Fitch returned to Philadelphia and began to form a joint-stock company like the one which had financed his surveying expedition to the Northwest Territory.

In Philadelphia of 1786 there were few very rich men. There was Robert Morris, who had acquired the title of "financier of the Revolution" by adding $70,000—at six per cent—to the millions of francs lent the United States by the French Government and by forming a bank to disburse the money. He and his partner, Thomas Willing, owned a fleet of ships and several warehouses on the Delaware. He was a great speculator in money and land. Until he finally overreached himself and was jailed in Prune Street prison for fraud, he was regarded as a financial wizard and he had begun to build a house 120 by 60 feet with towers, marble-encased windows, entablatures, architraves, pieces of sculpture, angles of porches, fragments of porticoes and scraps of colonnades, with an immense mansard roof and prominent skylights.

There was also William Bingham. Bingham owned more ships than Morris, was richer but less spectacular in his dealings. He had made the bulk of his wealth by running privateers from the West Indies during the Revolution and when he returned to Philadelphia he "appeared in the streets attended by a mulatto boy bearing his umbrella." He worked closely with the Government and, like Morris, he belonged to the informal but powerful Society for Political Inquiry. This organization, which included Washington, a few Pennsylvania politicians and the richest men of the metropolis, met frequently in Franklin's library where their realistic attitude toward capitalist government was so depressing to the liberal-minded Franklin, whose views were already discredited, and Paine, who occasionally attended, that these two patriots of the Revolution were forced into silence. Bingham's mansion, on Third Street above Spruce, was set in the midst of a park which was barred to the public by wide, wrought-iron gates. Inside, the walks, statuary, shade and parterres covered not less than three acres. The huge house was entered "by a single step upon the wide pave of tesselated marble" and the hall disclosed "a self-supporting stairway, broad, of fine white marble—the first of that description, probably, ever known in America—leading to the second story" which "gave a truly Roman elegance to the passage."

Like Morris, Bingham got himself elected Senator from Pennsylvania under the Federal government and this enabled him to increase his fortune in many ways, among which was the acquisition of a two-million acre tract in Maine through William Duer and Henry Knox.

Either of these men had money enough to squander on the steamboat. With the backing of their wealth and influence, Fitch's invention could have been completed within a short time, would have benefited by the monopoly which Robert Fulton was twenty years later to obtain through the power and wealth of Chancellor Livingston, and stood a chance of being operated profitably, on the Hudson and Mississippi. But whether through fear that he would be crowded out by them or through awe of their greatness, Fitch never urged either of the city's two great capitalists to become his patrons.

Instead, he went among the members of the growing middle class. There were many professional men and small merchants who could afford to make an occasional modest speculation. They formed a large intelligent body which was already acquainted with the fact that machinery reduced wages, that a man at a machine, and at no more cost than at a handicraft workbench, could produce ten, one hundred, two hundred times as much as by hand. And it had been proved to them that the wages saved in this enormously increased method of production would pay for the cost of machinery and continue to yield a profit.

As early as 1772 a writer in the *Pennsylvania Gazette* had tantalized his readers with the information that "a person who has for many years past been a master of several large manufactories for linen, cotton and calico printing, likewise cutting and stamping of copper plates for the same, intends some time this month [January] to leave England for America with six journeymen and all the machinery for carrying on the said business, previous to which, and unknown to the English manufacturers, he has shipped sundry machines, some of which will spin ten and others from 20 to 200 threads at one time, with the assistance of one hand at each machine."

At the risk of two hundred pounds fine and confiscation by the British Government, these machines and others as well were smuggled to America where they were bought and operated by stock companies, shares of one of which increased seventy-five per cent in three years. The year after Fitch formed his stock company to build a steamboat, Tench Coxe organized the "Pennsylvania Society for the Encouragement of Manufactures and the Useful Arts," which, in spite of its benevolent title, was a joint-stock manufacting concern whose object was to produce the greatest possible quantity of cotton at the lowest possible wages. And as the handweavers in England, made desperate by machine competition, had wrecked the looms, frames and spinning jennies which could produce so much for so little, Coxe's Society profited by the example and declared that their machines were for the benefit of "the industrious poor."

Beginning in the middle of April, 1786, Fitch had organized his joint-stock company within a week. There were to be forty shares, half of which were to belong to the inventor for his patent and for the labor he was to expend in bringing it to perfection. The remaining number were to be sold at twenty dollars each.

Among the first subscribers was Richard Wells, who was later a member of Coxe's manufacturing company. Wells sold various goods at his shop on Third Street and afterward became cashier of the Bank of North America. Another was Benjamin Morris, retailer of wines and groceries on Dock Street. A third was Joseph Budd, the hatter, who had become interested in Fitch through the map of the Northwest. Magnus Miller, John and Chamless Hart, Thomas Palmer, Gideon Wells were all either merchants or tavern keepers.

But the stockholders were not all representatives of the cash drawer and the counting house. There was Thomas Say, who was styled by the Philadelphia census taker as "Gentleman" and by the city's antiquarian as "that singular, pythagorean, cynical Christian philosopher" who, in 1742, appeared at a meeting of the Society of Friends and broke his wife's china, piece by piece, as a protest against the use of tea. There was Israel Israel who kept the tavern at the Sign of the Crosskeys and claimed to have been saved from an "ignominious death" during the Revolution because his British captor discovered him to be a fellow Mason. There was Thomas Hutchins, Geographer-general of the United States; Richard Stockton, whose father had signed the Declaration of Independence; Dr. John Morris, Dr. Benjamin Say, Edward Brooks, the ironmonger, and Stacy Potts, the Quaker farmer from Trenton.

Though all the subscribers signed the agreement willingly enough, Fitch found it impossible to collect more than three-fourths of the amount pledged. With three hundred dollars he was expected to manufacture a steam engine, fitting it and the necessary machinery into a boat.

Fitch and most of the members of the company had never seen a steam engine. But most of the stockholders had heard of John Nancarrow, who had a steel furnace in the city and was known to have worked in Cornwall, before he came to America, on steam cylinders for the coal mines. Nancarrow was interviewed;

he said he thought he could make such an engine. He was given the order and for thirty days Fitch stood first on one foot and then on the other, till Nancarrow finally produced his drafts. "Old fashioned," Fitch said and rejected them. The plans were too much like the descriptions of engines in 1732, of the atmospheric type and requiring weights to raise the piston.

One of the members suggested they hire Mr. Hornblower, who had put up the engine at General Schuyler's copper mine at Passaic. But the only Hornblowers connected with steam invention were the family of Cornish engineers of that name and though one of them may have come to America in 1750 to set up Schuyler's engine, all those who experimented with steam remained in England.

Richard Wells suggested Christopher Colles, the brilliant Irishman who had delivered lectures before the Philosophical Society on "Pneumaticks, illustrated by a variety of curious and entertaining experiments in an air-pump." Colles had built a model of a steam engine and had exhibited it before the Philosophical Society in 1773; and Wells, as one of the committee appointed by the society to report upon it, had seen the engine "perform several strokes (tho' some of the materials not being sufficiently strong and large, owing to his attempting the execution at a very low expense,) it did not continue long in motion."

Colles was then in New York. While the stockholders were trying to decide whether to send Fitch to see him, the inventor found exactly the man he wanted. Once he had found him he would have none other.

Henry Voight, a plain-spoken Dutchman, "handsome and of good address," made clocks and watches on Second Street between Race and Vine. He was a man of "high Passions, confident in his own abilities, flushed to excess with the prospect of suckcess and equally distressed with a Disappointment." He was also "familiar, friendly and sociable to all and a truly honest man in his Trade, but the most Gripeing, Mizerly wretch on earth for the honors of invention." But this was excusable, for Voight was "the first mechanical genius," Fitch "ever met with in the whole cours of" his life and he firmly believed that "a superior Mechanical Genius" to Henry Voight "was not to be found on earth."

It was lucky for Fitch to have met Voight at that particular time.

So far, Fitch's single contribution to the science of steam propulsion was his revolving chain and paddles which were to drive the boat through the water; either that or the paddle wheel which Nathaniel Boileau had whittled under his direction during the summer of 1785 in Warminster. At first he had believed that the thought of a steam engine was original with him—until the Rev. Irwin had shown him descriptions of engines which he now considered old fashioned. Afterward, he had clung to the revolving chain and paddles, offering it and its connection with steam as his justification as an inventor. It had been chain and paddles, chain and paddles that he had talked to Congress, to the state assemblies, to Patrick Henry and to Benjamin Franklin.

But three months after his first interview with Franklin, that benign old philosopher had introduced a paper into the minutes of the American Philosophical Society. Presented by Mr. Hopkinson, the paper was regarded by the Society as "a Dissertation written by Dr. Franklin, containing a great number of curious and useful observations and discoveries relative to voyages and maritime affairs" and the Society moved that their thanks "be returned to his Excellency for this valuable and entertaining communication."

Purporting to be a letter written aboard the British packet, *Captain Truxton,* to one David Leroy of Paris, the good doctor whiled away a dull evening rehashing, among other things, the plan of Bernouilli for boat propulsion through water. Without making any reference to steam navigation, he described Bernouilli's boat, which had a tube "in the form of an L, with an upright funnel opening at the top, convenient for filling it with water, which, descending and passing through the lower horizontal part, and issuing from the middle of the stern of the boat, under the surface of the water, should push the boat forward." This, obviously, had its drawbacks, which Dr. Franklin proposed to remedy by adding another tube of the same shape, but with the horizontal end protruding from the bow. Both upright ends, which would meet in the middle of the boat, were to be joined together and fixed with a pump worked by a handle which would draw the water in from the bow and carry it through the pipe to the pump, which was then to force it out through the second tube to the stern and thus gain the necessary power.

Coming from any one but the learned doctor, this nonsensical scheme would have evoked the amusement it deserved. But Franklin was the foremost man of science in America. Weighted by his name, his curious design stamped itself upon the fumbling minds of hopeful inventors. It impressed itself upon James Rumsey down in Maryland and it caused Arthur Donaldson of Philadelphia to bring the plan forward as his own. Donaldson was one of the contractors who had been given the job of cleaning out the Delaware after the Revolution, hauling up the junk, *chevaux-de-frise* which had been dumped there to prevent enemy ships from sailing into Philadelphia. Later, he had invented a dredging machine which he called the *Hippopotamus* and on his application to the Pennsylvania Assembly he had been given what amounted to a patent on the machine for several years. Now he promptly announced another invention—the steamboat. His drafts duplicated Franklin's plan, but he petitioned the Pennsylvania Assembly for the exclusive right to manufacture steamboats. Though the petition was not granted, it prevented the delegates from acting on Fitch's application and both were referred to a committee made up of George Clymer, the politician, Dr. David Rittenhouse, the scientist, General William Irvine and the two assemblymen, Grey and Whitehill.

But the most ludicrous result of Dr. Franklin's oddity out of Bernouilli was its effect on Fitch. To the struggling inventor the name of Franklin was the epitome of scientific achievement and he tried time after time to gain his support. He had called on him when he had begun to form his joint-stock company in the hope that Franklin would become one of the subscribers. When Franklin, refusing, had handed him "five or six dollars" as a mere charitable contribution, Fitch was so in awe of the Doctor that he realized only as an afterthought that he should have "treated the insult with the indignity it merited and stomped the poltry Ore under" his feet. And now, along with Rumsey and Donaldson, Fitch adopted the Bernouilli-Franklin contraption and was ready to abandon his own original plan of a revolving chain and paddles.

But by this time he had met Henry Voight.

The stubborn Dutchman determinedly "beat" Fitch "out of the Franklin design" and encouraged him to try the method he had first conceived. This meant that they must build a steam engine, beginning with the construction of a model.

The company had rented an old warehouse at the edge of the Delaware and here they took their fine assortment of tools. They set to work upon a miniature engine with a one-inch cylinder. All the parts were made by hand: the piston, the condenser, the boiler and the firebox. It was the first model of a steam engine either Fitch or Voight had ever seen. Exactly what it was like has never been determined. All Fitch's drawings and papers were deposited with the American Philosophical Society, from the archives of which they have long since disappeared. The engine he offered to sell the Society was rejected by the directors and his model and drawings filed in the United States Patent Office were destroyed by fire in 1836. But undoubtedly the engine was of a more effective design than any that had been built outside the Watt and Boulton ironworks in Soho.

The history of the steam engine is long. Like all major inventions it was produced by the collective mind of the race acting upon its environment, seeking easier ways to create the means of production. Through the pages of steamboat history runs a chain of names—von Guericke, who first suggested the vacuum engine; Desaugliers, who wrote general treatises on the use of steam; Papen, who worked on condensation of steam; Newcomen, who produced the highest type of atmospheric engine; Smeaton, who sought to produce a greater economy in the use of steam by changing the proportions of Newcomen's engine; Matthew Wasbrough, who first applied the crank to the steam engine as a means of gaining rotary motion; John Wilkinson, who invented an efficient cylinder-boring machine; James Watt, who conceived the idea of using a separate condenser and, with his partner Matthew Boulton, and their assistants, John Southern and John Murdock, carried the invention as far as the manufacturing method of his time could make use of it.

Among all those names only Watt's is popularly associated with the steam engine. The reason for this is that Watt obtained the basic patents for the construction of such engines. Under the patronage of Dr. John Roebuck, a wealthy industrialist, Watt was enabled to make a scientific study of the steam engine and to gain legal protection in the form of patents as early as 1769. These patents were extended by Act of Parliament in 1775 and for twenty-five years longer Watt, working with Boulton, who had acquired Roebuck's interests in the patents, had such a monopoly that, as Watt himself admitted, all further invention in England was killed off until 1800.

In addition to Watt's protective patents, which blocked the way of the British inventor, there were the restrictive laws of Great Britain which prohibited machinery from being shipped abroad. And yet when Fitch and Voight began to make an engine in Philadelphia they carried the invention to a line with Watt's achievement by designing a double-acting piston. This, "the idea of using steam to press alternately on the opposite sides of a piston, and thus to enable the engine to make a power stroke in both directions, was a great stride in the development of the steam engine" which Watt, after working fifteen years, had discovered in 1783, but did not make generally known until 1786. Yet in that same year, after completing their model at a cost of three Pounds, Pennsylvania currency, Fitch and Voight were "fully convinced" that "the steam engine might be worked *both ways* at once."

Their first model was successful in theory but disappointing in practice, for the cylinder was too small to develop sufficient force to overcome the friction. Fitch, with bleak determination, and Voight, with cheerful energy, began to make a new engine with a three-inch cylinder.

Meanwhile, they had ordered a small skiff to be made with Fitch's rowing apparatus attached. The skiff was completed before they had finished the engine. When it was delivered they were both anxious to try it. The paddles and chain looked cumbersome and weak. The question was, would the contraption drive the skiff through the water or not? Hopefully, they lowered the skiff into the Delaware and got inside. Taking hold of the shaft, Fitch started to operate the rowing apparatus by hand.

Lounging sailors and people passing along Front Street stared at the skiff with the strange protuberance on its side. A curious-eyed crowd gathered at the wharf. Fitch worked the shaft, uneasily at first, then in growing consternation. The skiff floated with the absurd helplessness of a wounded duck. Voight glanced at the crowd and flushed unhappily. Why had he ever got himself into such a business as this! He, a good, reputable clockmaker with a wife and a horde of children to provide for! It was a crazy invention. Those loafers on shore would never let him hear the end of it, but would make him the town's laughingstock the rest of his life.

In bitter humiliation, Fitch took up the oars. The crowd, particularly the boatmen, "scoffed and sneered" as he rowed back toward the wharf. To the Yankee inventor this was hardly a novelty. He had been sneered at by all classes of people for his efforts to lead a rational life. But Voight's "spirits seemed to be much depressed" and this disturbed him more than the ridicule.

They landed. Voight "stole off" through the crowd as quickly as possible and disappeared. In the face of the delighted skeptics, Fitch heavily took care of the skiff and locked up the machinery.

Though Fitch "esteemed" himself "to be more cool and dispassionate than Voight," he now "felt cruilly Distressed." He had worked for more than a year with nothing but the thought of his invention in his mind. He had badgered rival claimants and had pleaded before a host of scientists and politicians. He had neglected his Kentucky lands, which were being overrun by squatters. Instead of earning money from the sale of his map, he had given it barely enough attention to keep himself from going hungry and ragged. And all these sacrifices had been to no better purpose than to make him the enormous, gangling butt of hostile jeers along the waterfront.

Shambling back toward Jacob Scheuffel's boarding house, he stopped in at a grog shop and made himself "pretty free with West India produce." He lurched out with a bottle of rum past the respectable darkened houses and boxed street lamps to his cheap lodgings and drank himself to sleep.

Next morning he woke early as usual, but he was too humiliated by his groggy condition and his sense of failure to leave his room. He lay wondering how he "could get clear of the scheme with honor." Nearly sixty Pounds of the Company's money had been spent and there was nothing to show for it but the model steam engine. Every step in the bare hall outside his door made him fear that Voight had come to upbraid him for imposing on him with his presumptuous scheme and his mind sought everywhere, to even the scantiest rathole through which he could crawl from under the toppled structure of his plans.

Night came and he sat in cold desperation. He got back into bed, but lay staring up at the ceiling, his eyes wide open and dry. Every effort he made to escape drove his thoughts to the steamboat again. There was no release from the maddening circle until "at about 12 oClock the Idea struck" him "of Cranks and Paddles." Considering this, he grew cool and sober and could almost visualize the effect the new apparatus would have on the boat.

Out in the warm, silent street the watchman of the night patrol cried, "One o'clock!"

Fitch sat up abruptly. Cranks and paddles! It was "a thing of such importance that" he "ought not to risk a single hour of" his "life, for fear it might be lost to the World." Swinging his long, rheumatic legs to the floor, he shuffled through the darkness toward his worktable and felt about for the candle. He made a draft with his quill and became "still more delighted with it," for the drawing "Brightened" his "Ideas of the Scheme." He sat an hour in contemplation of this new contrivance, feeling "as ellivated" as he had been "depressed before." When he went back to bed he was smiling and he lay sleepless, impatiently waiting for dawn.

Daylight was as welcome as if he had been in "the most distressed storm at sea." Fitch jerked off his nightcap. In his old breeches, stockings and striped coattee, he tiptoed downstairs into the quiet street. Around the corner on Second Street, between Race and Vine, he stopped before a house with a clockmaker's sign and called in a low, exultant voice, "Harry!"

Voight came tumbling down from his bed. He had spent the day in anxious avoidance of Fitch, but if his friend called him out of bed at this hour it must mean that he had good news. As he opened the door Fitch burst in and "acquainted him of" their "relieff."

The skiff was launched again toward the end of July, 1786. Voight bent over and began feeding wood into the firebox, while Fitch grasped the tiller. As soon as they had got up steam the piston began to churn, the axletree to rattle and the oars on the side to cleave the water with strong, regular strokes. The skiff chugged bravely up against the current of the Delaware.

In Fitch's first draft of the rowing apparatus the lower arms of the paddles were attached to cranks and the upper arms ran "thro holes in a fraim above" to keep them in place. When the boat was in motion the sound of the wooden handles knocking against the holes through the frame made a frenzied rattling, which Fitch admitted was a "Very disagreeable Nois." It also caused considerable friction. But Fitch soon remedied this in a "very Simple manner, Viz, with Armes acting on gudgeons as we now use them, which took off both the friction and Nois."

In his enthusiasm Fitch prepared a description of the invention for the *Columbian Magazine*. It would be good advertising and it would make Dr. Franklin, with his dissertation on a pumping boat, look foolishly far behind the times. Rewritten and garbled in its first account by the editors, the *Columbian* later printed a corrected version:

"The steam engine is to be similar to the late improved steam engines in Europe. The cylinder is to be horizontal, and the steam to work with equal force at each end thereof. The mode of forming a vacuum is believed to be entirely new; also of letting water into it, and of letting it off against the atmosphere without any friction. The undertakers are also of opinion that their engine will work with an equal force to those late improved engines, it being a twelve-inch cylinder. They expect it will move with a clear force, after deducting friction, of between eleven and twelve hundred pounds weight; which force is to be applied to the turning of the axle tree on a wheel, of 18 inches diameter. The piston is to move about three feet, and each vibration of the piston turns the axle tree about two thirds round. They propose to make the piston to strike thirty strokes in a minute; which will give the axle tree about forty revolutions. Each revolution of the axle tree moves twelve oars five and a half feet. As six oars come out of the water, six more enter the water; which makes a stroke of about eleven feet each revolution. The oars work perpendicularly, and make a stroke similar to the paddle of canoe. The cranks of the axle tree act upon the oar about one third of their length from their lower end; on which part of the oar the whole force of the axle tree is applied. The engine is placed in about two thirds of the boat, and both the action and reaction of the piston operate to turn the axle tree the same way."

This description, though later carried into effect, was then no more than a prospectus. Fitch and Voight had tried the engine with the three-inch cylinder and it had worked successfully. The principle was established on the skiff and, with a larger boat and larger engine, they were certain of sufficient power.

But Fitch and Voight had to do more than invent the steamboat; they had to make it profitable to the stockholders.

Fitch realized from the beginning that the Delaware was unfavorable as a river on which to carry out his experiments. Short, broad and deep-channeled, it was navigable to deep sea vessels and sailing packets. Along its banks, particularly on the New Jersey side, lay a number of populous towns. They had been settled for many years and were connected by roads which were the most passable in the country. Along the New Jersey shore opposite Philadelphia, from Camden up to Burlington and from Burlington through Bordentown and Trenton, a rapid stage service had developed. The stages carried freight and passengers and made the entire journey in five hours, including the numerous stops along the road. The usual stage was a light spring wagon with four benches holding twelve passengers. Relay stages traveled as much as ninety-six miles a day and "the frequency of these carriages, the facility of finding places in them and the low and fixed price" positively "invite[d] Americans to travel."

Excepting the route from his native Windsor to New Haven, Fitch could not have met with such competition anywhere else in the United States. There was no road that ran conveniently along the Potomac and there was no brisk stage service along the rocky-shored Hudson. Circumstances over which he had no control had determined that he make his experiments on the Delaware or, very likely, carry his invention stillborn to his grave. For the Ohio-Mississippi route, which was perpetually in his mind, had been barred by the treaty with Spain. Philadelphia was the only city in which he knew men who had sufficient money and scientific interest to support the undertaking.

But even these men wanted to be assured that the invention would be profitable. At the stockholders' meeting the day after the successful experiment with the skiff boat, the questions were, How big a boat would Fitch have to build to pay dividends? Would it go fast enough to compete with the ten-shilling-to-Trenton stages on the Delaware? And, above all, how much would it cost?

From his trial with the three-inch cylinder Fitch believed that one of twelve inches diameter would drive a boat of "20 Tons Burthen 10 Miles per Hour, if not 12 or 14—I will say fourteen in Theory and Ten in practice."

The stockholders were pleased with themselves because the skiff had breasted the Delaware. They interestedly examined the ingenious contrivances: the heavy firebox and separate boiler, the single tube condenser fixed between the cylinder and air pump. Certainly, Richard Wells maintained, a full-sized boat should be made; and they gladly voted two extra shares to be given Henry Voight for his share in the work.

But the treasury was nearly empty. The stockholders shied at the prospect of a new levy. Fitch pleaded earnestly that he and

Voight could make a boat which would be profitable to all of them. He begged his friends and harangued his acquaintances to vote the necessary money, but the meeting ended and the directors had made no plans to replenish the treasury.

Other meetings were called, but fewer members attended. An engine with a twelve-inch cylinder and a boat that would carry twenty tons might cost a thousand pounds or more. Fitch appealed to them individually, beginning with Stacy Potts. And Potts answered from Trenton that while it afforded him "great satisfaction to find that the invention of the Steam-Boat is likely, now, to be applied to useful and valuable purposes, to the benefit and advantage of mankind in general, and the emolument and aggrandizement of the Proprietors in particular," nevertheless he felt that since he lived so far away from the other stockholders he had better drop out. Yet he hoped "that if the company should hereafter conclude to divide the care of the different departments of the plan, when extended to its greatest expanded usefulness, some part thereof may perhaps come with propriety within the compass of my convenient attention, when I should be glad to be considered, one of its friends and promoters." In other words, Potts was willing to rejoin the company when it was earning dividends, but until then Fitch could expect nothing more from him.

Unable to raise money in any other way, Fitch tried to sell the model. He wrote to Dr. Franklin as head of the American Philosophical Society, "Sir—In a conference that I had the honor of with your Excellency, I heard you mention that the Philosophical Society ought to be furnished with a Model of a Steam Engine, and having completed one on a small scale, would be exceedingly happy should it meet your Patronage, so far as to recommend the purchase of it, to the said learned Society, of whome Honoured Sir, you are President.... This Engine which we would wish to dispose of, cost us about One Hundred Dollars, but notwithstanding, whatever may be offered by the Society, will be thankfully accepted of...."

Days passed. Fitch's chagrin was deepened by the fact that no answer from Dr. Franklin came and that no action was taken by the learned society of lofty philosophers.

But he would not give up. He had been maligned and sneered at ever since he became a grown man; the steamboat was to become the one great justification of his existence. Undiscouraged, he sent a vehemently persuasive plea to the Pennsylvania Assembly. It had recently subsidized Whitehead Humphreys' steel furnace; if it had lent Humphreys three hundred pounds, couldn't it lend the Steam Boat Company one hundred and fifty pounds?

"Since the steamboat scheme is approved by all men of science who have examined it, and there has never been one, even of my most bitter enemies, that has ever attempted to point out how it will miscarry— Then I query whether the Assembly of Pennsylvania could not with great propriety take notice of the scheme, so as to give it proper incouragement? On the other hand, provided they should not, what could be said of us in other Countries? Would they not say that there was a poor fellow in America that proposed a plan that would inrich America at least three times as much as all that country N. W. of the Ohio, as it would make that country four times as valuable, beside the inconceivable advantages to the settled portion of the Continent —and this he demonstrated as clear as one of Euclid's problems; and not only that, but assertained it in miniature, so as it could not admit of a doubt—and notwithstanding he applied to Congress, and to each of the Middle states, they would not give him a single souse to exicute his plan, because that they thought he could do it by beging, and save them the expence. May heaven forbid that such a stigma should be placed to the acct of the Country that gave me birth!

"Permit me, Gentlemen, to inform you of the prospects we

have before us. Mr. Voight and myselfe are sure that we can build an Engine; nay, we are vain enough to believe that we can make one as good as they can in Europe.

"We know that an equal force applied to the turning an axil tree will row a boat faster than the same force applied to an Oar. These, Gentlemen, are indisputable facts, and have been assertained in miniture. Could I by any means raise sufficient money, I would not ask it from the Legislature; but there is such a strange infatuation in mankind, they would rather lay out their money in Beloons and Fireworks, and be a pest to Society, than to lay it out in something that would be of use to themselves and Country.... Pardon me for mentioning it, but on the other hand, provided the House should lend me one hundred and fifty Pounds, what reflections or discredit could the House suffer by it? Could anyone say that the House threw away one hundred and fifty Pounds on the whim of a mad projector? No! Because it is supported in this opinion of upwards of forty principal Characters in the Middle States, and on that which will be of public utility...."

Referred to Clymer, Rittenhouse, Whitehill, Irvine and Grey —the same committee which was considering Fitch's early petition for an exclusive right to manufacture steamboats—this application was favorably reported on and it was "Resolved, that a Committee be appointed to bring in a Bill to authorize the Supream Executive Council to direct payment of Mr. John Fitch's drafts, to any amount, not exceeding in the sum of one hundred and fifty Pounds, on proof made to them that the money so drawn for, has been applied to the purpose of compleating his Steam Boat—they taking his security for repayment thereof, in twelve months."

This was the closest Fitch ever came to receiving aid from either state or federal legislatures. When the Assembly met the report of the committee was voted down, thirty-two to twenty-eight.

What fools they were! Nay, he had a boat that would not only make the "Mississippi as Navigable as Tide Water, but would convert our vast territory on those waters into an inconceivable fund in the Treasury of the United States." He had a boat that would take the place of stages, packets and even armed vessels, a boat that would always be able to veer off a lee shore, make a quick, safe voyage and overtake, far out at sea, "any of the Pirattical cruzers on the Coast of Barbary, so as to give them proper chastizement!"

XI

Months after the trial of the skiff boat had proved his invention's ultimate success, Fitch was as humble before the stockholders as if he and Harry Voight had produced a failure. When meetings were called fewer and fewer members attended. Richard Wells, Benjamin Say and the others who came sat and looked at the engine in testy perplexity. Three hundred dollars had been put into the experiment, but it was worth so little that the American Philosophical Society would not accept the model even at their own price.

Fitch looked guiltily at the stockholders. He still had their interest, but he felt that if he badgered any of the faithful few for additional funds they would drop away like the others. "If levies had been made" at any of the meetings, the stockholders "would have esteemed the money as taken by" Fitch "and would much prefer a common beggar to come to their door than" himself. "All the hardships" he "had ever experienced," his apprenticeship to the Cheneys, his capture on the Ohio and his seasick voyage from Prison Island to New York, "were nothing to the distress of feelings in raising money from" his "best friends. Could money have been extracted from my limbs, amputation would have often taken place, provided the disjointed parts could have been readily joined, rather than to make the demands which I have."

He had one hope left. New Jersey had granted him the exclusive right to manufacture and operate steamboats on its waters for fourteen years. If the assemblies of other river states gave him similar privileges he would possess a monopoly like that held by Boulton and Watt on the steam engine in England. Members of the company would appreciate the value of this; safe from the fear of competition, they would be likelier to contribute more money toward the development of the invention.

Before starting out on his campaign, Fitch again petitioned the Pennsylvania Assembly for protection and in the middle of November, 1786, a bill was brought in "giving to John Fitch, his heirs and assigns, the exclusive right to all boats propelled by fire or steam." At this point Arthur Donaldson reappeared for the last time in Fitch's path by petitioning that the inventor "should be restrained to steam navigation as he is now attempting it."

To this Fitch replied tartly that he demanded a basic patent. "The propelling of a boat with steam is as new as the rowing of a boat with angels; and I claim the first thought and invention of it. It is the *force* and *power* that I contend for. Is it reasonable to suppose that a man in my station of life would throw away two years of the prime of his days, and encounter the difficulties that I saw before me, when I knew at the time I ought to exert every faculty to keep myself from the jaws of want?"

With a bundle of maps to pay his way he went down to the capital of Delaware and on February 3, 1787, gained his first victory of the new year. For the assembly at Dover passed "an act, for granting and securing to John Fitch, the sole right and advantage of making and employing the steam-Boat, by him lately invented" for a period of fourteen years.

From Dover he went confidently to New York where he presented his petition on February 24. It was referred to a committee of three of which Alexander Hamilton was chairman. That small martinet, son-in-law of the rich General Schuyler and friend of the Philadelphia manufacturer, Tench Coxe, was not blind to the fortunes lying in wait for the owners of machinery and was an eager champion of monopoly. Three days after Fitch arrived, Hamilton's committee brought in a favorable report and on March 19 New York followed Delaware in passing an act which gave Fitch exclusive rights to manufacture and operate all boats propelled by fire or steam within their jurisdiction. And on March 28 the Pennsylvania Assembly, dismissing Donaldson's complaint, gave Fitch "the sole and exclusive right and privilege of constructing, making, using, employing and navigating all and every species or kind of boats, or water craft, which may be urged or impelled through the water by the force of fire, or steam in all creeks, rivers, bays and waters whatsoever, within the territory and jurisdiction of this state, for and during the full end and term of Fourteen Years, from and after the present session of the Legislature." And the penalty for any infringement was confiscation of the rival vessel and a fine of one hundred pounds.

With these patents, which were so sweepingly basic as to make any future inventor despair or await the coming of 1801, the Steamboat Company began to revive. Joseph Budd, the hatter, Israel Israel, the tavern keeper, Henry Toland, the grocer and old Dr. Say, the cynical, pythagorean philosopher, reappeared at the meetings. When the example was set by Richard Wells and Dr. Say the others were willing to pay for the construction of a full-sized boat.

Describing their work as "An Indenture for Reciprocal Advantages," the stockholders drew up a paper under which the Company was reorganized. There were to be five directors and a treasurer. No member, no matter how many shares he might obtain, was to have more than three votes. Meetings and elections were to be held periodically. The inventor was to have no greater authority than any other member. Inasmuch as Henry Voight had helped to build the skiff and was expected to assist on the new boat, five shares were to be given him from those originally granted to Fitch. The company was not to be capitalized, but the expenses would be defrayed by the members according to the number of shares each held.

Brooke and Wilson, the ironmongers and shipbuilders, were engaged to make the boat. It was to be forty-five feet from stem to stern, with a forty-foot keel, an eleven-foot beam and a draught of three feet, eight inches. The cost was to be fifty dollars, including a coating of "stuff."

Meanwhile, Fitch and Voight worked on the machinery, trying to realize the bright prospectus Fitch had published in the *Columbian Magazine*. At every turn the stockholders would insist that the engine must be made as cheaply as possible. Their tools, though adequate to make a model, became no more than toys when confronted with the greater task of producing an engine for a forty-five foot boat of twenty tons capacity. They needed a forge and a foundry; they needed a machine to bore cylinders like the one John Wilkinson had invented in England. Instead, their workshop was an old warehouse. The parts they could not make themselves had to be entrusted to one or another of the workmen of the town who had scarcely heard of a steam engine.

Brooke and Wilson delivered the boat in April. It lay like a small, flat-decked barge beside the wharf where it excited little comment until Fitch and Voight began to build the furnace on the deck, when passing townsmen and sailors along the waterfront stopped to jeer and pester them. For what could have been more ridiculous than a pile of thirteen hundred bricks, weighing seven thousand pounds, mortared together on top of a boat?

In spite of the most careful economy the cost of the engine continued to rise. By April 1 the Company had received bills of more than four hundred Pounds. The stockholders whistled and looked grave. When would the engine be finished? Why wasn't it finished now? What more did Fitch and Voight have to do on it?

There was a score of difficulties. For the sake of cheapness they had made the cylinder caps of wood. But even the strongest wood, shaped by the most expert whittler, was of little use in confining several pounds of steam. The old-fashioned horizontal cylinder was no good, either; which meant that the machinery had to be torn down in order to replace it with a perpendicular cylinder. Then the condenser was unsuitable. Voight irritably jerked it out and threw it away. Fitch watched him nervously while he set to work on a different principle to make what he called a "pipe condenser," a round, straight piece of metal without joint or elbow that connected the tubes running from the air pump to the cylinder. But no sooner was this completed and found to work than the steam valves choked. Again Voight came to the engine's aid; he invented a double cock "through which the steam could pass to the cylinder, and when it had done the work of moving the piston, to repass said cock to the condenser."

Meanwhile, those of the stockholders with a scientific flair amused themselves in seeking other uses to which the engine might be put. If it possessed so much force, why couldn't it be used to throw projectiles in place of gunpowder? Why couldn't a weapon of warfare be made out of it? Richard Wells and Richard Stockton made a special kind of gun and on April 18, "with about 12 ounces of water, 30 musket balls were shot successively with force sufficient to mark deeply a pine board at five yards distance." Later experiments showed them that "in two minutes 24 balls could be thrown," and that a regular machine gun could be developed, A few days afterward, with more steam, George Turner shot a hole through a pine board at a distance of twenty feet.

May came and the engine was still unfinished. More money was needed and the stockholders were growing alarmed. Fitch recollected that Thomas Hutchins had not yet paid for his shares and he wrote to him pleadingly. But Hutchins answered that he was growing poorer every day, that the money Congress owed him had not been paid and therefore he was unable to pay his share of the Company's expense. Fearful of all the bills that were being brought to the treasury, Fitch sold four of his shares and for a while paid the bills himself. The money also helped him to settle his account with Peggy Patterson, who had colored his maps, and to pay what he owed at his boarding house.

By the middle of June the engine was in readiness. Boat, rowing apparatus, furnace, boiler and cylinder had been completed at a total cost of five hundred and thirty Pounds, Pennsylvania currency. There it stood, ready for trial, to the intense derision of the greater part of Philadelphia. Fitch and Voight waited in sharp expectancy. For the John Fitch Steamboat was to have a gala showing, a more important audience than had been assembled in Philadelphia since the signing of the Declaration of Independence.

For eleven years the American states had lived independently of the laws by which England had bound their commercial development. They had won their battle for self-determination. But what were they do with the victory?

In spite of the Revolution the country's economic system remained the same. Large plantations worked by Negroes for white owners sprawled through the south, shouldering the small farmers into the mountains. Fishing fleets manned by white men for white owners tacked along the New England coast. Little farms and big farms patched the inland plains of Connecticut and Massachusetts. Great tracts still grasped by the descendants of Dutch Patroons kept the land along the Hudson in feudal bondage. The coal and iron of the middle states had yet to be mined. In the seaports wealthy shipowners depended on carrying the country's produce to England, France, Spain, the West Indies and beyond the Barbary Coast.

Even then the small farmer, woodsman, miner and mechanic was unable to buy back the equivalent of what he had produced. It was noted as a chronic situation as early as 1750 that "in plentiful years the Product so far exceeds the Consumption as to overstock all the Markets far and near." Trade with Europe was indispensable. "If we hear of a Market, if we can come at it by land, we run, ride and drive, till we have overstocked it; by

Sea, we are all afloat, sailing till Provisions may be purchased cheaper there abroad than at home."

But Europe, with England in the lead, was also driving for world trade. Every country with a possible hope was fighting to export more goods than it imported and thus acquire capital. This was the aim of America as it was of France, England and Spain. Kept by the profit system from the people who had produced it, the wealth of the world was beginning to pile up and the rulers of nations fought and bargained for the privilege of extending their trade, of selling to another country what was needed in their own.

As a dozen small states on the far side of the Atlantic, America not only lacked bargaining power, it stifled its foreign trade in a mass of contradictions. A treaty that opened a market for Virginia tobacco was likely to bar Pennsylvania pork, Georgia rice, South Carolina indigo or New England whale oil. A foreign commercial arrangement of equal benefit to all sections was impossible.

Internal trade was also hampered by economic differences between the states. The old Continental currency which Congress had issued during the war had dropped in value to a few cents on the dollar. The states were printing their own money and there was no stable, uniform medium of exchange. There was inflation in Rhode Island, deflation in Massachusetts, a tight group of determined creditors and a great host of impoverished debtors everywhere.

Apart from the fact of contiguous boundaries, all the states had one bond in common. They all had rich and poor. Virginia had the Carters, the Byrds, the Washingtons, the Lees and slavery. Massachusetts had the Otises, the Cabots, the Derbys and thousands of poor farmers with mortgaged lands. New York had the Schuylers, the Clintons, the Livingstons, the Duanes, impoverished farmers and city slums. Pennsylvania had the Binghams, the Morrises, the Willings, city slums and a ragged frontier.

In the spring of 1783 General Washington had persuaded the enlisted men of the army to go home without being paid for their services during the last two years of the war, but gave all the officers five years' full pay. The soldiers disbanded, but not without showing their grievance. Many of them could look back on seven years of the most gloomy hardship, of perpetual hunger and raggedness. They had been so poorly fed and clothed that in January, 1780, the Pennsylvania Line, the hardest fighting regiments in the Continental service, had revolted, killed a captain and several other officers who tried to stop them and marched on Congress where they paraded their indignation, with such a united air that Congress granted their demands. After a forty-five-day furlough most of them had reënlisted and had later fought at Yorktown. But when the war was over and they were cut loose from the army with nothing in their pockets but their discharge papers they grew indignant again. Army contractors like the highly respectable Otis of Boston had sat at home in comfort, earning a hundred per cent profit from every deal in the war, while they had been out in the fields marching, drilling, fighting, spending years without a roof over their heads or a floor under their feet. And another march of rebellious veterans was begun on Congress.

Congress was frightened. It fled to Princeton like a scattering of old women. Afraid to call out the militia, who were sympathetic to the march, Congress appealed to General Washington for Continental troops. Anthony Wayne and his Pennsylvania regiments, which had been campaigning in the South, were then approaching Philadelphia, but it was the opinion of the generals who remained in the capital that as Wayne's troops were returning from active service, hungry, worn and ragged, they might join in with the clamorous veterans instead of accepting orders to put them down. Wayne was sent home around by Lancaster and General Washington ordered a thousand men from headquarters, choosing those who had suffered least hardships, to drive the back-pay marchers out of Philadelphia.

Three years later another soldier led a rebellion. This time it was directed against the courts, through which the rich note-holders were squeezing poor mechanics and small farmers. After a period of inflation which enabled the wealthier citizens to acquire still more wealth, came sudden deflation and money was so scarce that people went back to barter for a living. Debts which had been contracted at forty cents on the dollar were ordered to be repaid at full face value. Added to this tricky juggling of the currency were the poll tax which the poor man had to pay for the right to vote, the increase of taxes and the government's tightening hold on money.

The masses of people in Massachusetts put up with falling prices, severe unemployment and scarcity of currency while the legislature put through several sham reforms. When these accomplished nothing, the farmers, mechanics, small shopkeepers and mechanics called on their "fellow-sufferers to resent unto relentless blood." Led by Daniel Shays, a former army captain who had stormed Stony Point with Anthony Wayne and had fought in the people's army at Bunker Hill, about one-fifth of the population began to march.

General Washington stammered "such a formidable rebellion . . . I hardly know how to realize it." Elephantine old Henry Knox, the Secretary of War, hurried up to the scene. Major General Benjamin Lincoln, who had meekly surrendered his sword to the British in Charleston, thundered to the troubled ground with an imposing force where he killed two rebels and took eighty-four prisoners. Other forces, sent against these men who were fighting for a chance to live, fired into the ground.

The Governor of Massachusetts appealed to Congress. He wanted sixty fieldpieces to shoot down the insurgents. It was a desperate moment. The sacredness of private property was being questioned by bloody men. But just as the New England delegates had voted against Virginia's motion to send two companies of United States infantry to protect the settlers on the Ohio against the Indians, so now the Southern delegates voted against the use of United States artillery to put down "Shays' Rebellion."

And when affairs had brought the country to such a condition that the men of property of one state would not vote to protect the men of property of another state it was time to form a strong, central government.

The convention had been arranged in 1786 by Washington, Hamilton and Madison, at Annapolis where delegates from five states had met to bargain over internal boundaries and trade relations. Hamilton had proposed another meeting to be attended by delegates from all the states to form a constitution under which the wealthy men from every section would willingly coöperate. The delegates had agreed to this and Congress had sent out invitations to a convention at Independence Hall, Philadelphia for May 14, 1787.

Fifty-five delegates, representing all the country except Rhode Island and the disputed territory of Vermont, sat in the stiff, low-backed benches of Independence Hall. They were well arrayed in satin breeches and brightly colored coats with laced stocks ruffling their breasts above their fancy waistcoats. They wore silver buckles and powdered hair and most of them lodged at the Indian Queen tavern where there was a host of liveried flunkeys. In the whole hall there was not a pair of linen overalls or a linsey-woolsey coat or a scent of bear-grease plastered hair or a coonskin cap to jar their sense of propriety. And their dress reflected the content of the document Hamilton, Madison and John Jay had worked over since the last meeting and which was about to be adopted as the Constitution of the United States.

It is true that Hamilton was dissatisfied with the provisions of government, for it was his belief that the Chief Executive should be elected for life and be given greater power than the King of England or Louis Fourteenth. Still, the document provided for federal taxation, tariffs and other subsidies to the mercantile and manufacturing interests, the right to declare war, the establishment of a Supreme Court whose members should be chosen for life, the Presidential veto, the saddling of taxpayers with a huge public debt and the impossibility of the voters to recall more than a third of their representatives in a time of crisis. Wherever the document recognized the governed class specifically, it bound the farmers, mechanics, apprentices and indentured servants still tighter. Slaves, apprentices or indentured servants "held to service or labor in one State" and escaping into another were to "be delivered up on claim of the party to whom such service or labor may be due." In case of mass protests against any laws Congress had the right to order out the militia to "suppress insurrection." And within ten years all of these efforts to chain the people were to result in higher taxation than had been levied under the King, the enrichment of speculators in public funds, armed attack on farmers protesting against high Federal taxes; and gifts, paid with these same farmers' money, to infant industries such as Tench Coxe's "Society for Manufactures."

From their deliberations at Independence Hall, or from their lodgings at the Indian Queen, or the Bunch of Grapes, most of the delegates strolled down to the Front Street wharves to see the strange invention which "walked the waters like a thing of life." And several of the Constitutional delegates allowed themselves to be cajoled aboard the ungainly monster.

Though the machinery of the steamboat was still imperfect, it bucked the current of the Delaware at a rate of two and a half miles an hour. Governor Edmund Randolph and most of the Virginia delegation were "pleased to give it every countinence they could." Oliver Ellsworth of Windsor came down to see the boat and his native pride was mildly stirred when he learned that it had been invented "by Mr. Fitch, of Windsor, in Connecticut." Dr. Samuel Johnson, later President of Columbia, also appeared greatly interested and impressed. After an experimental journey around to Gray's Ferry in the Schuylkill, he went back to his tavern and forwarded Fitch a polite note by his servant:

"Dr. Johnson presents his compliments to Mr. Fitch and assures him that the exhibition yesterday gave the gentlemen present much satisfaction. He himself, and he doubts not, the other gentlemen, will always be happy to give him every countenance and encouragement in their power which his ingenuity and industry entitles him to."

Rembrandt Peale, who had hoped that some of the distinguished gentlemen at the convention might want their portraits painted, reported that "hearing there was something curious to be seen at the floating bridge on the Schuylkill at Market Street, I eagerly ran to the spot, where I found a few persons collected, all eagerly gazing at a shallop at anchor below the bridge, with about twenty persons on board. On the deck was a small furnace, and machinery connected with coupling crank projecting over the stern to give motion to three or four paddles, resembling snow shovels, which hung into the water. When all was ready and the power of steam was made to act, by means of which I was then ignorant, knowing nothing of the piston except in the common pump, the paddles began to work, pressing against the water backward as they rose, and the boat to my great delight moved against the tide, without wind or hand..."

But there was always something wrong. On that journey the rudder proved itself too long for quick maneuvering and the boat "ran aground at an angle in the river."

Until cold weather Fitch and Voight gave exhibition runs up and down the Delaware and into the Schuylkill. It was puzzling that General Washington had kept away from the scene of his experiments. A testimonial from the future President would have been of great assistance, but Fitch generously ascribed Washington's absence to a "too great delicacy of his own honour," which was working into an absurdity because he had given James Rumsey a certificate for his pole-boat. Another absentee was Dr. Franklin who, in spite of his interest in scientific experiments, would never give Fitch a written opinion on the steamboat or come aboard. It was curious. Fitch could not understand it.

Dr. Rittenhouse and Dr. Ewing were less hesitant. They cheerfully certified that they had "frequently seen Mr. Fitch's steamboat, which with great labour and perseverance he has at length completed," and had been "on board when the boat was worked against both wind and tide, with a considerable degree of velocity, by the force of steam only."

Fitch collected many such testimonials that summer and fall, but no money. His experiment had made the development of steamboats inevitable; and as if to clinch the matter, chance had placed the man who was to resurrect the invention and acquire all the credit within a few yards of where Fitch's boat lay at anchor. The man's name was Robert Fulton and he was listed in the Philadelphia directory as a miniature painter living that year at Second and Walnut Streets.

But each new trial showed Fitch the tremendous work ahead before the steamboat could compete with stage and packet. Another boat would have to be made and equipped with more powerful machinery. The twelve-inch cylinder was too small to create sufficient pressure; two miles and a half an hour was not enough. And that absurd weight of brick and mortar around the furnace; he had already discovered he could do away with this by placing the furnace directly under the boiler.

Late in the fall, when Philadelphia was quiet again, Fitch laid his proposals before the stockholders. When he said a new boat would have to be built most of them looked pained and clapped their hands over their pockets. Confronted "with almost the whole expence of another engine, the scheme became in a very Tottering situation," even though Fitch and Voight promised the stockholders they would build a boat that would go to Trenton in five hours. The old boiler had spouted water in a torrent and Voight promised to build a new one on a different principle. And Fitch had a scheme for using rollers to remove the friction from the oars. The stockholders were still reluctant and Fitch, in a frenzy of anxiety, burst out:

"But why these earnest solicitations to disturb my nightly repose and fill me with the most excruciating anxiety? And why not act the part for myself, and retire under the shady Elms on the fair banks of the Ohio, and eat my cours but sweet bread of industry and content, and when I have done, to have my body laid in the soft, warm and loomy soil of the Banks, with my name inscribed on a neighbouring Poplar, that future generations when traversing the mighty Waters of the West, *in the manner that I have pointed out,* may find my grassy turf and spread their cupboard on it, and circle round their chearful Knogins of Whisky, with three times three, till they should suppose a son of misfortune could never occupy the place."

Richard Wells and Dr. Say, who had continued to support him, prevailed on the other members to stand an equal share of the cost of the new enterprise and began by paying Fitch's expenses to Warwick Furnace in New Jersey with plans for an eighteen-inch cylinder to be cast.

But the Company was not to escape difficulties by sending Fitch across to New Jersey. There was no foundry in America equipped to make a satisfactory cylinder. The piece cast at Warwick Furnace was so weak that the inventors had to choose between rejecting it and reënforcing it with copper; and while they were trying to decide which to do the proprietors of the furnace became discouraged with their own product and smashed it up for pig iron.

Fitch had returned to Philadelphia when he learned of this. Instead of giving the order to another foundry he and the directors decided to try the old cylinder on a narrower boat. Their present craft with its twelve-foot beam presented too broad a surface to the current. Brooke and Wilson began to build an eight-foot boat, with the paddles at the stern instead of at the sides. Also, the furnace would be seven thousand pounds lighter. With these improvements they expected to increase their speed without extra power.

Months passed before the Delaware thawed, flooded with spring freshets and ebbed again into a steady, quiet river on which a temperamental steamboat could be tried. Fitch waited anxiously through a lean winter and spring. He had given up trying to sell his maps and was gradually becoming destitute. There was nothing to be got out of the thousands of acres he had surveyed in Kentucky and the Northwest, not even a clear title. He had to be contented with his determined faith in his invention and the long, disputatious evenings with Harry Voight.

Both Fitch and Voight were Deists, that is, they were unwilling to declare themselves atheists, but had found no religion to satisfy their inquiring miinds. When it came to the worst, when the ignorant townsmen's jeers followed Fitch to his boarding house, when the boarding house keeper looked on him with suspicion and the stockholders regarded him as a thieving impostor, Fitch and Voight would sneak off along Second Street between Race and Vine to the Sign of the Buck. There, with an occasional noggin of whisky or rum, they would try to straighten the maze in their minds and square religious precepts with their day-to-day existence. It went without saying that they "denied Jesus Christ," but, Fitch could never get it properly answered, were "there any punishments or rewards after this life?" And does it make a man happier or more miserable to believe in an after-life? Or Voight, being warm blooded and a scientific materialist, would shock his hearers by demanding "are not men and animals composed of the same kind of matter?" And sometimes Fitch, his dark face growing long and dour, would ask, almost in a way that robbed the words of any question, "Can suicide be a Noble act in any case whatsoever?"

But when spring came they set to work again. The new boat was made and fitted according to the new specifications and it was a slimmer, fleeter-looking craft. Instead of the old furnace there was a small firebox directly under the boiler. The rollers Voight had invented reduced the noise and friction of the paddles. The new pipe condenser made the cylinder more efficient and the paddles at the stern promised greater driving power. Early in July, 1788, they believed they had solved the last of their minor difficulties and at the first stockholders' meeting that month it was decided the steamboat was ready for a public trial —with Burlington, which was halfway to Trenton, as their modest goal.

When this proposed journey became known, everybody from the jeering sailors on the ships at anchor in the Delaware to the skeptical residents of Frankford County, of Dunk's Ferry and Burlington prepared for the day in the hope that the performance would deserve their loud, derisive yells. Even among the stockholders only Richard Wells and Dr. Say had heart to risk the ridicule of the voyage and when they came on board it was with a certain grim defiance.

Fitch had piled half a cord of hickory on the deck by the firebox. He and Voight went seriously at the business of getting up steam. There was no such thing as a gauge or safety valve in all America, hence no way to know when the boiler was crowded. So far in their experiments the difficulty had been to get enough steam; probably neither of them imagined too much was possible.

Fitch grasped the rudder and Voight stood by the pile of hickory cordwood. The firebox crackled and steam began to form. As the pressure mounted the axletree shook and the oars dipped into the water, driving the boat upstream. Voight looked warily at his pipe condenser, but it was working well. At the stern the paddles splashed and seesawed rhythmically.

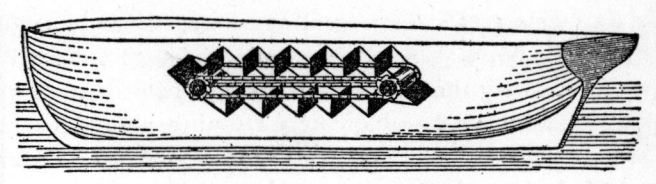

THE MODEL OF SEPT., 1785, WITH ENDLESS CHAIN AND FLOATS AND PADDLE-BOARDS.

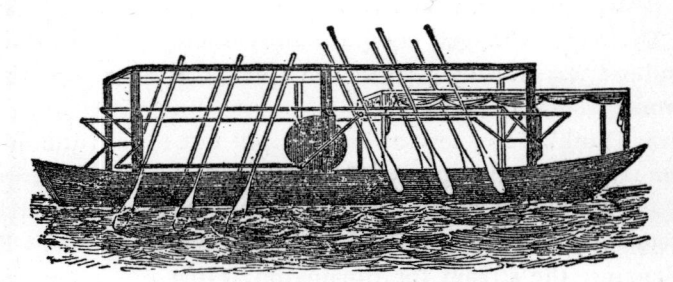

THE *Perseverance*, PHILADELPHIA, 1786-'87.

The Steamboat, PHILADELPHIA, 1788-'90.

The four men passed Point-no-Point where it seemed to Fitch that the whole population of Frankford and upper Philadelphia County stood along the banks. As the boat steamed past they saw a ripple of women's handkerchiefs running among the men's cocked hats. Cheers came faintly squeaking over the water and reached Fitch through the noise of the machinery. Voight opened the firebox and heaved in hickory sticks. He wiped his forehead and glanced at Fitch, who was beginning to exult. Richard Wells and Dr. Say exchanged congratulatory smiles, noting that the steamboat was moving against the current at about four miles an hour.

Near Dunk's Ferry several bateaux put out toward the middle of the river to be close as possible when the amazing contraption chugged past. And as at Point-no-Point women's handkerchiefs fluttered gayly as the boat moved steadily on, past Dunk's Ferry and against the stream for Burlington: Fitch was tense with a somber, wary pride. It had been three years since he had conceived the idea of a steamboat. He had given up everything, had endured insults and poverty to perfect it. Now, it seemed, he was coming into his own. A little above Dunk's Ferry another assemblage waited on the Delaware bank. They were from Bucks County, Fitch's adopted home. Suddenly gunpowder roared. One of Fitch's old friends had fired the cannon which had been left there since the night Washington surprised Colonel Rahl and his Hessians at Trenton that Christmas Eve of 1776.

Farther upstream on the green banks of Burlington a greater crowd waited. The town wharf was black with people. Voight opened the firebox and heaved in hickory. The steamboat churned steadily on.

They were opposite Burlington and making for the landing when the boiler hissed through an enveloping cloud of steam. Voight backed toward Fitch and they stood helplessly while the boat slowed, stood still, then began to drift backward with the current. Fitch threw over the anchor. On the wharf the waving hats and handkerchiefs of the welcoming committee drooped uncertainly.

A bateau rowed out to discover why the steamboat had stopped. Because they had wanted it! Dr. Say and Richard Wells snapped their chagrin. But Fitch flung out the truth. A weak boiler was nothing to be ashamed of.

Hiring the boatmen to put them on the Pennsylvania shore, the directors left Fitch and Voight to drift down with the tide to Philadelphia. When they were alone Fitch turned to Voight, to the river, the woods and the July sky and relieved himself with loud, Yankee railing. "The god of Fortune," he declared, was "a Blind, whimsical Jade! Here she got Job canonized for a Saint whilst I must bair the Ridicule of the World; and if the Devil had only had sense enough to put him in mind of building a steamboat at that time, he would have been of the same opinion as his wife!"

XII

THAT September day in 1784 when General Washington, stopping overnight at the Liberty Pole and Flag, viewed James Rumsey's pole-boat experiment at Bath, Maryland, encouraged a long train of blunders which worked hardship on many and were of advantage to none.

It was the West again that supplied the motivating force, the cheap, fertile land beyond the Blue Ridge and Alleghenies into which farmers and mechanics were escaping from the taxes, mortgages and unemployment of the East. In 1784 John Fitch had already noted "the thousands of Kentucky"; and within six years their numbers were to increase till a hundred and fifty thousand people had homesteads along the westward flowing rivers.

As Fitch persistently dreamed of the Ohio and Mississippi bearing heavily laden boats to sea from these western farms, so Washington determinedly planned that western produce should be shipped past his front door. Even Pennsylvania was not to share in the profitable business. "The advantages," the General had written while Congress was considering the treaty with Spain—"with which the inland navigation of the Rivers Potomac and James are pregnant, must strike every mind that reasons upon the subject." But as to "the consequences which may flow from the free and immediate use of the Mississippi," "My opinion of this matter has been uniformly the same and no light in which I have been able to consider the subject has been able to change it. It is, neither to relinquish nor push our claim to this navigation, but in the meanwhile to open *all* the communications which nature has afforded, between the Atlantic States and the western territory, and to encourage the use of them to the utmost. In my judgment it is a matter of very serious concern to the well-being of the former to make it the interest of the latter to trade with them; without which," and here he raised the same bogey of secession that Lord Cornbury had used in 1715 to keep the Colonies dependent upon England, "the ties of consanguinity, which are weakening every day, will soon be no bond, and we shall be no more a few years hence to the inhabitants of that country than the British and Spanish are at this day; not so much, indeed, because commercial connexions, it is well known, lead to others and united are difficult to be broken and these must take place with the Spaniards if the navigation of the Mississippi is opened.

"Clear am I that it would be for the interest of the western settlers as low down the Ohio as the Big Kanawha and back to the lakes to bring their produce through one of the channels I have named; but the way must be cleared and made easy and obvious to them or else the ease with which people glide downstream will given a different bias to their thinking and acting.... It may require some management to quiet the restless and impetuous spirits of Kentucky of whose conduct I am more apprehensive in this business than I am of all the opposition that will be given by the Spaniards."

Washington's scheme was to join the rivers of the West to the rivers of the East by canals, particularly by one canal which would link the Ohio with the Potomac. He had already helped to form a company for that purpose. By bargaining with influential Virginians like Thomas Jefferson from the western part of the state so that they were granted a similar right to dig a canal from the James toward the Blue Ridge, the Potomac Company was organized with a state subsidy and an imposing list of shareholders.

With a waterway extending to the Alleghenies the Potomac

would become a busy river. Towns would thrive along its banks and the price of land would soar accordingly. Stockholders would derive a permanent income from the tolls paid at the locks through which the cargoes of wheat, corn, tobacco, pork, lumber and furs would have to pass on their way to sea. Speculators anticipated the benefits of the Potomac Canal. Lighthorse Harry Lee, Washington's friend and neighbor, bought up land around the Great Falls where the locks were to be built and laid it out in town lots in preparation of the expected boom.

All rational engineering opinion of that time agreed upon the artificial canal as the means to employ for long distance transportation. It was the system used in England. Benjamin Franklin had recommended it to America before the Revolution. Christopher Colles, though he was to end his days as janitor of a New York museum, had written a pamphlet in 1785 on canal navigation in which he laid down the principles that were followed by De Witt Clinton in building the Erie Canal.

But General Washington had met James Rumsey. His slow fancy had been quickened by the sight of Rumsey's pole-boat. Here, close at hand, was the exact medium to help him carry out his plans for navigation of the Potomac as far west as the Alleghenies. He gave his certificate of the boat's performance cheerfully. Rumsey was a fine man. There was no nonsense in him about building steamboats on the Mississippi and robbing the Potomac landowners of their rightful trade from the West.

The next summer the directors of the Potomac Company met to consider extending the waterway west of the Great Falls, where they were going to begin the work. A superintendent would be needed and General Washington suggested Rumsey, "the most skilled mechanician in two states, a man of genius, industrious and an inventor," or so the directors had been informed. And on July 14, 1785, as there were no other applicants "after some deliberation it was resolved to proffer the position" to Rumsey.

Rumsey courteously accepted the job and its salary of two hundred pounds a year, Virginia currency. But instead of making plans to dig an artificial canal with locks to regulate the height of the water, he plunged blindly into the wasteful task of deepening the Potomac's channel. Some of the directors remonstrated, pointing out that at low water the river would be no deeper than before the expensive channel had been cut and that during freshets the flood would be ungovernable and might destroy the locks. But Rumsey was insistent and General Washington "gave him the whole weight of his support." For the ex-tavern keeper was his particular protégé and "with the characteristic gesture he used towards all those to whom he gave his confidence at all," he would have backed Rumsey's attempt to cut a channel through the Rocky Mountains.

Thus after the ungainly Fitch had stumbled into Mount Vernon with his plans for a steamboat, Washington sat down and wrote a partisan warning to Rumsey: "Sir:—if you have no cause to change your opinions respecting your mechanical boat, and reasons unknown to me do not exist to delay the exhibition of it, I would advice you to give it to the public as soon as it can be prepared conveniently. The postponement creates distrust in the public mind, it gives time also for the imagination to work, and this is assisted by a little dropping from one, and something from another, to whom you have disclosed your secret. Should a mechanical genius therefore hit upon your plan, or something similar to it, I need not add that it would place you in an awkward situation, and perhaps disconcert all your prospects concerning this useful discovery.... I will inform you further that many people in guessing at your plan, have come very near the mark, and that one who has something of a similar nature to offer to the public, wanted a certificate from me that it was different from yours. I told him that I was not at liberty to declare what your plan was, so I did not think it proper to say what it was not...."

While Rumsey's genius was undimmed by the ultimate failure of both the channel project and the pole-boat, while his stubborn insistence, backed by the "dominant personality" of Washington, had yet to prove that he was destroying all hope of uniting the West to the East by water, he was connected by the Potomac Company enterprise with still another man of influence.

Thomas Johnson, former Governor of Maryland, to whom Fitch had appealed for support and who had at first received him amicably, was an official of the Potomac Company. He was also part owner of the Catoctin Iron Works which had made the machinery for Rumsey's pole-boat. So between the fall of 1785 when he wrote enthusiastically that Fitch's boat could be propelled *"in any kind of water,"* and the winter of 1787 when Fitch next saw him, he had become much more cautious of implied comment on Rumsey's invention, for the pole-boat was effective only against the current.

With such respectable connections, which were afterward enlarged on a grand scale and formed into the Rumseian Society, James Rumsey belatedly sought to apply that force of which "he had mentioned something of the sort" to General Washington in 1785. It is clear that the boat he showed on the river at Bath was not a *steam* boat but a *stream* boat. All references to it stressed its mechanical means and were silent as to the use of steam. It is equally clear that any efforts which Rumsey made to apply steam after he received Washington's cautionary letter were unsuccessful until at least the fall of 1787, fifteen months after Fitch propelled a skiff by steam on the Delaware and several months after the delegates to the Constitutional Convention had been passengers on Fitch's shallop.

Fitch's success was like rowels digging into Rumsey's flanks. There is little doubt that Rumsey had contemplated the power of steam, perhaps even in connection with a boat. But so had William Henry of Lancester and Thomas Paine before him. Though he lived in the country, away from any practicing mechanics, he was ingenious enough to construct an hydraulic steam jet and an engine for turning grist mills. Whether steam had crossed his mind in connection with boat propulsion, it seemed such a natural, simple idea, once it had been formulated, that he must have felt he had every right to it. Without Fitch's example, he, too, might have struggled for years and covered virtually the same ground so painfully explored by Fitch and Voight between 1785 and 1792.

Since he too possessed strong mechanical aptitude, it became as important to Rumsey to develop steam engines as it was to Fitch. And in the spring of 1786, a few months after he had received General Washington's admonitory letter, he set to work for the first time with the definite idea of completing a steamboat. He went to Charles Weir and Company at Baltimore and ordered brass cylinder cocks. He went to Fredericktown where he had copper work and tinsmithing done. He went to the Catoctin Iron Works where he ordered a cylinder cast. But then he began to discover that there was more to a steamboat than a number of parts. His difficulties in finding the proper proportions were greater than those of Fitch and Voight and December came before the boat was ready for trial.

That winter the Potomac was frozen over most of December. It was just as well; for though Rumsey appeared disappointed because the ice prevented him from making an experiment, his invention was still in its delicate infancy. And there it would always remain until he struck out on a new course. For the basis of motion on which he depended was nothing more valuable than that curious contrivance which had been resurrected by Dr. Franklin and published in the minutes of the Philosophical Society where Rumsey had read it.

With trunks to draw water in at the bow and eject it at the stern, the boat was not launched on the Potomac until December, 1787, Rumsey having spent the intervening year in an effort to make the hydraulic steam jet which was to supplant manual labor at the trunk pump. The boat moved about a quarter of a mile upriver to Swearingen's Run and came back to the wharf. General Washington was not present, but Major General Horatio Gates was there, also the Rev. Robert Stubbs of Shepherdstown Academy, Abraham Shepherd, William Brice, David Grey, John Morrow, Henry Bedinger, Thomas White and Charles Morrow. All these men gave their certificates that they had seen Rumsey's boat "move against the current of the Potomac, on the 3d December, 1787, with two tons on board, exclusive of the machinery, at the rate of three miles an hour, by the force of steam, without any external application whatever."

That winter Rumsey extended himself into the Rumseian Society. Thus far he had been helped by his silent partner, James McMeekin, a doctor in Berkeley County, Virginia, but after the trial on the Potomac he went to Philadelphia and began to acquire celebrated sponsors. He visited Franklin, who was pleased that Rumsey had made use of his little plan, had even improved on it, in fact. The use of the hydraulic steam jet was extremely ingenious. And so, by the implied flattery, Rumsey succeeded where Fitch had failed and Franklin willingly gave the weight of his great name to the enterprise.

From Franklin, Rumsey went to Major General Arthur St. Clair, the home guard commanding officer of the Pennsylvania Line during the Revolution. St. Clair knew nothing about machinery, but he was never blind to the main chance and the names of Washington, Franklin and ex-Governor Johnson were recommendation enough.

Small but imposing, the list of Rumsey's well-wishers continued to grow. He appealed to William Bingham and enlisted him as a member of the Society. Samuel Magaw, Secretary of the Philosophical Society, Miers Fisher, the lawyer, John Wilson, the boatbuilder, Benjamin Wynkoop, the merchant, James Tunchard, John Jones, Levi Hollingsworth, George Duffield, Woodrop Sims, Joseph Sims, Adam Kuhn, Charles Vancouver,

Burgis Allison, John Vaughan, John Ross, William Turner as well as the business firms of Reed and Forde and William Redwood and Sons all joined.

Once he had formed his society, Rumsey abandoned his trunk boat to rust on the banks of the Potomac and sailed for England in an old-fashioned packet. His two brief experiments had apparently convinced him of the utility of the Bernouilli-Franklin contrivance. He had a manner so convincing to others that they were impressed by his verbal descriptions and in London, where he gained more patrons, he made a long, futile attempt to acquire a patent on steam navigation in Great Britain. He began to construct a trunk boat on the Thames, which occupied him till the day before Christmas, 1792, when he was seized by a fit of apoplexy, fell off a chair in his boarding house and died "in a sudden manner" after eight years of puttering with setting poles and steam jets. He had acquired nothing but the whimsical distinction of having been the only person who seriously attempted to make a steamboat on the eccentric Bernouilli-Franklin principle, but before he sailed for London in the spring of 1788 he opened the Rumseian Society's attack on Fitch, whom he charged with plagiarism.

Insolently ignoring the fact that Fitch had built three boats and that one of them was in operation at the time, Rumsey published a pamphlet in the spring of 1788 entitled "A short treatise on the application of steam; whereby it is clearly shewn, from actual experiments, that steam may be applied to propel boats, or vessels of any burthen, against rapid currents, with great velocity." The support of General Washington gave him this audacity. As commander-in-chief of the army which had won America's independence, Washington's popularity was strong enough to carry the vast amount of owning-class legislation which the Federalist party pushed on his shoulders. Whenever the acts of government roused the people's resentment, the Federalists silenced them by crying treason against Washington.

Rumsey followed the tone of all men who had reason to hide under Washington's cloak in the beginning of his pamphlet. Claiming that the use of steam was a secret of his and quoting letters from Washington to show that Greatness was privy to his design, he then wrote:

"I was under many disadvantages arising from my remote situation, and could gain truth only by successive experiments, incredible delays were produced, and though my distresses were greatly increased thereby, I bore the peltings of ignorance and ill nature with all resignation, until I was informed some dark assassins [Fitch] had endeavoured to wound the reputation of his Excellency and the other gentlemen who saw my exhibition at Bath, for giving me a certificate."

The knife-thrusts of these dark assassins at his Excellency's character gave Rumsey "inexpressible uneasiness;" in fact Washington's name was so dear to him that he "should certainly have quitted my steam-engines, though in a great state of forwardness, and produced the boat for which I obtained their certificate the pole boat, for their justification and my own, although I had actually made several experiments on a boat with steam, but Mr. Fitch came out at this minute with his steam-boat, asserting that 'he was the first inventor of steam, and that I had gotten what small knowledge I had from him, but that I had not the essentials.'"

All of which would have been unimportant if Rumsey had gone no further. But his aim was to acquire the patents which had already been given to Fitch and to accomplish this he had to show the priority of his own invention. And this, in turn, required the manufacture of a considerable number of lies.

Charging that Fitch had pilfered his "secret" through Captain Henry Bedinger in 1784 when both Bedinger and Fitch were supposedly in Kentucky, Rumsey attempted to hide the real date of his first experiment with steam, but laid his deception wide open by admitting that it was not until he had heard of a letter by Daniel Buckley of Philadelphia that he "proceeded with ardour in perfecting the steam-engine." This letter of Buckley's had been written to a friend in Berkeley County and Buckley had stated in it with regard to Dr. McMeekin, one of Rumsey's partners, "I am sorry he [Dr. McMeekin] has been deluded by a person [James Rumsey] who I have reason to believe is a deceiver, as Mr. Fitch, of Philadelphia, says Mr. Rumsey 'got what small knowledge he had of him.'" This was larded into the pamphlet so as to make it appear that the letter was written in the spring of 1785 and that directly afterward Rumsey had "performed his mighty deeds." However this was disproved by Buckley himself, who certified that the letter was written "when Mr. Samuel Briggs was making patterns for Mr. Fitch's castings" in the summer of 1786.

Rumsey would lie only indirectly. But his two brothers-in-law, Charles Morrow and James Barnes, were so jealous of the Rumsey family honor that they were willing to forfeit their own. Morrow swore to a long, circumstantial account of how, in the beginning of 1785, Rumsey had disclosed his plans for building a steamboat, that the boiler, pumps, pipes and cylinders had been cast in Shepherdstown and that by the first of December the boat was ready for a trial run. However, he averred under oath, the river had frozen over and Rumsey had had to wait till spring. Meanwhile he had invented several improvements but the workmen had put them together so badly that the actual demonstration was delayed till the spring of 1786 when, with Morrow on board, the boat went against the current until the steam escaped from the boiler.

This was the most useful lie of all, for it stated under oath that Rumsey's experiment antedated Fitch's by several months. It was confirmed by Joseph Barnes, who added the realistic detail that the machinery "made many powerful strokes, and sent the boat forward with such power that one man was unable to hold her." When Rumsey sailed for England these two men were left to carry on the battle against Fitch through pamphlets, through the press, in the courts and, if need be, by their fists.

Fitch first heard that Rumsey was building a steamboat through William Askew who came to Philadelphia in the winter of 1787 "and told so many unaccountable stories" among the shareholders "that he gained but little credit with the Company as to the truth of the main story itself." Still believing that Rumsey was pursuing his pole-boat and knowing from hard experience that the construction of a steamboat was a difficult, hazardous pursuit, Fitch "could not credit it, but suspected Askew to be a man that wished to tell great stories."

But when Rumsey's pamphlet, first published in Virginia and then reprinted by Joseph James in Chestnut Street, appeared and was widely distributed by the Rumseian Society the members of the steamboat company became frightened and many of them sourly treated Fitch as an impostor who had swindled them out of several hundreds of Pounds.

Richard Wells, Fitch's chief supporter during the past year, was especially dismayed. The name of Washington, the sponsorship of Dr. Franklin, Arthur St. Clair, the rich William Bingham, even Sam Magaw, the printed words of Rumsey's charges, the sworn statements by Charles Morrow and James Barnes—what could Fitch say to justify himself against so powerful an array of tacit accusers? Richard Wells coldly closed the door.

Fitch slunk back to his boarding house and locked himself in his room. His bill for lodgings was overdue again and both his landlord and landlady watched him with prowling suspiciousness. In spite of his well-meaning industry it seemed that he had roused the whole world against him. But he was determined not to let Rumsey's attack go unchallenged. Ever since he had dedicated himself to steamboat building he had kept certificates and testimonials of all important events connected with his progress. Just as in his apprentice days he had carefully checked the hours stolen from him by the Cheneys. Now he had a whole portfolio to draw on, from the statements of Nathaniel Irwin and Cobe Scout to the affidavits of the delegates to the Constitutional Convention.

A few hours' study of Rumsey's pamphlet showed him the weakness of Rumsey's argument. If Rumsey, as he pretended, had had his boat in such "a great state of forwardness" in the spring of 1785, why had he spent two years before exhibiting it to his brothers-in-law, especially since his own boat had appeared in the meantime? No, "This boat, which grew like Jonah's Gourd the first season of 1785 withered down to about one week's work for the two following years, when it may be reasonably supposed that the last part of the time there would be more strenious exertions, as they knew we were going on and was forward with ours." The reason was, it was obvious to Fitch, that Rumsey had been depending on the pole-boat until 1786 and then, when it had failed, he had followed Fitch in the employment of steam and was now guilefully using the statements of Washington and the other gentlemen, which had been given for the pole-boat, to make it appear that they were for the steamboat.

Rumsey claimed that he had written Washington in March, 1785, saying that he had "taken the greatest pains to perfect another kind of boat" and that he had become convinced that boats of passage may be made to go against the current of the Mississippi and Ohio Rivers, or in the Gulf Stream (from the Leeward to the Windward islands) from sixty to one hundred miles per day." However, "the principles of this boat," he was "very cautious not to explain, as it would be easily executed by an ingenious person." And he asserted that Washington wrote in reply "It gives me much pleasure to find by your letter that you are not less sanguine in your boat project than when I saw you in Richmond; and that you have made such further discoveries as will render them more extensively useful than was at first expected." Fitch doubted this. Neither Rumsey's nor Washington's letters mentioned steam and he correctly believed that Rumsey had invented his own letter and was now attaching the earlier genuine note from Washington to it to make it appear as a direct reply.

General Washington remained silent throughout the battle of the pamphlets. But unless he realized that Rumsey had never written him such a letter his mind must have subjected him to a curious oversight. For, five days after Rumsey had supposedly informed him that he had a scheme to propel boats through the Gulf Stream, Washington wrote to Hugh Williamson, Congressman from North Carolina, describing the pole-boat only: "The counteraction being proportioned to the action, it must ascend a swift current *faster* than a gentle stream, and both with more ease than it can move through *dead water*." And nearly a year later, when Washington again referred to Rumsey's invention, he spoke only of the *mechanical* boat and made no reference to steam. Thus, while it might be argued that Washington was withholding Rumsey's "secret" from Williamson, the argument can scarcely be stretched to include his withholding it from Rumsey himself.

Four days Fitch kept close to his room, arranging his material for defense. To Rumsey's charge that he had learned of the Potomac Company's Superintendent's invention "through Captain Henry Bedinger while at Kentucky," he replied that he had not been in Kentucky in 1784—he had been in the Northwest Territory during that year, as his diaries in the Library of Congress prove. And as to the date of Daniel Buckley's letter being 1784 or 1785, the receipt of which Rumsey claimed had caused him to proceed "with ardor in the completion of the steam-engine," he proved by affidavit from Buckley himself that the letter was written in the summer of 1786.

Against the few and obscure experiments which Rumsey alleged for himself, Fitch put forward the result of his own efforts. He had affidavits from Bucks County to show he had conceived the idea of applying steam to vessels in April, 1785; he had copies of letters in favor of his scheme written by Dr. John Ewing, William Houston and Samuel Smith in August, 1785. It was a known fact and could be proved by the minutes that the drawings of his boat, models and tube boiler had been deposited with the American Philosophical Society in September, 1785; likewise that, in November, he had applied to the Virginia Assembly for encouragement in the use of steam as applied to boats and that he had executed a bond to Governor Patrick Henry, conditioned on the sale of his maps, to raise money for that purpose. And on December 20th he had advertised for aid in building the steamboat in the *Maryland Gazette*, which circulated through the territory in which Rumsey claimed to have been at work. He had also petitioned the Maryland Assembly for assistance and there had been a public hearing, favorable to his invention, on January 19, 1786. Why, then, had Rumsey waited a full two years before bringing in a counter-claim to the invention? Because, until the winter of 1787 he had had nothing to show.

Fitch took his writings to Richard Wells. Wells read them and his suspicions disappeared. Convinced that Fitch was the epitome of "injured innocence," he offered to help arrange the arguments in logical form and publish them in a pamphlet.

Fitch accepted gratefully. And "whilst this was doing" he set out to demolish Rumsey's claims with a thoroughness that would leave no basis for dispute. He marched directly into the enemy's territory.

Ex-Governor Johnson had already shifted his ground. Though he had enthusiastically encouraged Fitch in 1785 and had made the damaging admission in a letter to Governor Smallwood that the scheme of propelling boats "in any kind of water" was a novelty that belonged to Fitch, he now declared that at the same time he had written the letter for Fitch he had an order from Rumsey to cast cylinders for steam at his Catoctin Iron

Works. He attempted to explain his previous admission by claiming that he had considered himself "under an obligation of secresy till in the progress of making copper cylinders in Fredericktown some time afterward" he had found that "the designed cylinder was a subject of pretty general conversation."

Obviously, either Johnson's "memory or his candor was at fault," Fitch replied and demanded to know how Johnson could have recommended his boat to Smallwood when Rumsey's was within six days of completion?

Governor Johnson wriggled, claiming that he had felt bound to secrecy.

But, Fitch persisted, if the entire steam engine was completed by December 1st, as Rumsey claimed, then the cylinder must have been finished by November 25, the day Fitch visited Johnson and therefore his "obligation to secrecy" was already removed, because the purpose of the cylinder, according to Johnson himself, was then "a subject of pretty general conversation." And if Fitch's boat was in direct conflict with Rumsey's how could the ex-governor recommend Fitch so warmly to Smallwood? No, he had either acted hypocritically to Fitch and false to Rumsey in 1785 or else he was lying in 1787.

Fitch went on through Fredericktown. He found Michael Baltzell who had turned the works for Rumsey's first machinery. Baltzell declared that this had been done in the spring of 1786, not in 1785 as Rumsey alleged. Fitch continued to gather affidavits. All of them proved his contention that Rumsey had depended exclusively on the pole-boat until, after learning of the Franklin-Bernouilli trunk-boat proposal, he had thought of making a trial of it and of using a hydraulic steam jet instead of a hand pump. Frederick Tombough stated that he had made the copper pipes for Rumsey's boat in March, 1786; John Peters swore that he had done the tin work at the same time. John Frymiller, Tombough's apprentice, and Joshua Minshall, another coppersmith, substantiated this. And from Fredericktown

Fitch went on to Baltimore where Charles Weir declared that he had made brass cocks for Rumsey in the spring of 1786.

With these proofs Fitch returned to Philadelphia. "The Original Steam-boat Supported; or a reply to Mr. James Rumsey's pamphlet, Shewing the true Priority of John Fitch and the False Datings of James Rumsey" was published that summer and, after giving it as wide a distribution as possible, Fitch resumed his work on the steamboat, hoping that Rumsey and his backers would be driven into silence by his array of proofs.

But the chief purpose of the Rumseian Society was to carry on the fight until Fitch's patents were revoked and new ones were issued in Rumsey's name. Rumsey had anticipated a long dispute when his first pamphlet appeared and before he left for England he wrote to his brother-in-law, Charles Morrow:

"I beg, Sir, that you will Leave no Stone unturned to Detect fitch in his Villiney. You shall have one of his pamphlets sent you as soon as they May come out you may then judge what sort of proofs is wanted and can forward them to our Secretary and Committee of Correspondence."

A few months after Fitch's pamphlet appeared the Rumseians returned to the attack with another, "Remarks on Mr. John Fitch's reply to Mr. James Rumsey's Pamphlet, by Joseph Barnes, formerly assistant, and now attorney in fact to James Rumsey."

In this pamphlet Barnes published retractions from Charles Weir and his partner Cuasten, from Christopher Rabord and from Mrs. Zimmers, the widow of Frederick Tombough's partner. Charles Morrow, Rumsey's other brother-in-law, reiterated his statement that the boat had been ready for trial in December, 1785, but that the ice had prevented navigation. Conrad Byers swore that he had made brass or copper cocks for Rumsey in the fall of 1785 and Francis Hamilton gave oath that in December, 1785 "James Barnes and James McMechen, [Rumsey's partner] brought a boat of about six tons burthen, with a variety of machinery on board, to the Shenandoah Falls," that ice and faulty machinery prevented a trial until March, 1786, when "the boat moved against the current, though not with much success." But Tombough, Peters, Baltzell, Morris, Minshall and Frymiller were not so willing to perjure themselves and, in spite of Barnes' persuasiveness, they refused to change their statements.

It is a curious fact that during this long dispute Dr. James McMeekin remained silent. Like Charles Morrow, he was one of Rumsey's partners. For a quarter interest in Rumsey's inventions Dr. McMeekin advanced three hundred Pounds. According to Francis Hamilton he was aboard the steamboat when it was taken to the Shenandoah Falls in December, 1785. Then why is it that only Rumsey's two brothers-in-law, Barnes and Morrow, persistently claimed that the boat had been propelled by steam at that time?

The answer to this is contained in the suit of McMeekin vs. Rumsey in 1800. It presents another and final proof that Rumsey placed no dependence on steam at the time he began his experiments. The petition of "James McMeekin of the County of Berkeley" states that "some time in or about the year 1784 a certain James Rumsey and your orator entered into articles of agreement for the purpose of prosecuting and receif[ing] profit by an Invention of constructing boats to sail up Rapid streams." And the petition further mentions that "James Rumsey, being a man of abilities well versed in the doctrines of Hydrostatics, central forces and Laws of gravitation, aspired to other objects of invention which were extremely useful to the world, such as Rumsey's improvement on Dr. Barker's mill and Rumsey's steam boiler," but no mention is made of Rumsey's steamboat, and no claim is laid to it as one of the "other objects of invention" in which Dr. McMeekin had a partnership!

But these facts, like the Washington letter, came to light years after Fitch had died a disappointed man. In the meantime the powerful Rumseian Society was endeavoring to influence the various state legislatures against Fitch and in favor of Rumsey by writing such letters as the following, which was sent to the Virginia Assembly:

"James Rumsey, an ingenious Gentleman, a Native of Maryland, but lately from Virginia, in December last exhibited before a number of respectable characters of Maryland and Virginia the effects of Steam in propelling a boat of considerable burthen against the current of the River Potowmack, and models of machines for the raising of water to a great Height and in large quantities by the force of Steam, in both which a boiler upon an entirely new construction invented by himself is used with the greatest apparent probability of far exceeding all others heretofore known, not merely in point of force but in the smallness of the Quantity of Fuel necessary to generate the steam." And therefore it was the duty of the delegates to annul the patent given to the ungentlemanly, anti-Federalist, Deistic Fitch and protect the interest of Mr. Rumsey and his powerful associates.

With tireless persistence and energy Fitch fought every pretension of the Rumsey agents. When Barnes' pamphlet was published he went down to Fredericktown again and began to interview the inhabitants. He found Jacob Sandrel who had seen "the Tin works made by John Peters for Mr. Rumsey's steamboat made in the front room of my House in the spring of the year" 1786. He found Benjamin Harris who, in the fall of 1786 "worked for one month in the Potomac Company for Mr. James Rumsey and in the fall after worked on the banks of the Potomac about one mile below Harpers Ferry where he Saw Mr. Rumsey's boat coming up the river, being worked by Mr. Barnes and Robert Harper and some others who was setting it up with poles near the shore. He found Englehart Cruze who reported that Rumsey had told him his boat was damaged by ice not in the winter of 1785 but in December, 1786. He found Leonard Smith who testified that he had steered Rumsey's boat in the spring of 1786 and that it was not propelled by steam, but by the setting poles such as Benjamin Harris had seen. Altogether, Fitch collected the affidavits of twenty-one residents of Fredericktown which showed that Rumsey had not begun to use steam before the spring of 1786 and had not made a successful trial before the winter of 1787. And as Barnes had charged in his pamphlet that Frymiller was drunk at the time he swore he had worked on Rumsey's machinery in 1786 and not 1785, Fitch patiently collected the names of six witnesses who declared that Frymiller had been sober. He would have canvassed every house in the town, but by that time Charles Morrow had got busy and Fitch had to leave suddenly or prepare for a beating from Morrow and his friends.

This left Barnes with exactly four alleged witnesses to the steamboat experiment of 1785—himself, Morrow, Conrad Byers and Francis Hamilton. Yet the zeal of the brothers-in-law was so great and the prestige of the Rumseian Society was so persuasive among the legislators that Fitch was kept busy defending himself for the next six months. In an effort to intimidate Fitch, Barnes informed him that "Mr. Rumsey's agents intend[ed] to make application to all the Legislatures of the United States for the exclusive privelige of using steamboats upon the plan by him intended.

"I therefore think it my Duty to give you particular information that the Legislature of Virginia sits for the Dispatch of Business on the 21st day of this instant, in order that you may give instruction to make what opposition to it you may think proper."

This letter was given to Clement Biddle, who carried out the legalistic trappings by declaring before a notary public that on "the 14th day of October [1788] he went to the Dwelling or Lodging of John Fitch and speaking to a Woman of the House requested to know if Mr. Fitch was within, her answer was that he was not then within but expected him home at one o'clock."

Beginning in Virginia, the Rumseian Society's efforts to have

Fitch's patents repealed failed by a vote of one hundred to fifteen. Next an attempt was made in New Jersey, which was followed by another in New York. Finally, in the spring of 1789 the Rumseians massed their forces for an attack in Pennsylvania. Thomas Fitzsimmons, one of the Federalist speculators who grew rich from the knowledge that the Government intended to redeem soldiers' back pay certificates at their face value and bought them up wholesale at a few cents on the dollar, and George Clymer, another Pennsylvania politician, presented a scheme for the appointment of commissioners to grant patents for the state and the legality of the question was submitted to the Judges of the Pennsylvania Supreme Court:

"Can this House, consistent with the principles of law and justice and the Constitution of this State, enact a law upon the principles reported before this House, in the case contested between John Fitch and James Rumsey?"

Miers Fisher, a member of the Rumseian Society, took the affirmative, and argued the case of Rumsey. Richard Wells appeared for the steamboat company and protested against the commission.

Chief Justice McKean, like all biased judges, argued that if Fitch's patent had been obtained by deception it might be repealed and in the next breath strongly suggested that there had been deception, therefore the Legislature had the right of repeal.

Judge Bryan saw a dangerous precedent set in case the law was repealed and flatly opposed it. A third judge gave no written opinion, but the committee of the house, composed of Lewis, Downing, Neville, Hoge and Clymer, declared that it was "inexpedient" to set up a patent commission at that time—evidently because the Federal Congress would convene in the fall and matters of patents, copyrights and other methods of protecting inventors and authors would be legally formulated.

Failing in this, Fitzsimmons presented another bill, which would have given the patents for a steamboat to Rumsey. Like the previous underhanded scheme, this also was ruled out but Fitch, in a fury, addressed himself to the two Rumseian politicians, both of whom had been elected to Congress where they would be actively in support of Rumsey.

"Gentlemen, Clymer and Fitzsimmons:

"I think proper to tell you that I have felt the full force of all your endeavours to injure me, in the State which has sent you to Congress; but notwithstanding every exertion you, as members of Assembly, have been able to make, my rights in Pennsylvania remain yet unshaken. The attempt made by you, Mr. Fitzsimmons, to introduce a bill into the House, to take them by surprise, and was purposely intended to hurt me, was treated by the House as it justly deserved, and you were not permitted to deliver it to the Speaker.

"The active and unnecessary part which you, Mr. Clymer, took to endeavour to get another law passed, that was intended to ruin me, you will be mortified to have it known to the world that you failed in your design, but I think I ought not to suffer it to pass in silence.

"You are now going to Congress, and wish to have it known to your fellow citizens that I deem you my professed enemies on this subject, and that you will leave no stone unturned to hurt my interest with that honorable body."

Fitch had already petitioned Congress for a law which would "preclude subsequent improvers on his principles from participating therein until the expiration of his granted rights" which he had received from the several states. But Congress had a phrase that dealt with such legislation even then and every time Fitch's petition came up for discussion they "Ordered the said petition to lay on the table."

Small wonder Fitch wrote in a frenzy of despair—"reflecting how I had ruined myself to serve my Country, and how many sleepless, restless nights I had suffered to bring about one of the greatest events, and such exquisit tortures of the mind, and had placed myself on a base dependence of my friends, it effected me beyond measure. Could I have been dependant on my township only for sustenance I could have supported it much better, or could I have recalled my life back for four years, I would gladly have offered my neck to the common executioner."

XIII

"Under the auspices of the god of nature" Fitch made several trips up the Delaware in his steamboat that summer of 1787 after the leaky boiler had been repaired and strengthened. But to most of the people the steamboat was still a fearsome or ludicrous object and the passengers to Burlington preferred the stage, which went to Trenton in five hours and cost ten shillings. Thus the steamboat must approximate the speed of the stage before it could even begin to compete by cutting prices. And this meant an average of eight miles an hour.

On October 12 Fitch and Voight lured a crowd to the wharf with an offer of free grog and sausages, packed thirty people aboard and, going against the tide which set at the rate of two miles an hour, they careened from the Philadelphia Front Street wharf to the Burlington town landing in three hours and ten minutes, a fact which was duly certified by Andrew Ellicott, the mathematician, Richard Chase, John Poor and John Ely of the Pennsylvania Assembly. As the distance from Philadelphia to Burlington was twenty miles, they averaged better than six miles an hour.

Four days later, with a more distinguished company aboard, Fitch and Voight tried to drive their craft still faster. Besides Ellicott there were Dr. Ewing and Robert Patterson of the University, David Redick, vice-president of Pennsylvania, John Smoley of the Supreme Executive Council, Dr. David Rittenhouse, Timothy Matlack, Charles Pettit, J. B. Smith and redfaced, blustering Jonathan Hart, Captain of the First Regiment of United States Infantry. Captain Hart testified after the trip that he was "fully convinced that the same force applied to a boat would be sufficient to carry it against the most rapid waters between the mouth of French Creek on the Allegheny and the mouth of the Muskingum on the Ohio, and that on an average it would carry it between three and four miles an hour on any of the western waters." But so far as travel on *eastern* waters was concerned, this last trip was less successful than the previous one, for the boat moved only "at the rate of four miles an hour."

The present boat was too slow for the Delaware. A new one would have to be built. This called for more money, which the smaller stockholders could not afford. Joseph Budd, the hatter, Henry Toland, the grocer, Israel Israel, the tavern keeper, Thomas Palmer and Magnus Miller, the merchants, and also Thomas Hutchins the geographer, resigned their shares. To go on with the experiments after sixteen hundred Pounds had been spent was, as usual, the privilege of the wealthy.

When the poorer stockholders began to desert the company, Voight likewise sought a way out. He was losing his customers. He needed money for rent. He had a wife and half a dozen children to feed and clothe. Besides, he grumbled, Fitch had ten shares in the enterprise whereas he had five; and furthermore, Fitch got all the glory.

Fitch denied this promptly. He reminded Voight he had taken "every opportunity in all Companies and amongst all ranks of men to extol his great mechanical ability"—which many of his letters and petitions prove. But Voight, under pressure of supplying the needs of his family and also with a sense of guilt at abandoning his friend, continued to wrangle his way out. Working at odd times while waiting for money to carry on the steamboat, they had made a new invention which was to utilize the paddle wheel but which, instead of being driven by steam, was to be propelled by horses ambling in a perpetual circle around the deck. And though Fitch had already given up his claims to this to the stockholders, Voight made an issue of the pending patents.

"Mr. Voight is better acquainted with machinery than he is with mankind," Fitch later observed, "otherwise, after his long acquaintance with me he would not have offered me so serious an affront as he did. For when I was about to take out my Patent he, probably being agitated by some of his Friends, called upon me pretty early one morning and demanded in a pretty positive manner and with considerable warmth that his name should be inserted with mine in the Patent and further said that the scheme would become half ours and that he would assign the half of his half to me. I must confess that this indignity roused my Resentment to think that I was capable of bribery in preference to honor, but knowing his temper I had prudence enough to inform him, 'You know, Harry, that it has been my study to do you the Strictest justice and I have carried out my desires to excess and you cannot think I would wish to injure you now. But this is a thing that is new and requires Consideration, but will propose this: that we get our friends Robert Scott and Isaac Hough both Deist cronies whome we both esteem as men of honor as well as men of sence to meet us this evening and consult them what ought to be done.' Which he received kindly and went off satisfied.

"Accordingly we met agreeable to my proposal and in the evening I proposed this and said, 'Harry, I wish to give you equal honors with me in the invention and you know it has been my study to do it, but to do it by fraud I cannot; if you will assign your half to the Company in the same manner as I have done I wish your name to be inserted with mine. But to rob the proprietors of their just right, I never will consent to it.—And on these conditions only will I admit your name to stand with mine in the Patent. Which proposition appeared to the refferees to be just. And he seemed to be pacified. But some of the Company, when I mentioned it to them, was opposed to it and sayed that he was a headstrong, obstinate Dutchman and would not consent to it, as it would give them much trouble. Which, I must confess, gave me disgurst to the members of the Company for such unreasonable suspicions."

The upshot of this was that Voight went back to his clockmaking and left Fitch single-handed with the task of raising money and designing another boat. After puzzling for some weeks he decided that the only way to fill up the treasury was to issue new shares. Forty shares at ten pounds apiece would bring in four hundred pounds, which would be sufficient to build a new boat. Subscribers to the new shares were to have the first hundred pounds of "neat profit," after which all earnings were to be divided equally between the old shareholders and the new ones.

"Every individual is as capable of judgeing as myself," he informed the stockholders,—"whether a steamboat that could travel from Philadelphia to Trenton in five hours would earn money or not, whether passengers would prefer going in a Boat in five hours at five shillings, or in a waggon in four hours for ten shillings. If they would prefer the boat, and the number of passengers to Trenton may be estimated at 8 per day at 5 s, and 12 per day to Burlington and Bordentown at 3 s 9 d each, going and coming, it would amount to 8 Pounds, ten shillings per Day. Now if we should allow thirty shillings per day for expenses, the clear profits would be seven Pounds per day. This, in 250 days in a year, would be 1750 Pounds which will justify the continuance of the experiment."

Not only was the treasury empty, but the Company was in debt for the steamboat of 1787 and when Fitch took this estimate for a new boat among the stockholders he was treated "more like a slave than a freeman... Not only that; I have been continually teized with duns from our workmen, and inbarassed with Constables, for debts; and I was of so bare and mean an appearance that every decent man must and ought to dispize me from my appearance. Not only that, but dare not scarsely show my face in my own Lodgings; which occationed me never to remain in them longer than I could, with the greatest expedition, swallow down my food which always in the evening drove me off to a tavern, and altho I always kept good hours, at my return drove me to my bead. Not only that; altho they were worthy, rispictable people, I dare not find fault with anything, which I might do with propriety could I have paid them weekly, but was obliged to suffer just indignities from my lanlord and be henpecked by the women. Added to this, there was the Most Powerful combination against me, who thought that they could not serve God or themselves better than by saying every illnatured thing they could of me; which made me heartily curse my Barberus Captors for staying the savage Blow."

But the malign demons whom Fitch had come to feel were keeping him alive for their private sport, now interposed in his favor. Dr. William Thornton became one of the new stockholders and the steamboat company was revived.

William Thornton was one of those active, intelligent liberals produced in so great a quantity during the latter half of the eighteenth century. Like Franklin and many other members of the Philosophical Society, like the manufacturer, Tench Coxe, like the statesman, Alexander Hamilton, Thornton glimpsed the practical connection between science and industry. He could see that man, by acting upon his environment, creates his own means of production, and that with the aid of mechanical invention the wealth of the world was being rapidly multiplied. Arkwright's spinning frame, Hargreave's jenny, Watt's steam engines had quadrupled the scientific means of production and there was no reason to doubt that such inventions could be extended indefinitely. All this was in the air, like bright sunlight beyond the threshold of a musty room.

Dr. Thornton had a satisfactory income. His family was of the British colonial governing class and his mother owned a large plantation in Tortola where Thornton was born in 1761. Profit from slave labor was large enough for young Thornton to be educated in England and Edinburgh, where he was graduated from medical school in 1784, and for him to continue his studies in Paris, where he became an intimate friend of the Countess Beauharnais and of Count Andriani, the naturalist, with whom he traveled on the continent.

When he arrived in Philadelphia in 1788 Thornton seemed "by his vivacity and agreeable manners, to belong to the French nation." He also carried a private sorrow for the slaves who provided his income. Instead of "hardening his heart to the fate of the Negroes, as most of the planters do," he had "acquired that humanity, that compassion for them with which he is so tormented." And he "should have set his slaves at liberty if it had been in his power; but not being able to do this, he" conceived a vast project "for their benefit. Persuaded that there never can exist a sincere union between whites and blacks, even in admitting the latter to the rights of freemen, he proposes to send them back and establish them in Africa."

But meanwhile, Thornton continued to enjoy his income. He bought a comfortable house on Callowhill Street near the Ridge Road, married Ann Brodeau, who had organized a cultural academy, joined the Philosophical Society, painted, wrote verses, studied philology and architecture, contributed papers on medicine, astronomy, philosophy, government and art. He designed the Octagon House for John Tayloe, Montpelier for James Madison and produced the plan and drawings which form the nucleus of the Capitol at Washington. In 1800 he kept a stable of thoroughbreds, with an average value of two thousand dollars a head, which he had imported from England and Barbary. In 1802 Thomas Jefferson appointed him Superintendent of the United States Patent Office, which position he still held in 1814 when the British troops besieged Washington. On August 25 it is said he met their cannon and destructive torches with the words, "Are you Englishmen or Vandals? This is the Patent Office, a depository of the ingenuity of the American nation, in which the whole of the civilized world is interested. Would you destroy it?"

Thornton was "a wit, a scholar and a gentleman, with a well-earned reputation for letters and taste"; "and his company was a complete antidote to dulness." But for all his culture, his liberalism and humanitarianism, he continued to derive a good share of his income from the slaves on his Tortola plantation; and just as this slave power was the basis of his culture, so was the drive for profit the basis of his connection with Fitch. But of all the men whose belief in the practical value of scientific discovery led them to buy shares in the steamboat company, Thornton was the friendliest to Fitch and the most useful to the scheme. He had inventiveness and enthusiasm and he bought sixteen of the new shares.

Of the remaining twenty-four shares, Richard Stockton took six. The rest were divided among Richard Wells and Dr. Say, all who remained of the early investors, and a number of small business and professional men. Isaac Morris had a brewery on Pear Street; Richard Morris was a High Street merchant; Robert Scott, one of Fitch's fellow Deists, was an engraver; Sam Wetherill was a druggist; Wood Lloyd was a tailor in South Water Street; and Francis White, though a "dealer in public securities," was no more than an agent for such men as Senator William Bingham, Senator Robert Morris, Congressman Thomas Fitzsimmons and Congressman Jeremiah Wadsworth of Connecticut, who knew in advance what securities the government would redeem and acted accordingly.

The new stockholders took over the management of the Company in January, 1789, under an agreement that when they had constructed a boat that would move eight miles an hour they would pool their shares with those of the original holders and all would share alike in future expenses and profits. It was a further condition that the boat should travel from Philadelphia to Burlington and back again in five hours and a half and repeat the journey for twelve successive days.

At Fitch's insistence, it was decided that an eighteen-inch cylinder should be made. In March the order was given to the Drinkers of Atsion Furnace, who accepted it with grumbling foreboding. It was too large for their foundry, they protested; they hadn't the means and it would be a makeshift job.

The cylinder was completed, but not until June. Then it had to be bored and set up in the boat with the newly proportioned machinery. Taking the place of the guiltily skulking Voight, Dr. Thornton invented a new kind of condenser which was expected to transform water into steam more quickly than Fitch's old pipe condenser. It was made of thin sheets of copper and at first sight of it Fitch vehemently protested that it was not half strong enough to withstand the pressure. But Dr. Thornton was a talented man beside whom Fitch looked like a backwoods ignoramus and his objections were disregarded. The new condenser was tried. It "crushed in like an eggshell." While Thornton began to make another of thicker copper, Fitch resurrected the old condenser and tried it.

The old condenser worked, but in spite of the increased size of the cylinder the boat went no faster than before. By this time it was August. A few weeks later Dr. Thornton's strengthened condenser was ready for trial. It successfully resisted the pressure, but failed to increase the speed. The stockholders grew impatient and Fitch stalked around in a frenzy.

Finally, Fitch appealed to Voight, who came reluctantly, bringing along a new design for a pipe condenser. This also failed. Then Voight invented a forcing pump which, instead of making a water jacket around the condenser, drove a jet of steam directly into it. And when that failed they were all convinced that the trouble must be somewhere else, that the old condenser was as good as any improved ones they had made.

Of all the machinery for the enlarged cylinder, only the air pump had not been increased in size. Now they removed this and, after more delay, replaced it with a larger one. Meanwhile December came. In a few more weeks the ice would stretch over the Delaware and navigation would cease until spring. When the new air pump was installed, Fitch, Voight and the interested directors gave the engine a hurried trial, when it was found that the alteration "brought the action pretty nearly to perfection." But they were still dubious and they decided that a more rigorous trial must be made before they could be certain that they had increased the engine's power.

But now the "elliments" took a hand in thwarting them. In the middle of the morning after they had got up steam a gale blew off the Pennsylvania shore and the Delaware chopped and frothed like a stormy lake. With the steamboat rocking and the wind lashing at the bow there was no use trying to make headway. Fitch opened the door of the firebox and raked out the hickory coals, then went gloomily back to his boarding house.

At midnight he was wakened by some one yelling in the street outside his window. The steamboat was afire. A watchman had seen it while passing the Front Street wharf. Fitch pulled on his ragged clothes and ran anxiously into the December night. He saw flames as he crossed the cobbled streets. Pushing past the bystanders, he ran out on the burning deck. On either side of the firebox the wood was charred to the water's edge and the blaze was spreading. He cut the boat loose and called for help to sink it and save the machinery.

A grog shop was still open when he turned back from the wharf. With hot buttered drams he repaid his helpers and made his own despondency endurable.

Later in the month the steamboat was raised, but when the deck had been repaired it was too late in the winter to make further trials. The steamboat was run up into drydock until the following spring. The directors of the company went back to their businesses and Fitch, after a thoroughly unsuccessful year, was left to face the winter months with nothing in his pockets and debtors besieging him from all sides.

Toward the end of December he appealed to the stockholders. Taking care to extol his collaborator as "that Exalted Genius, I mean my Friend Mr. Voight," and to point out that "the indignities thrown on me by the public I am as callous to as the woodchopper's hand to an axe," he had to admit that for the pleas of the creditors he felt a "Bleeding Heart" and he begged the directors to call a meeting and appoint a committee to examine the accounts and make proper payment. As for himself, he reminded them that he had spent four years on the project, that every shilling was gone, that he was ragged almost to the state of nakedness and that he wanted to escape from his boarding house but that his landlord, Peter Beek, would not let him go before he had paid his bill. Under these circumstances, couldn't the directors do something "to relieve the anxieties of the most distressed man on earth?"

While the directors remained in their comfortable houses, Fitch left his lodgings and tramped up to Bucks County in the hope of finding some clocks to clean. He had to do something or starve.

Cleaning clocks earned him no more than pocket money. After ten days spent among the Longstreths, Dr. Irwin and Cobe Scout, Fitch was drawn back to Philadelphia by his anxiety over his invention. He walked the streets with a budget containing fewer and worse clothes than he had brought home from his Indian captivity. Going down North Second Street toward Harry Voight's clockmaking shop, he passed The Sign of the Buck where he and Harry and Michael Kraft, the tavern keeper, had drunk many a glass. Michael had died a year or two before and now his widow, Mary, was taking care of the customers. Fitch owed a small bill there and had no money to pay it, but he opened the door and went inside.

Mary Kraft was the greatest pattern "of honesty, generosity and noble sentiments" Fitch had ever met. She was also lively and capable. Since her husband's death she had provided for six or seven children as well as he had been able to do. The Sign of the Buck was neat and comfortable. There was a glow from the hearth and a homely gleam from the brass and pewter.

Gaunt and ragged, but with that overpowering determination which had driven him through one disappointment after another, Fitch sat talking to Mary Kraft. He was discouraged and nearly every door in the city was closed to him. Mary listened, understanding how poor he was, seeing there was no place else for him to go. She was not rich like the steamboat company directors, nor even like the small business men who owned a share or two apiece. She was poor, but her answer was simple and direct as Timothy King's had been when Fitch had needed to be found in clothing in order to be apprenticed to Benjamin Cheney: "You can live here, John, and go on with your invention and pay me when you can."

XIV

THE year Fitch went to live at The Sign of the Buck his steamboat achieved its greatest justification while he reached new gradations of torment and poverty.

Having lost most of his shares in the original company and having acquired none through the reorganization he was in a position to be treated as a nuisance by the directors when the year began. True, the steamboat was his invention, but he had accomplished nothing during the past twelve months and now the directors had among their own members a man who was more capable of carrying on the experiments. Dr. Thornton determined to make still another condenser. Twice as large as any of the old ones, it would solve the problem of speed. And Fitch was to be pushed aside.

Fitch was furious. "When in easy circumstances my temper of mind made me modest to excess and [I] would put up with almost any indignities, and resent them no other way but by a familiar levity; but when in wretchedness [I] was haughty, imperious, insolent to [my] superiors; yet exceedingly civil in both instances till indignities were offered [me], when the greater the man, the more sweet the pleasure in retorting upon him in his own way." And now, when the Company began to make Dr. Thornton's oversized condenser Fitch railed sardonically at each stage of the process. It was not a larger condenser that was needed, but a smaller one; for the smaller the condenser, the more perfect the vacuum!

With Thornton's condenser, Fitch pointed out, a vacuum was impossible. He made a rough drawing of it and showed it to the directors, explaining how the entire mechanism from the air pump, through the condenser and on to the base of the cylinder would fill with air. And driven one way by the piston and the other by the suction, it would "skulk in the bottom of the Condensor for security, where it cannot be dislodged until the steam is destroyed, when it rushes out and does the same injury again."

But the directors insisted. The Thornton condenser was made and fitted to the boat in time for a trial on Easter Monday. A fire was built, steam was formed and they all stood waiting on deck in a high state of expectancy, looking over the bow which was pointed upstream.

The result was exactly what Fitch had predicted it would be. Churning in the air-choked cylinder, the piston developed barely enough power to move the boat against the tide.

Dr. Thornton was astounded and the rest of the directors were palsied with discouragement. It was the seventh condenser that had been tried and the least successful of all.

Fitch came triumphantly forward with his own proposal—to make a small condenser composed of a single straight tube. The advantage of this, he explained, was that instead of furnishing a pocket for the air to lurk in, it would provide a direct passage for the steam to drive the air all the way from the cylinder through the condenser to the air pump and expel it through the valve. And while this method might not be absolutely successful, "the quantity of air remaining would be inconsiderable to what [it] would be in a large Condenser; consequently, less capable of injuring us, and much more perfect vacuum formed."

At the end of their scientific resources, the directors finally ordered a new condenser to be made according to Fitch's design. It was begun at once and Fitch stalked restlessly around the workshop until it was finished. He and Voight were cronies again and nearly every evening Voight would come up the street to The Sign of the Buck and sit with Fitch and Mary in the taproom. At nine o'clock, when the watchmen began to make their rounds, Fitch would go upstairs to bed, leaving Voight and Mary Kraft sitting there while he tossed in torment with his hopes. For the last five years he had thought of nothing but his steamboat. The loss of his Kentucky lands had vexed him and sentimental recollections of his children in Windsor had often plagued him, but it was for the sake of the steamboat that he had gone through poverty and scorn. Looking back, he could reflect on the difficulties he had overcome, the penuriousness of the shareholders, the false claims of the Rumseians, the method of propulsion, the weight of the furnace which he had reduced by six thousand pounds by placing it in a firebox under the boiler. And now the condenser!—his principle was right and it must be made to work.

The new condenser was tried a week after Dr. Thornton's failure. A strong northwest wind was blowing down the Delaware from the Pennsylvania shore, making the trial a severe one. The boat was the old hulking failure of the year before, with patched deck and sides where it had been burned in the accidental fire. All that was new about it was the boiler, which was stronger than its predecessors, and Fitch's newly designed condenser.

Dr. Thornton and Richard Wells came down to the Front Street wharf while Fitch and Voight were getting up steam. It was a fine April day except for the gusty wind which blew the directors' ruffles and flapped Fitch's ancient rags. As they stepped aboard even these enthusiasts must have had a sense of now-or-never, a kind of reckless skepticism in which to cloak the losses of their time and money. For everything had been tried that could be tried.

Under the rising steam the piston began to churn, the axletree to shake from side to side and the oars at the stern to cleave the water. With the wind on his left cheek, Fitch headed for the current, then steered upstream. The machinery was working violently, with surprising force. They all had the feeling that they were going at a swifter rate than ever before, but while they were tentatively estimating their speed a pulley snapped and the oars rattled down to a standstill.

For once there was a favorable omen in their misfortunes. If the eighteen-inch cylinder and straight tube condenser could work the machinery with such force as to break a pulley it meant that the steamboat had increased its speed surprisingly. As they came to anchor the crews of passing sailing ships leaned over the sides to jeer and hurl hearty curses at these cranky competitors of the men before the mast. And when one of the directors called for help to get to shore the sailors reached new heights in their derisive answers. Philosophically Fitch took up the oars and waited to drift back toward the Front Street wharf with the tide.

The triumph which was promised in this first trial run was fulfilled four days later when, with a stronger pulley, Fitch and Voight "tried our Boat again; and altho the wind blew very fresh at the northeast, we reigned *Lord High Admirals of the Delaware.*"

That day "no boat in the River could hold its way with us, but all fell astern, although several sail boats, which were very light, and with heavy sails that brought their gunwales well down into the water, came out to try us. We also passed many boats with oars, and strong manned, and no loading, and they seemed to stand still when we passed them. We also run round a vessel that was beating to windward in about two miles, which had half a mile start of us."

Cavorting up and down the river past crews which had been jeering at their efforts for the last four years, they returned at last with all their machinery in working order, "fully convinced that what we had persued so long with imbarassment" was now a complete success, from which "we concluded that our troubles were at an end."

That evening they went around the town, inviting all the members of the Company to be at the wharf at two o'clock the next afternoon to see their performance repeated. Beaming, Voight locked his shop door at noon and bustled to The Sign of the Buck. Fitch and he walked down to the Front Street wharf, looking up at the overcast sky and feeling the wind growing stronger.

By two o'clock the wind had beaten itself into "a perfect storm" and nobody had come except Dr. Say, but as he was eager for the experience they fired up the boiler and scudded out into the current again where they went "amazingly swift" before the wind for an hour or more.

The successful exhibitions continued along the Delaware and Fitch's joy overflowed into his journal: "Thus has been effected, by Little Johnny Fitch and Harry Voight, one of the greatest and most useful arts that has ever been introduced into the world; and although the world and my country does not thank me for it, yet it gives me heartfelt satisfaction."

Besides the members of the Company, Dr. Ewing, David Rittenhouse, Dr. Robert Patterson, General Irvine and Mr. Gray of the Assembly came aboard as distinguished passengers. On the second Sunday in May Fitch and Voight reached Burlington with a number on board and two days later they received their first notice from the press. Under a Burlington date line of May 11, 1790, the *Gazette of the United States* printed the following paragraph in its staid narrow columns, which was reprinted in newspapers and magazines from Charleston to Boston:

"The friends of science and the liberal arts will be gratified in hearing that we were favored, on Sunday last, with a visit from the ingenious Mr. Fitch, accompanied by several gentlemen of taste and knowledge in mechanics, in a steamboat constructed on an improved plan. From these gentlemen we learn that they came from Philadelphia in three hours and a quarter, with a head wind, the tide in their favour. On their return, by accurate observations, they proceeded down the river at the rate of upwards of seven miles an hour."

As Fitch and Voight continued to display the steamboat's prowess without any embarrassing moments the directors decided that it was time to establish a regular packet service between Philadelphia and Trenton and that the first step should be the building of a well-appointed cabin for the passengers. All the stockholders wanted the cabin to be elegant. Dr. Thornton, as the chief authority on architecture, took over the task of drawing plans. He worked for several days and then presented his drawings, which were of a lofty and commodious design.

Fitch stared at the drawings and objected vigorously.

But weren't they elegant? the shareholders protested.

Too high, Fitch said; "and a high cabin, though elegant, will slow up the boat. Therefore I say, if it must be elegant, make it low and line it with Gold!"

So far, all the passengers who had been persuaded to come aboard were men of influence whose names could be used for publicity purposes. There had been scientists, merchants, army officers and a few government officials. But early in June they prepared a stroke to make the steamboat famous. They visited the Governor and all the members of the State Executive Council with invitations for them to make a journey in the steamboat in a body. This was accepted and on June 16th, 1790, Governor Thomas Mifflin, Samuel Miles, Zebulon Potts, Amos Gregg, Christopher Kuchner, Frederick Watts, Abraham Smith, William Findlay, John Hartzell and Charles Biddle, Clerk of the Assembly, marched aboard the steamboat in all their legislative majesty.

It was a fine day. Amidst the pleasures of "walking the waters like a thing of life," of being regaled with beer and sausages and of listening to the witty, instructive discourse of Dr. Thornton, the legislators became mellow and well-pleased with their outing. It was a great invention, they decided, and deserved every encouragement. When they were landed at the wharf they drew off by themselves to consider the best means of showing their esteem.

The steamboat had no flag, one of them observed. It ought to have a set of colors to fly fore and aft. The members of the Council nodded. After speaking to Governor Mifflin, Charles Biddle turned to the waiting Fitch and informed him that he was thereby authorized to buy a suitable array of flags and present the bill to the gentlemen of the Council.

Fitch stiffened with joy and thanked the Governor and Council with a look of wild, stern gratitude. Like Voight, he craved nothing so much as the marks of honor and the flags of the State of Pennsylvania would be like an official benediction upon his past struggles and future triumphs.

The flags were made with great care while he looked forward to the presentation ceremonial. They cost five Pounds, six shillings and eleven pence. The day that they were delivered he wrote to Governor Mifflin to inform him that everything was in readiness, and carried the flags to the state house.

Governor Mifflin didn't answer. Fitch was disturbed. Mifflin was noted as a shrewd politician; could it be possible that he was afraid to be officially associated with the steamboat because it was still unpopular? Doubtless it was. Fitch enclosed another letter to him in a message to Charles Biddle.

Biddle's acknowledgment was encouraging. "I will deliver your letter to the Governor Mifflin, President of the Executive Council tomorrow morning. Anything in my power to serve you in this, or any other business you may have with the president or council, I will with pleasure." But the days multiplied into weeks and still there was no answer from Mifflin and no presentation of the colors.

On September 4 a letter arrived. It was from Biddle again. "Gentlemen," he addressed Fitch and Voight, "With pleasure I deliver to you an ensign for your Steam Boat. As it is not at the expense of the state, but the voluntary contribution of the President and of Messers Miles, Gregg, Rucker, Wall, Smith, Potts, Findlay and Hartzell, members of the Supreme Executive Council, and of the Secretary, it must not be considered as presented by me officially." However, "I sincerely hope that your ingenious labours may redound to your honor and emolument in proportion to the advantage the Public may derive from them and that your striving against the stream may neither prove useless to the world or unprofitable to yourselves."

At this cagey trick of dissociating themselves from official presentation of the flag, Fitch slumped again into bitter disillusionment with American lawmakers.

He had also lost his dispute with Dr. Thornton, who had made the passenger cabin high and elegant. But in spite of this obstacle thus offered to the wind, the steamboat was still the swiftest packet on the Delaware.

According to the agreement of January, 1789, the holders of the forty additional shares were to turn over their stock to the original company and all shares were to have an equal value when it was proved that the steamboat was capable of moving against the current at the rate of eight miles an hour. This was concluded with appropriate ceremonies in June when "a mile was measured in Front Street... and the bounds projected at right angles, as exactly as they could be, to the wharves, where a flag was placed at each end, and also a stop watch. The boat was ordered under way at dead water, or when the tide was found to be without movement. As the boat passed one flag it was struck, and at the same instant the watches were set off; as the boat reached the other flag it was also struck, and the watches instantly stopped. Every precaution was taken before witnesses; the time was shown to all, the experiment declared to be fairly made, and the Boat was found to go at the rate of Eight miles an hour, or one mile within an eighth of an hour; on which the shares were signed over with great satisfaction by the rest of the Company."

This great satisfaction arose because the stockholders now had hopes of dividends. They could not beat the running schedule of the stages, but they could lower the rates. In direct competition with the shallops which went to Burlington, Bordentown and Bristol and the stages which went to Trenton and Chester, the Company established a base at the foot of Arch Street by the Ferry and began to advertise regular trips.

"The Steamboat," it was announced, "is now ready to take passengers, and is intended to set off from Arch Street Ferry, in Philadelphia, every Monday, Wednesday and Friday for Burlington, Bristol, Bordentown and Trenton, to return on Tuesdays, Thursdays and Saturdays. Price for passengers 2/6 to Burlington and Bristol, 3/9 to Bordentown, 5 shillings to Trenton." And on Sundays it was planned that the boat would carry passengers back and forth from Chester.

During that summer of 1790 these advertisements were published frequently in both the *Federal Gazette* and the *Pennsylvania Packet,* but not in Franklin's *Gazette.* This was a mistake, as the directors soon must have realized, for not only would the feelings of any newspaper publisher have been wounded by such neglect of his advertising columns, but Franklin's *Gazette* was edited by the late philosopher's spiteful grandson, Benjamin Franklin Bache. Bache had inherited his grandfather's shares in the Rumseian Society, also and though he had "taken many trips in the boat, on his own business, to Burlington and other places, without offering a single souse for the favor," and had likewise "made himself pretty free on board in wine and porter which was provided by poor Mr. Voight" and Fitch, he nevertheless ridiculed the steamboat in his best unsigned manner:

"A boat on this construction, barring all accidents of breaking paddles, cranks, gudgeons, watchwheels, chains, Loggerheads, cocks, valves, condensers, pins, bolts, pistons, cylinders, boilers and God only knows how many more useful parts, would *almost* stem the tide of the Delaware; and the net proceeds of the monthly expenses would not exceed those of the income above ten Pounds; so that in one year there must be a clear saving of 120 Pounds—no matter to whom, so that it is saved.

"And to compleat the machinery of a Boat on this plan, of ten or fifteen tons Burthen, and keep her in tolerable order, may be done at a very moderate expense; as one master coppersmith, with three or four journeymen, a master Blacksmith, with as many Journeymen, aided by an ingenious watch and clock maker, provided they are industrious, will be amply sufficient for the purpose."

All these absurdities Bache had conjured out of half a dozen minor accidents; the axletree broke twice, the grate burned out and had to be replaced and once they overcrowded the boiler. In August, after the boat had been running for two months, an enthusiastic correspondent reported to the *New York Magazine:*

"Fitch's steamboat really performs to a charm. It is a pleasure, while one is on board of her in a contrary wind, to observe her superiority over the river shallops, sloops, ships, &c., who, to gain anything, must make a zigzag course, while this, our new invented vessel, proceeds in a direct line. On Sunday morning she sets off for Chester, and engages to return in the evening— forty miles. ... Fitch is certainly one of the most ingenious creatures alive, and *will certainly make his fortune."*

Only in his prediction of Fitch's future was the Philadelphia correspondent mistaken. On the upriver run to Burlington, Bristol, Bordentown and Trenton the company lost money with every journey On May 11th, which was a better than average business day, only seven passengers came down to the foot of Arch Street to go aboard. Two were bound for Trenton, ten shillings; one for Bordentown, three shillings, ninepence; one for Bristol, two shillings; and three for Burlington, which amounted to seven shillings, sixpence. The total comes to a little over twenty-three shillings, while the minimum expense of the trip was thirty shillings.

Between the middle of May and the end of August a great number of trips were made to Trenton during the week and to Chester on Sundays. To lure the passengers away from the shallops and stagecoaches the directors offered beer and sausages, rum, porter and the comfort of their elegant cabin. They proved that on short runs the steamboat was swifter and steadier than the shallops and that on the run to Trenton they could make the journey within an hour and at half the expense of the stagecoaches. Nevertheless, the deficit continued to grow.

In the hope of reducing their expenses and increasing the number of passengers they competed with the regular ferry that carried Saturday holiday Philadelphians around to Gray's Gardens on the Schuylkill, which was a summer rendezvous for all classes and colors drawn by dancing, outdoor drinking and long promenades through the shaded dusk. The steamboat charged "a quarter of a dollar for each person thither," but they soon gave it up because they were unable to fill the boat even at that price.

The steamboat had traveled eighty miles in a day. It had carried passengers between two and three thousand miles from the middle of May to the end of September 1790. It had proved itself mechanically by going so much faster than Robert Fulton's *Clermont* was to go in 1807 that, "Had they started together, over the same course, at the same time, Fitch's boat would have reached Albany fifty-two miles in advance" of the *Clermont*. But between Philadelphia and Trenton, without the beneficent tricks of subsidy and franchise, without a wealthy, influential backer and an assured monopoly, the steamboat drained the pockets of its supporters and doomed its inventor.

Ever since he had begun his experiments Fitch had bent determinedly toward the grand scene in which the steamboat was to be developed during the next seventy years. As early as the summer of 1786 he had planned for the use of a steamboat on the Ohio and Mississippi. When Jonathan Longstreth, the son of his old friend in Warminster, went out to Kentucky that July he had carried the news that Fitch meant to build a steamboat at Philadelphia or Pittsburgh for the inland rivers. And Brigadier General James Wilkinson, one Colonel Edwards and several other early Kentucky plantation owners were "very impatient for the boat to arrive."

When the hope of this had been blotted by the treaty with Spain, Fitch had persisted in his belief that a boat might be operated on the Mississippi, arguing that "It may be said the Spaniards will not allow us a trade *down* the River. They cannot refuse us one *up*, and I believe at or near the Falls of St. Anthony may be nearly as good a stand for the fur trade as Hudson's Bay, which is worthy the attention of the most potant Emperor."

In this Fitch was anticipating events by only fifty years. It was not till 1840 that St. Paul, at the Falls of St. Anthony, and St. Louis became the main fur trading posts between the Mississippi and the Rocky Mountains. Meanwhile, "pardon me, generous public, for suggesting ideas that cannot be dijested at this day," . . . but "A Boat that would go at the rate of 4½ miles per hour, could be applied on them Waters to advantage and it would make ½ mile per hour against the strongest Freshes, and by the advantage of Eddies might ascend at the rate of more than one mile per hour, and in common seasons would ascend that River sixty miles in 24 hours, and four men that could Navigate a boat of fifty tons Burthen, 60 miles per day up the

Ohio would be much the cheapest transportation that could be used, because no Machinery whatever is so expensive as the labour of men."

"Our boat as she is," Fitch wrote in the winter of 1789, "would answer a very valuable purpose on the Ohio," but whereas "Rumsey's patrons are men of fortune and give as much attention to his project as if it was a scheam of 100,000 Pounds a year, the gentlemen who support me are generally men of business and give little attention to it, which makes the Ballance of Influence amazingly against me."

On the inland rivers, from Pittsburgh to New Orleans, there was a great trade waiting, and no stagecoaches to compete with, no "invidious rivermen" to influence the people against him with their jeers because they were afraid the steamboat would take their business away from them. With this in mind Fitch wrote to Magnus Miller, addressing him as the most enterprising and first merchant of Philadelphia, proposing that he build a boat that would use sail at sea and the steam engine on the rivers, carrying salt shad and pickled herring around to New Orleans and ascending the Mississippi for a valuable cargo. "The Chiney and Glass Trade cannot be carried on any other way to that country." And while the fact that "the Spaniards will not let us pass" was a "principle objection," he believed they would do so for the following reasons: first, it would encourage an art of such magnitude to their Nation; two, they would wish the Americans to be at the expense of the first experiments; and, three, they would be in fear of offending their "Kentucky Neighbours." But if all else failed "they could not stop us without they could Ketch us, for we could pass forts in the night and outrun them by day!"

Nothing came of his proposal to Miller and he again appealed to the directors of the company. He was destitute, as they knew, but if they would pay his barest expenses he would go to New Orleans and arrange for the rights of navigation of the Mississippi for his boat. If he didn't succeed, they needn't worry about paying his expenses back to Philadelphia, for he would set up as a silversmith in New Orleans.

Every attempt to reach the Mississippi failed. In the fall of 1790, however, the directors were forced to make some provision for western navigation or forfeit the legal monopoly granted by the state of Virginia. It had been provided in his Virginia patent that Fitch was to have two steamboats in actual use on Virginia waters before November 7, 1790; otherwise he would lose his patent by default. So far as transportation on the Potomac or James was concerned, this ruling was unimportant; but at that time Virginia's territory extended westward along the banks of the Ohio to the Mississippi. Therefore another boat had to be built and both boats conveyed to Virginia waters within the next two months or the company would lose its most important single patent.

Since the summer of 1786 four thousand Pounds had been spent on Fitch's experiments. No profit had yet been made. The members of the company were anxious to preserve their Virginia rights, but reluctant to pledge further sums and much more reluctant to give money outright. This produced a series of half-hearted agreements which accomplished nothing but the slow drag of wearied hopes.

In September the stockholders met. They levied ten Pounds against each member. Listening perturbedly, Fitch heard nothing proposed as to when or by whom the money was to be collected. He protested to Edward Brooks, the ironmonger who was now the company's treasurer, that it was well enough to make levies, but that he had too much experience with duns and constables to start building a boat before the money was on hand. The case was critical, he reminded them. A new boat must be ready within two months; work could not be held up while he went around begging the stockholders to fulfill their pledges.

All the directors wanted the boat made, but all of them continued to shy from an immediate levy. Let the vessel be contracted for, they said; they would pay for it later.

This was precisely what Fitch had always tried to avoid. He knew from past experience that the stockholders would baffle his endeavors, that they would overrule him at every critical turn and order the cheapest machinery possible for the boat. And he tried to avoid the difficulty in the only way he knew how, which was by appealing to outsiders who would be expected to benefit from western navigation. He besieged the Pennsylvania representatives from the counties adjacent to Pittsburgh, Albert Gallatin and James Findlay from Fayette, John Hoge from Washington and General Gibson from Allegheny, for assistance in raising subscriptions among the western farmers who had sent them to office.

More than any other people of the United States the farmers from these counties were in need of transportation. Living in scattered neighborhoods along the Ohio, Allegheny and Monongahela Rivers, they subsisted by growing wheat and corn, raising cattle, shooting and trapping game, making their own clothing from hides or rough homespun. Separated from the commercial towns and cities by the Allegheny range, prevented from a downriver trade by the closed port at New Orleans, they were forced into an economy of barter. On corn and wheat, their two chief crops, transportation costs over the mountain were prohibitive and their only means of getting money was in exchange for whisky which they distilled from the grain and carried over the Alleghenies to the eastern towns by pack-horse. All that was needed to prove how dear their few dollars were to them was an excise tax on their only commodity; and when the Federal government began to swell the treasury by laying a tax on whisky they drove the internal revenue officers back over the mountains. And when warrants were issued against their leaders the whole district came together to shout the farmers' protests.

By August, 1792, Gallatin, the immigrant son of an ancient

Swiss family, who managed to be at the same time a Rousseauesque believer in the charms of the wilderness and a hardheaded property owner, found himself pushed up at the head of several thousand belligerent farmers. They had resolved that the laws of Congress were hasty and oppressive, that the salaries of officials were outrageously high, that the interest of the national debt was unreasonable, that the redemption of the Continental notes at face value when the original holders had sold them to the government speculators for a few cents was outright theft, and that "a duty laid on the common drink of the nation, instead of taxing the citizens according to their property, falls as heavy on the poorest class as on the rich." By the fall of 1794 the merchants, speculators and manufacturers who formed the government regarded Gallatin as an "arch-fiend" whom they sought to indict in Federal court and the insurrection had been vanquished by an expeditionary force composed of Secretary of the Treasury Hamilton, President Washington, Governor Lee of Virginia, and fifteen thousand militiamen at the cost of eight hundred thousand dollars.

But in the summer of 1790 when Fitch called on the western delegates for aid in building a boat which would carry their farmers' crops, they received him as a ridiculous crank. He visited them at Major Boyd's, where Gallatin, Findlay and Hoge lodged that session, and spoke first to Findlay. Findlay, who was "not the great Findly, but little Hump Back Findly," put him aside with vague encouragement, refusing to sign his petition. Fitch went on to Gallatin's chamber, where the lean aristocrat of the wilderness silenced him with brusque disdain.

Only General Gibson received him seriously; Fitch grasped at this wisp of hope. General Gibson was to consult with himself whether he could "patronize the scheme for 20 shares, or in partnership with another, so as to build a boat for that place [Pittsburgh]." He also informed him that "som of the Gentlemen from your Country, whome I waited upon to obtain their

Certificates and Countinance, would not even deign or show the least desire of informing themselves of the principles which I ment to go upon; as if they were affraid that they should be convinced that it was their duty to support me.... Such base injustice to the man who has spent his whole fortune, with five or six years, to serve these very men, and the world of mankind at large, must be sensibly felt by a man of fealings; yet, Sir, I dispise such petty imbarrassments.... But should we say that your Country should be deprived of so valuable a machine for Fourteen years, the resentment would be just? But it is not that part that I mean to act, but upon more noble principles; and convince the little, suspicious minds that I am not capable of injuring myself for the sake of injuring others."

But General Gibson decided not to take twenty shares, or ten shares, or five shares. Meanwhile the second boat, which was appropriately named the *Perseverance,* was at last being built. Fitch was fretting at the empty treasury; the directors were countermanding orders and substituting schemes of their own to keep expenses at a minimum. Though the old boat housed the machinery for a successful model it was difficult to duplicate the proportions when all the work had to be done by various journeymen. The stockholders confined themselves to their shops again and nothing could be got out of them in spite of the fact that the Virginia patent would expire in November. As Fitch wrote, the company was "convulsed and everything was thrown in a most tottering situation." And he pleaded "Would you, Gentlemen, so far countinence my application as to support me here for only three months,—for my all is now expended, my last Certificate is sold and gone...."

The next misfortune occurred on the night of October 13th, when a storm broke the new boat from her moorings and drove her out into the Delaware to be washed up on Petty's Island. And before the *Perseverance* could be drawn off, repaired and brought back to the Front Street wharf it was October 22.

Fitch wrote frantically to the Virginia Assembly "that your petitioner after several years' unremitted attention and at an amazing expence [has] compleated his steamboat which he has had in use as a passage boat on the River Delaware during the last summer; that as soon as he had assertained the utility of his boat from actual use he immediately began another boat for the application of steam; not only to comply with the condition of the law of your state, but to navigate her waters—but that in a storm on the night of the 13th Instant, his new boat broke from her moorings... which renders it impossible for him to compleat her in time to comply with the condition contained in the Law of your State."

Referred to the Committee on Propositions and Grievances on November 4, the petition was reported on December 7 by Lighthorse Harry Lee, the committee's chairman: Resolved, that it is the opinion of this committee that further consideration of the petition... be deferred to the 31st day of March next,"—which merely added to the general uncertainty of the undertaking.

Meanwhile, winter was "crowding on like an army with bayonets" and Dr. Thornton, who was the most dependable contributor among the stockholders, had sailed with his wife to the pleasant warmth of his Tortola plantation. The mechanically successful steamboat and the unfinished *Perseverance* were both docked until after the ice went out of the river. Seventeen-ninety was coming to its end and except for his position at The Sign of the Buck, Fitch was worse off than ever. Mary Kraft, "the most Noble Spirited woman on earth," never gave him "a sower look on account of Bad pay, but treated me the same as if I paid her weekly."

Fitch spent Christmas day writing a joint proposal to Robert Morris and to Oliver Pollock, Morris' business associate in New Orleans, that they each advance two hundred and fifty pounds toward the construction of the *Perseverance* and, reserving a tenth share for himself and a twentieth for Henry Voight, that they "have an equal share in this boat, according to the money advanced, with all the advantages and immoluments which may be given by the Government or Governments for the taking a boat from this city to the Rapids of Ohio." After which, Morris and Pollock were "to be permitted to build any number of Boats they shall see fit, in proportion to their shares in the Boat Perseverance by allowing the original shareholders one half of the neat profits after deducting the prime cost of the Boat or Vessel." The object was, he explained in a letter to Morris, to open a "Trading House at New Orleans; and doubt not but if Mr. Morris should patronize it, Mr. Leamy, the Spanish Consul, would give it Countinance and probably Support." Even then "not less than ten or fifteen boats would do the business for that river," he estimated; and "these boats, by carrying back the people at reasonable rates who transport the produce down the River, must soon make an amazing ods in the Trade of that Town..."

But the treaty by which the rich men of the East had bound the development of the West still blocked the way. Before they could establish a trading post at New Orleans, Morris and Pollock answered, Fitch would have to get a permit from the Spanish Governor of Louisiana....

Fitch was now dependent on the charity of Mary Kraft. He had sold his last share of stock in the steamboat company, had collected all the small debts that were owed him and had spent the money frugally. Apart from shirts, shoes and stockings his entire wardrobe consisted of a pair of breeches which had begun "to break in the Crotch; four stocks, in constant wear about three years...One coat" of which "I cannot tell the exact age and constant wear of it, but it is broke in every part, especially the lining, elbows, about the wrists and under the armes; an old second handed hat, now worn by me about two years; one Greatcoat, three years old; one pair of Cours Indian legings and one nightcap, 2¼ years old but very good."

Voight, too, had virtually pauperized himself. He had neglected his business for the last three years and most of his old customers had grown impatient at finding his door so often locked. Others had left him because of his disreputable Deistic ideas or on account of his cranky notions respecting steamboats. And he was further embarrassed by the fact that he had a wife and seven children to support.

But they were both still determined to continue work on the steamboat. As there was no money to be had from the stockholders they decided to apply for jobs with the government. Congress was moving to Philadelphia from New York that year; there was also the Pennsylvania Assembly and if they found a position at either place they believed they would be able to carry on their steamboat building during holidays and in the evening.

They began by collecting testimonials to their fitness and respectability. The Pennsylvania Assembly, under their new constitution, was to have a Sergeant at Arms and, backed by recommendations from Dr. Ewing, David Rittenhouse, Andrew Ellicott and Dr. Patterson, Fitch modestly petitioned the Senate that he might be the favored applicant. He was promptly rejected even "for such a petty office, bearly for my support," which made him "truly ashamed for my meanness of soul to think of the like... and had I at that time had my writings in such forwardness as I have at present I certainly should have died in the Speaker's chair and should have thought it to have been a greater honor to the state than to have Peters die there."

He next appealed to Robert Morris to help him become "Supervisor of Roads or Surveyor of Roads and Rivers"; and when that failed both Voight and he applied for positions in the Federal Mint. "John Fitch is a goldsmith by trade," their joint petition boldly read, "and flatters himself that he could render essential service to his country as assay-master. Henry Voight is perfectly acquainted with the process of coinage, and of all machinery for the business, and can make the instruments himself, having worked at it in Germany for several years." Dr. Ewing, who gave Fitch a personal letter to President Washington, was silent on his accomplishments as a goldsmith, but said truthfully that he was "an ingenious man, and a gentleman of the strictest integrity and diligence in his business, executing any trust committed to him with the greatest fidelity, and believed his modesty is such that he would not undertake an employment which he was not persuaded he had sufficient ability to execute."

Fitch failed in this appointment as in the others. But there was something about Voight's stocky self-assuredness and his claim to foreign experience that was as impressive as the representations of the self-ennobled Kalb and Steuben whom Congress made General Officers upon their own recommendations. Voight was made Chief Coiner in the United States Mint.

A more shattering disappointment broke over Fitch in the following spring when after months of postponement Thomas Jefferson, Henry Knox and Edmund Randolph, who had been appointed Commissioners for the Promotion of Useful Arts, settled the Fitch-Rumsey dispute by giving patents to both of them!

Fitch remonstrated before each of the Commissioners. When he brought his papers to Thomas Jefferson the Secretary of State shook his unwigged red head, pursed his lips and waved Fitch's old portfolio aside, saying "it was too much like tampering with judges out of doors."

"I have an undoubted right to petition," Fitch persisted.

Jefferson objected that Henry Remsen, his clerk, was away and that he could do nothing till he returned. Finally he glanced at the paper and dismissed Fitch with, "I can say nothing till after the board meets."

To add to the insult the patent granted Fitch described not his own successful boat, but the boat which Rumsey was never able to move more than a hundred and fifty yards! It reads "For applying the force of steam to trunk or trunks, for drawing water in at the Bow of a boat or vessel," all of which distinguished the Bernouilli-Franklin-Rumsey contrivance.

When the Commissioners destroyed all the financial value of his invention by giving Rumsey as much right to it as he had himself Fitch determined to quit Philadelphia. He wrote a long explanatory letter to Dr. Thornton and, to save postage to Tortola, carried it around to Thornton's house. When he arrived Mrs. Brodeau, Thornton's mother-in-law, handed him a note she had just received in which Thornton had ordered that Fitch be paid a hundred Pounds to continue working on the boat. And as though this was not enough to tempt him back into the struggle, an hour later he heard from Richard Stockton that the Governor of Louisiana had sent a permit for the steamboat, its operators, their families and household goods to enter New Orleans!

He went back to work in May and labored till September on the *Perseverance*. During this time one of the directors had ordered a wooden case for the boiler. It was found to be too short and to save money they tried to piece it. This looked well enough but at the first surge of steam from the piston the water gushed out as if from a hydrant. Instead of buying a new jacket, the directors decided that the air pump was at fault and that there was probably something wrong with the condenser. These were taken out and before they were replaced the treasury was again empty.

In the midst of this mass of confusion and failure, and with his mind taken up by machinery, God and the welfare of the world, he slipped, almost without realizing it, into a tragic and "delicate dilemma" . . . "the most serious part of my life" . . . for which "I ought almost to suffer by the common executioner."

For several years he had been living at Mary Kraft's Sign of the Buck, at first unable to make any payment. He had been astonished at the kindness of her welcome.

"I for 22 years have never saught after woman, but rather chose to avoid them and have in that time frequently treated the Sex unbecoming a man for which I ask their Pardon. I have in this time kept a solemn Lent for more than seven years together, which I look upon to be too scrupiously unreasonable in either sex.... I have never saught after tham to this day, but should I see one going into the Histericks and throw herself in my way I would lend every friendly Aid in my power to relieve her...."

His marriage had been brief and disastrous. Of his wife he said, "I cannot say that I was ever passionately fond of the woman, but for the sake of promises, I determined to marry her." Nowhere does he express for her or for any other woman as deep an affection as he felt for his friend Voight. Perhaps there were reasons why his wife Lucy turned into a shrew, which Fitch did not understand. But he understood friendship, and in the light of this understanding of friendship and failure to understand love, this singular story which he tells here becomes credible. "I give this to you in the Strictest confidence you are not at liberty to let anything be published that will hurt the feelings of my friends or their Children and strictly forbid the whole truth to be made public in less than thirty years in which time probably they will be dead and their children married."

"I once had two friends, a male [Henry Voight] and a female [Mary Kraft]. The female was a wido and kept a public house where my male friend met me every evening and many friendly hours we Passed without ever being interrupted by jarrs or different sentiments, as our sentiments were the most uniform of any two men I ever saw, altho our persons and passions were as different as any two.

"I always kept early hours and was never out much after 8 oClock and seldom ever failed of being at home and in bead by

9 oClock in the Evening and always left my friend with my other Friend and a long time passed before I suspected their friendship but to be as pure as my own and unmixed with any designs. But after a year or two's time I began to suspect their Friendship was carried to excess and finally the productions of love appeared. I was much allarmed for them as both of them had valuable Familys of children of six or 7 each; and to see the destruction of those families, who were the only friends I had in the World, wrecked my Tortured Soul to the Centure.

"After about one week consideration I told my male friend that I would relieve him and said to him, 'I never design or intend to marry, therefore what I am about to propose can be no inconveanance to me'; John Fitch calmly made this extraordinary statement and proceeded to follow it up with a unique offer: 'and to save your and her reputation I will marry the woman and Pledge my word of honor never to bead with her.'

"He seemed to be possessed at that time with that degree of gratitude as was due for such a generous offer and when we mentioned it to her at the same time told her that I would not be burthensome to her, but that I would live with her and pay my bord the same as another Border and ask no favours from her.

"She, being a shrewd, sensible woman, probably thought that there was some trap laid for her and treated the offer not only with contempt but with considerable resentment, when heaven knows there was nothing but the purest and undefiled friendship designed. I did at this time pledge my Plighted faith of honor to do everything which lay in my power to save the reputations of my friends and their families and made no reserve to myself, being conscious that I had committed no crime against the laws of my Country...

"She was obliged to quit a good run of business which she had and closit herself in an obscure house to protect herself. I did not nor could not forsake her and carryed my friendship even to madness, far beyond the limits of prudence... At the birth of the Child, it being on a Sunday evening and the porches in the front of the House crouded with people, there luckily came on a thundergurst and drove the people in and I believe the crys of the Child was not heard. I took the child in my arms and carried it to a nurse who the midwife had prepared and was obliged to degrade the man and become a nurse; for all of which I feel a happiness that I have done it."

Afterward "I religeously preached up the Valuableness of their families and warned them that the meshurs they persued would certainly terminate in the destruction of Both. They frequently promised me that they would comply with my advice—but reason must and always will give to Love, especially in the female Sex. Their resolves cannot be relied upon no longer than their beloved object is absent; and men are not to be relied upon when the allurements of women and opportunities serve their purpose. In this situation they continued till the effects of Love promised further increase to their family.

"They both being allarmed, let me know their offense. She went from home four or five months. During that time happened to fall in with some of her acquaintance. And you may well think the predicament that she was thrown into! Not knowing how to protect her honor and thinking probably I was of an easy disposition and her sincear friend, run the Venture without my leave of throwing herself on me for protection and called herself after my name. This, when I heard it, not only allarmed me, but I thought it unkind usage and it was the first time I knew that one person could make a bargain . . .

"On her return home she was brought to bead about eight miles off and word was sent to me as her Husband. You may have some conception of the Convultions of my mind, though in a very imperfect manner; for to acknowledge one who had prostituted herself to be my wife was degrading the man too much and [I] could not indure the thought. But on the other hand I knew her goodness of heart and that she was led into her errors by the purest Love, that her connections with him had diminished her friends and that he was totally refuseing to give her any countinence and refuseing to go and see her in her distress. And to leave so Valuable a woman without a friend on Earth I could not.

"The woman who called me her husband being in such a deplorable situation thro her love for my Friend and being treated with such neglect, nay, baseness from him, required me to become her protector. I never denying what she had said, but rather encouraging the World to believe it, found myself Very seriously intangled. Of course I became obliged to become her Gardian and assume the direction of her family, as her distresses carried her to excess in Histericks and other Extravigencyes. Thinking by acting as her most intimate friend I possibly might wean the affections of her from the man who had treated her so basely, of course I at that time became more intimately acquainted with her than ever I had been before. I then had a design of making her my lawful wife as soon as I could be persuaded her affections were so far called off from him as that I could feal myself safe in the ingagements [and] of course delt with him according to the strictest turns of justice.

"Sir," Fitch wrote to Voight on November 1st, 1791, "I will yet call you my friend and hope that our friendship may never be dissolved, altho I have the greatest cause of complaints; but anything as to myself will never be resented by me— But, Sir, I have taken your once esteamed Nancy under my protection and mean to treat her as the Wife of your friend ought to be treated and believe me to be Base if I do not use her the same as I would my Old Friend Harry..."

"He being sensible of my determination, became much enraged; as if I had debarred him from his choicest pleasure. He came Drunk and kept on so all the next day. The abuses which he gave to her and me ought to remain unpardonable, but I have forgave him the abuses to myself, for which he took me round the neck and Kissed me. The offense he has given to my other friend has not been settled, neither can I see [that] any reparation can be made for the loss of Character which he caused Nancy in his wild Extravagance and by very falsly, as well as loudly, asserting to our listening Neighbors.

"After she had given herself out to be my wife and I had lived in the house so long, the world must suppose the last Child to be mine; and for me to deny it and forsake her then would undoubtedly set every honest man against me for ruining the woman and destroying so Valuable a family. Of course I was obliged to step forward and receive her as my Wife and give her every countinence which is due to a wife or be looked upon as a Damd Rascal. But by receiving her—if what was true should come to light—I must be esteamed as acting beneath the dignity of a man. But knowing the Worth of the Woman, I resolved to take her part, Rather choosing to be supposed guilty of meanness than rascality. At the same time I could not believe that the damdest Scounderal on Earth could be guilty of blasting a woman's character" yet Voight came yelling at the window that the child was his "and made me wish that the Devil had me rather than to have been so entangled. But after I was so intangled, if she had been the Devil himself was determined to make the best of it. But knowing her to be as good a woman as ever lived as well as a woman of fortune and a fortune in herself, this compelled me not to forsake her. And believe that I saved her life by my friendly Aid, which otherwise would probably have been destroyed by her freting.

"On the Whole I acknowledge that I have far exceeded Quixot in relieving Distressed Ladies, but hope that the imputations of windmills may not be laid to my Charge. On the Whole, if mankind had been as good as they ought to be, I do not know one instance of my life in which I should have acted differently and yet I have felt in Character much beneath the meanest Citizen from the experience. I hope the world will judge more candidly in future and not to suppose one mean or Base without full conviction.

"I do believe that the greatest torment that a man can have in this World is to be teised with a woman and have ever been of that opinion since I left New England. Not being a very handsome man and one of Very indifferent address and of no flattery, you might reasonably suppose that I have steered thro life upward of 20 years without the worst of ills befalling me.

"All I can say of the matter is this: I think this is a dam wicked world and when I get clear of it never wish to come back to it any more. I have frequently been apt to conclude it is a place where they transport Souls to from other Planets that is not fit to live in them, the same as Great Britain used to send Convicts to Virginia; and if I was sent here as a lunatick to Bedlam or for runing into Chymereal whims, I am sure my lesson of Caution will be sufficient to make me more cautious when I get back to Jupiter again."

Meanwhile Voight's loud, outrageous scenes at The Sign of the Buck had driven Mary Kraft from Philadelphia. In December, 1791, she fled to New York and lodged at 7 Chatham Street where she represented herself as Mrs. Mary Fitch.

But no sooner had she arrived than she began to worry about the children she had left behind. There was also business to be seen to with regard to the executors of her husband's will. And more than that, without the Sign of the Buck she had no means of earning a living. She wrote to Fitch, saying that she was coming back.

Fitch protested. Let her come back and settle the estate or "send orders to Esqr. Weaver to sell a certain part of your effects and then go to Charleston" of which his nephew, the son of Sarah and Timothy King sent favorable reports, "and get into some small way of business and live as becomes a good Citizen, which I have no doubt you would do, and save yourself and family.

"My dear Girl," he assured her, "the affairs of your family remain much as they was at your departure, otherwise than Michael has left his place and got another at [illegible]. The Executors have determined that the children shall have Guardians, which I think very proper in the case of Michael and Charlotte. Elizabeth and Hannah, I think, are well provided for and well satisfied and I can get Polly with Hannah at Mr. Young's at 3 shillings per week, where I think she will be properly satisfied. And I believe the Executors will not meddle with them, for two reasons—first, because they cannot better their situations, second, as you are left their Guardian by the will.

"Believe me Nancy this once to be an honest man and that I wish to live no longer than I can live independent of Michael Kraft's estate, but be assured that if you return to Philadelphia to live again you loose the patronage and protection of your John."

Baffled by Fitch from his "choicest pleasure," Voight retaliated by laying claim to the invention of the Horse-boat, of which "there was not a Stick, wheal, Gudheon or Rivet" but what belonged to Fitch. And this instance "of a plain, open, sociable Dutchman, and a man of such address that no one could suspect his integrity, to betray so sincear a friend as I was to him, and not only betray but try to destroy me that he might Rise by my falling," led Fitch to believe he had learned mankind so well "that the most contemtable wretch amongst them would deprive God Almighty of his throne."

He wrote bitterly to Voight, "Your ungenerous treatment of me in striving to deprive me of all kinds of merit in my schemes, notwithstanding what I have done to save your reputation and the destruction of your family, and altho I have given you much more than you deserve of our Inventions that you might stand on an equal footing with me, yet you have striven to deprive me of my just reputation.

"This conduct, Sir, of yours has roused me to a determination to procure justice, but however, I wish to do it in an agreeable manner. I intend to be at Mr. Flemings this evening, where I expect you will meet me to settle our affairs. It may not be improper to inform you that it is my most serious intention to enter a caveat against your patent unless you settle with me amicably. Your interest, therefore, will induce you to meet me."

Voight felt equally injured. "Sir," he replied, "as for taxing me with ungeners tretment towards you, is a thing, witch is diametrical the contrary: what you say, that I should or would do towards you, you have done against me: and I can prove the thing sir to your Face.... I hafe bin the looser quite sufficient on the Steam Boat on your account; and I hafe no doubt but you will try to seek to take every advantage; and take everything from me you can: but depend upon, you will fint it a hart task, believe me, my friend... If you hafe anything to say to me, you know where I live and my door has always been open to you; and I hafe walked a many a long trip on yr account, now I think you may as well come to my house in Second Street as me to go some place witch I don't know—I know no Fleming by name nor where it is, but you know Mr. Wells, and if you will come there this evening by 7 oClock I will be there and hear what you hafe to say."

They continued to bicker throughout the winter. Meanwhile Mary Kraft came back from New York and Fitch, as he had warned her, moved his few belongings to another boarding house. He left, reluctantly and aggrieved. From his new quarters he wrote accusingly:

"Nancy, I absolutely did hear 2 persons say and if I remember right it was you and Harry Voight that J. F. should never want whilst you had a shilling. Your words are verified for I never have wanted and this will inform you that I never will and also that you have lost the most Sincear friend you ever had.

"P. S. I do not want to hurt your fealings, but I wish you to have serious reflections. Fair Well."

He moved to the boarding house of another widow, Hannah Levering, and spent the winter there. When spring came the steamboat company had been abandoned by all but three or four members. With forty dollars which Richard Stockton had contributed, Fitch went to work again on the *Perseverance*. So small a sum was useless, since the piston plunger was too weak to work against over two hundred pounds of steam. Still hopeful, Fitch appealed to Edward Brooks, Stockton and Dr. Say, "Gentlemen, I wish that we may be governed by reason and not from inclination, nor to be turned out of the most juditious path which we ought to stear, thro fear of the frowns or smiles of the public. We have bore the Buffetings of the world a long time and since we are so used to it it can be no great hardship for us to stand it a month or two longer..."

But the stockholders would give no more. Let the boat be tried and the whole project stand or fall upon its performance, they said. In a last attempt to raise money for alterations in the machinery, Fitch begged Dr. Rittenhouse for an advance of fifty Pounds, promising to pay him a hundred in return by going to Kentucky and selling his land there. "My Friends have become disjointed, when the scheme is on the crisis of compleation, and can raise no more money. I am both in debt and in Rags; but could I compleat it by selling all my property in Kentucky at a great loss, I would gladly do it. I think with 50 Pounds I could cloathe myself, pay my debts and compleat the greatest undertaking, worthy the notice of Mr. Rittenhouse, and wish his name recorded, that he was the man, and wish the honor conferred on him."

When this appeal failed Fitch gave the *Perseverance* her final trial. Henry Voight leaving his office of Chief Coiner of the United States Mint bustled down to the Front Street wharf. Going close to the edge of the Delaware he smiled down at Fitch who was worriedly inspecting the sluggish piston. The engine strained weakly, and he knew the reason as well as his former partner, but the sight of the ragged, ungainly inventor laboring at his hopeless task made him expand with joy till he began to rock back and forth on his sturdy heels.

He wished the Devil would fetch away all steamboat builders, Voight proclaimed. No, he didn't either, he crowed slyly, because in that case the Devil would take him first! And he had a fine job and was a good, respectable citizen. He was also, he went on crowing, the only man who knew how to make the steamboat go; he could make the boat go nine miles an hour and could do it in less than three days! But he wouldn't tell Johnny Fitch how to do it. No, my friendt!

Fitch bent his head. This was the end of his experiments on the Delaware. Every penny he had earned from his map had gone into the steamboat; in the cause of the steamboat he had journeyed hundreds of miles on foot, had neglected his Kentucky claims, had written thousands on thousands of words in letters, petitions and pleas, had frayed away the last tough fiber of his Yankee ingenuity. And now, he believed, it had all come to nothing for lack of money to make a few alterations. This, added to Voight's triumphant revenge, made him feel as if he were "bound with chains and being beaten."

XV

EVER since his pinched, meager childhood Fitch had sought a way of life in which there was knowledge instead of meanness and superstition, community of interests in place of anarchical competition. From the long, dismal Sundays of his youth when he "dare not go into the gardain to Pick Currants or into the Orchad to pick up an Apple" because of local religious taboos he had rejected Presbyterianism. The business of living, he already knew, was hard enough without the church's efforts to cramp it further. As a young man he had deserted his wife rather than endure her nagging attempts to make him into a devout ignoramus.

Still to Fitch's mind some form of organized religion was indispensable. He believed his need for greater knowledge and for a government that would reflect the will of the people was inseparable from religion. He believed ardently that mankind had a mission to carry out, which was to "purify the life of the community and to uplift the state," that a man's duties were as important as his rights and that his social obligations were paramount. Like his forefathers, he believed that these were the tasks of a Christian. But where their convictions had hardened into dogma, into mumbled prayers and the protection of property rights, his were rampant and critical.

At Trenton during the Revolution he had joined the Methodists, hoping that among this newer sect he would find answers more applicable to the problems of existence. But he discovered that their materialist base was little broader than the Presbyterians' and that their sense of comradeship, of being banded together in a fight for goodness and democracy was inoperative before the individual tendency of each to benefit at the expense of all the others. He found the same inconsistency between purpose and practices in the Masons, which he joined when he came home from the wilderness. Their brotherhood of the Mystic Tie held forth the slogan but contained little of the reality of brotherhood and all he could write of them in his will was "as I have lodged seven or eight Pounds in the Masons funds I trust they will have generosity enough to give everyone present" at his funeral "a good Drink so as to make them feel Glad they are alive."

But like thousands of his generation he still dreamed of changing the world through socio-religious action, of uniting not only the people of America, but the people of all nations and races under the acknowledgment of a single Deity in a society that would punish "Breach or want of honour with greater severity than even Fraud itself." For in spite of the fact that the Northwest Territory had been parceled out to a few avaricious speculators and that he was growing bald in the unaided struggle of trying to perfect a socially useful machine, he could conceive no connection between private ownership and the increasing burdens of the poor.

Far from revolutionary as Fitch's ideas were, they were suppressed wherever they rose above a whisper. Though the Constitution protected "the free exercise" of religion, it was conveniently overlooked by the government in the case of Deists like Fitch and Negro Baptists of the South and was guaranteed, in fact, only when respectable pewholders could go home "Satisfied of a Sunday" with a "good Federalist sermon." For, as General Washington had warned his officers in his Farewell Address, "Of all the dispositions and habits which lead to political prosperity, religion and morality are indispensable supports." And without religion "where is the security for property...?" which took for granted that private property was sanctioned by nothing short of Divine Right.

Not long after Fitch and Voight met they both discovered they were "Deists by profession." And "there being great numbers of people coming to see us at the Boat, and we frequently getting middling glad in liquor, spoke our sentiments perhaps more freely than was prudant for us to do." Over a dram of grog or a noggin of whisky they would find another crony with whom they were agreed in "Mechanical, Philosophical and Religious sentiments."

In this way they were surprised to discover that "large boddies of people were of our belieff, altho too delicate to confess it." There were Robert Scott, the engraver, Isaac Hough, Mr. Parrish, Mr. Meminger, Mr. Goodfellow and Major Moore, who kept the livery stable at the lower end of town. And by the fall of 1789 they had increased the number of their heretical friends to fifteen or twenty who would drop in at their lodgings or stop at their workshop when the directors were not there. This "put a Scheam" into Fitch's head, "which was, to form a society for that body of people. I had two views in it. The first was for the benefit of mankind and the support of Civil Government." In the second he was "stimulated by pride and determined the world" should know that "contemptible as I was and despised by all ranks of People from the first officers of Government down to the Blaiburry Garls, I could call in all the world into my doctrins, the Jews with the fulness of the Gentile Nations and establish one Aery [era] through out the World."

"This scheme I thought I had pretty well matured before I mentioned it even to my friend Voight. My designs were that as I had found a large body of people in whome Religion or rather Christian Creed had no weight... to form a society... in which they should be bound in honor... and expelled for any improper conduct either to the society or others... and not only expelled, but to have their names published in some public paper ... which I thought would be more Terror to them than all the Tormants of Damnation Preached by the ablest Divines."

"I proposed in my own mind further after the Society was once formed and a Generous Constitution adopted to invite all Ranks of people to join us that we might not be looked upon as a Deistical society only.... I also proposed to have a friendly Society and, in short, in every respect to pattern after George Fox, excepting only that all questions should be freely discursed, even to the denial of the divinity of Moses, Jesus Christ and Mohammed.

"Upon this broad Bassis I had no doubt but we should soon form a Society ... that would produce some able speakers. As soon as that should be effected so that the questions on our files could be ably handled, proposed to make our meeting public and publish the questions weekly what was to be discursed the Sunday following.

"These Ideas with many more were the outlines which I had figured out to myself before I mentioned it to my friend Voight; when he approved of the plan and we agreed to try to form a Society. The next evening we saw Isaac Hough and he agreed to join us. The day following I called on Robert Scott and he was zealous for it. In the meantime Mr. Voight saw Mr. Parrash and we all agreed to meet the Sunday following. Accordingly we did at the hour appointed and Mr. Hough and Mr. Parrash were appointed to form a Temporary constitution and a week or two after presented it to us and after a week or two I got a parole of honor annexed to it, which was the first step I could introduce to my Plan.

"Our Society in the winter of 1790 increased Very rapidly and our numbers soon arrived to about forty and had we then thrown open our Doors to Christian Deists we should soon have had the Society crouded and many able speakers, that we could with credit throw open our doors for all classes of People to hear our debates." But the other members were fearful of becoming anything more than a "private society" which met with as little publicity as possible. This timidity exasperated Fitch and he would have stepped forward, but "my despicable appearance, my uncouth way of speaking, and holding up extravagant ideas and so bad an address must ever make me unpopular, but was I a handsom man and a good riter I could now do more than ever Jesus Christ or George Fox did."

Fitch was convinced that "more than half the wealth of Philadelphia was possessed by real Deists" and because of this he believed that a society could easily be formed which would lead a swift course through bigotry and superstition. That Deism was the secret religion of many of the rich and influential men was true. Its liberality was a reflection of a more luxurious way of living and of the scientific achievements which had made more wealth possible. It had been vaguely formulated by the leisure class philosophers, by Rousseau and Voltaire in France, by Hume, Bolingbroke and Gibbon in England. Until the end of the eighteenth century it was "rather an aristocratic movement" and had enlisted such tacit adherents in America as Washington, Franklin and Jefferson. Its basic idea, that religion sprang from the hearts of men and not from divine revelation was "generally accepted by educated men during the latter half of the eighteenth century. But "In America as in England respectability called for church affiliation, and there seems to have been a feeling among gentle folk that their liberal theological views were not for the poor and lowly." They felt that once the poor had realized their destiny was in their own hands they would no longer submit to oppression. "Very few rich men," one of the franker wealthy converts stated, "or at least men in the higher grades of society, and who have received a liberal education, care anything about the Christian religion. They cast off the yoke of superstition themselves; yet, for the sake of finding obedient servants, they would continue to impose it on the poor." [1]

Without understanding that class interest towered far above even the loftiest philosophical speculations, that rich Deists would inevitably join rich non-Deists in the fight to keep the masses in ignorance, Fitch believed that if Peter Yarnell, an outspoken Quaker from Montgomery County, or Nathaniel Irwin "should step forward and form a Society upon generious Principles and give public lectures on questions every Sunday and charge but a moderate price they would in the first place soon make a fortune. In the Second Place, they would do real and great good to mankind. Third, they would soon have connections with other Societies which would take rise throughout the continent from the original society" until they were strong enough to elect members of Congress "and finally a President of the United States and fix a new Era that all the world would remember when the names of Jesus Christ and Washington is lost."

Now, he informed Rev. Irwin, there was "the greatest opening for a man of Tallents equal to yours to make himself the Greatest which ever lived. Moses, Jesus Christ, Alexander or Mohamet would stand but cyphers to him." And although he admitted that this was "too delicate a matter to speak to a divine so freely as I have done, but wish to do all the good I can and I esteem you the fitest person in the whole course of my acquaintance to undertake it, could you be prevailed upon to ingage in the great undertaking"

"The person who undertakes this," he went on to assure Irwin, "must be a person of real Ability and of good Address and nothing else is wanting but a perfect knowledge of Masonry and of Foxes' and Westly's plans. And by compounding them all together, a most perfect sistim might be adopted. I would take the Legislative and Executive from George Fox, the Friendly

[1] Koch, G. Adolph, "Republican Religion."

part from the Masons, and perhaps something similar of making themselves known, and the Classes and Class meetings, with the prerogative of appointing Class leaders from Westly. I should wish in a particular manner for Classes that youths might be lernt not only the Art of Speaking, but also of reasoning on any subject; which would enable every genius to come forward and men of real ability not to lie concealed and all men more capable of judging of right and rong between man and man.

"On these Principles, sir, I wish you to forego a good name for a Short time and do the most good and make yourself the greatest man that ever Lived." "If not, sir, it will be my study to find out some other, that I may have the honor of being their Servant; and I wish the business not delayed."

The Reverend Irwin, however, was satisfied with his peaceful Neshaminy congregation which he entertained and instructed with ingenious discourse. He was one of the patrons of Halyburton's "Rational Inquiry into the Principles of the Modern Deists" when that attack on Deism was published in Philadelphia and even for the sake of rivaling "Moses, Jesus Christ, Alexander or Mohamet" he was not tempted to "forego a good name."

But a militant Deist was already striding toward Philadelphia. His name was Elihu Palmer and in the choice between his reputation and his convictions he was not the man to hesitate.

Elihu Palmer, a farmer's son from Canterbury, Connecticut, had worked his way through Dartmouth College by teaching school during vacations and with the aid of the founder's fund for the Christianization of the Indians. He had graduated in 1787, when he was twenty-three, and had been elected to Phi Beta Kappa. As a divinity student in search of a parish, he received a call a few months later from the Presbyterian congregation at Newtown, in Queens County, Long Island. On his way he preached a Thanksgiving sermon at Sheffield, Massachusetts, in which "Instead of expatiating upon the horrid and awful condition of mankind in consequence of the lapse of Adam and his wife," he heretically "exhorted his hearers to spend the day joyfully in innocent activity, and to render themselves as happy as possible."

As an inquiring student of religion, Palmer had been driven away from religious dogma through contact with the ideas of Locke, Newton and the great body of writings which opened men's minds to philosophical skepticism and logical naturalism. At Newtown the task of teaching the Presbyterianism which he had himself rejected became still more difficult because there he met a man of similar ideas, a Dr. Ledyard who was possessed of "talents and a freethinker." From the beginning Dr. Ledyard "amused himself by attacking Mr. Palmer on doctrinal points of religion." Anxious to hold his parish, but too honest to defend a position he had secretly rejected, Palmer compromised by admitting that he believed as Ledyard did but asking him to keep his heterodoxy secret.

But this was no help to Palmer in his wretchedness at having to say one thing while he believed another. At Mrs. Riker's one evening he raised his voice in bitter mockery, reciting Dr. Watts' lines on original sin:

> "Lord I am vile, conceived in sin,
> And born unholy and unclean;

"Then turning to Mrs. Riker he declared that he did not believe a word of it, no, not one word, he repeated with emphasis."

By the end of 1789 Palmer's position had become intolerable; his frankness soon lost him his congregation and he started down to Philadelphia to join the Baptists.

But Palmer's quarrel with religion was more than a rejection of dogma. He was the eighth child of hard-working parents; his twenty-five years had been a struggle with poverty and his mind was warmed by class consciousness. "The grand object of all civil and religious tyrants," he declared, "those privileged imposters of the world, has been to suppress all the elevated operations of the mind, to kill the energy of thought, and through this channel to subjugate the whole earth for their own special emolument." "In all the ancient world, Man, every where bending beneath the weight of a compounds despotism, seems almost to have lost the erect attitude assigned to him by the power of Nature, and to grovel upon the earth the most miserable victim of ignorance and tyranny." Let "Reason, righteous and immortal reason, with the argument of the printing types in one hand, and the keen argument of the sword in the other, ... attack the thrones and the hierarchies of the world, and level them with the dust; then the emancipated slave must be raised by the power of science into the character of an enlightened citizen; thus possessing a knowledge of his rights, a knowledge of his duties will consequently follow, and he will discover the intimate and essential union between the highest interests of existence, and the practice of an exalted virtue."

Like all Deists, Palmer believed in the perfectibility of man and he slashed at the Bible as at the shackles of a slave. "The destruction of the cities of Sodom and Gomorrah by fire and brimstone precipitated from Heaven in the form of rain; the blowing down the walls of Jericho with rams' horns, by the triumphant march of the priesthood round the city; the marvellous and frightful story of the witch of Endor; the woeful condition of Daniel in the den of lions; the hot, sultry situation of Shadrach and his two companions in the fiery furnace; together with the unnatural and hopeless abode of poor Jonah in the belly of the whale; all these are specimens of that miserable and disgusting extravagance with which this Holy Bible is every where replete."

Within a few months Palmer had gained and lost his Baptist pulpit in Philadelphia. Study had taught him the great benefits of science and experience had shown him the stifling effects of bigotry and suspicion. It was this determination to bring his knowledge to the masses that even Deistical property owners viewed as a crime. "Hume, Bolingbroke, and Gibbon," complained the Rev. Robert Hall, "addressed themselves solely to the more polished classes of the community, and would have thought their refined speculations debased by an attempt to enlist disciples from among the populace," but now infidelity "boldly ventures to challenge the suffrage of the people, solicits the acquaintance of peasants and mechanics, and seeks to draw whole nations to its standards."

One raw Monday in the middle of March Fitch left Hannah Levering's boarding house and shambled down Second Street toward the workshop where the machinery for the *Perseverance* was being built. At one of the narrow, cobbled cross streets he met his friend, the livery stable keeper, Major Moore. It was obvious from the Major's reserve that there was something on his mind; talking in monosyllables, he led Fitch into a nearby tavern and there, over a stiff bottle, he explained that on the previous Thursday the "Society of Universal Baptists had shut their door on Mr. Palmer and refused him leave to speak in their house any more, altho he had gained great applause amongst all ranks of people."

As a separate fact this was deplorable, but when Fitch linked it with his dwindling "Universal Society" it became "great news." Here was the man for whom he had been waiting, the apostle of goodness in men's hearts and reason in their minds. With the help of the Universal Society Mr. Palmer would be a scourge of superstition and a reformer of civil government. Fitch finished his drink and "went directly home" where he hurriedly collected all his writings and all the scientific and ethical questions which made thinking as hard as putting together an unfamiliar machine without drawings. He was "immediately resolved to make a nois in the world and do the greatest good" with the aid of Mr. Palmer.

With his ancient greatcoat, broken shoes and formidable walking stick, he waited on the militant Deist at his lodgings. Briskly reflective, Mr. Palmer thumbed Fitch's papers, nodding, smiling, frowning while Fitch waited anxiously. But he was soon relieved, for when they began to talk it was evident to Fitch that Palmer "was as well established in my belieffs as I was myself."

Fitch declared earnestly "that I had been prepairing the way in the wilderness for him, thro unbeaten paths." He assured him that he "could bring in 40 Generious, clever fellows into his Society in a lump." He "mentioned near 20 more whome I had great confidence in" and he asked Palmer to "take the helm."

Palmer was encouraged. His ideas and background were forcing him to oppose the rulers of society. Even then he must have felt the need for the kind of organization he later established, a society of Deists with allied organizations and periodical literature. Now Fitch's offer "strengthened his hand" and together they made plans for Palmer's next public address.

Fitch urged him to begin by speaking before his forty "generious, clever fellows" of the Universal Society, then throw open the doors to all citizens, Deists and orthodox Christians, from the "first characters of government" to the lowliest apprentices and indentured servants, when there would be "a fair discurtion of every question," to be joined in "by all sectaries of people and all classes."

But Palmer was "inclined to go on more prudent grounds." Many of the Baptists had stood by him in spite of the ruling of their officers; he was grateful for the support of Fitch and his forty-odd friends, but it would be better if he began by speaking under the auspices of his Christian followers.

During that week Palmer's Baptist friends hired a hall for him in Church Alley and on the following Sunday he preached from the book of Malachi, sixth chapter, eighth verse: "to love mercy, deal justly, Walk humbly with our God and publickly deny the divinity of Jesus Christ." All arrangements had been quietly made and though there was a "Crouded Audience" there were no interruptions from outside.

Emboldened by his success, Palmer prepared to address a larger audience with a more fiery sermon on the following Sunday. To Fitch's great satisfaction he accepted the Universal Society as his sponsor. One of the members who owned a large room agreed to rent it cheap for the meeting and Palmer published an advertisement in the "public papers that he should the Sunday following preach against the Divinity of Jesus Christ."

But the day the notice appeared, the Right Reverend Bishop White, of the Protestant Episcopal Church, in defiance of the first article of the Bill of Rights, paid a wrathful visit to the owner of the hall who was left quaking from the threat of having his doors bolted against Palmer and the Universal Society. So while the Deistic heads of government looked hypocritically on, Bishop White closed every hall in Philadelphia against Deism and roused the city with his outraged cries till Palmer's lodgings were besieged and he was driven out of town.

Thus ended abruptly the Universal Society in its "Anoque Dominy 2," by which Fitch and his co-heretics had dreamed of reforming the world. A few days after this defeat Fitch urged Palmer's "takeing the field, but he not being such a Vetren as myself was conquered on the first repulse and, I may say, by the advance gards only of the Broken Christians." To Fitch, in spite of the swift action of Bishop White, "the world was ripe for a Revolution in Religion," and it was merely that Palmer was not the man to bring it about. But here he underestimated Palmer as well as the "Broken Christians," for Palmer returned to Philadelphia in 1794 as a rampant Deist and continued to fight orthodox religion until he died.

It was at about this time that Fitch closed his autobiography and History of the Steam Boat Company, which he had begun the previous fall. He had started to write under an overmastering sense of injustice which had found outlet through the suggestion of Nathaniel Irwin that a "detail" of his curious and singular life would be instructive to future generations. Knowing he had been wronged, but without understanding how or why, he had a belief that a precise recital of individual acts was a powerful weapon of self-defense. He had been treated coldly by Washington, craftily by Franklin, with unfair abruptness by Thomas Jefferson, with scorn by Gallatin. His history of the Steam Boat Company, he believed, would "hand to the latest Ages the" brazen "conduct of the first officers of government, but not being on an equal footing with them," he felt "obliged to suppress" his writings during his lifetime. Therefore, they were to be sealed and deposited with the Library Company of Philadelphia with the unjunction to the "Liberarian" that the seals were not to be broken until thirty years after his death.

The manuscript was dedicated to his children, but it was addressed to the "Worthy Nathaniel Irwine of Neshaminey:

"Sir, was I a Biggot in your beliefs and doctorines which you so zealously and with the greatest ingenuity that I ever heard from a pulpit weekly support, I should think that the word Reverand would bearly do you justice; and for fear if I used that word it might be imputed to the function of a Christian preacher, I omited it. But, Sir, you may be assured that I revear you more than any man, but not because you are a Christian Preacher, but because I esteem you one of the most valuable Citizens of Pennsylvania and have frequently felt a Sweet Pain that such an Exalted Genius should be confined to the Pitiful business of Neshaminey Congregation whilst many of the first offices of government are filled by those less deserving."

The hardships Fitch had undergone as the spindling son of a poor farmer in an orphaned home, as an apprentice to the cruelly niggardly Cheneys, as a captive of the Indians and as a sick passenger on the British prison ship were as vivid in his mind as when he had experienced them. Those early days had stunted him with a sense of inferiority, complicated by his conviction of his ability to accomplish valuable things which the world scorned. At fifty, he was still as "crazey after learning" as he had been as a boy of ten when he had worked and waited a year for Salmon's Geography. But the world surged around him without core or point and it was impossible for him to make a satisfactory generalization. All he could understand of his life was that every episode was a repetition of the time he stamped out the flax to save his father's house from burning and had his blistered ears boxed in reward.

When the steamboat company abandoned the *Perseverance* in the summer of 1792, Fitch had little left of his self-respect. Jefferson's inconsiderate treatment of his claims had made him feel persecuted. Though he had been enabled to pay his lodging bill at the Sign of the Buck "in full to date of April 16" he had since gone in debt to Hannah Levering and he was "an indigent citizen." His high hopes of saving mankind had been exploded by the suppression of the Universal Society. Robbed of his last shred of merit he fell back on the meager comfort that he was descended "from the antient and noble family of Fitch of Braintry, Essex." He reminded people that his was a "Branch of an Antient Family whose fidelity could never be doubted." But he could not long accept this vicarious substitute for personal recognition and he began to look back on his life and submit it to devilish self-questioning. Tormented by doubts of his sanity he resorted to buttered drams and pondered suicide.

On July 13, 1792, Fitch called in three of his cronies, Levi Willard, Eben Kingsley and Jamie Chaplin. He told them he believed he was going to die and asked them to witness his will.

"O Lord my God I beseech thee now to enable me to make this, my last will, in a rational manner and conformable to the laws of Nature; and that it may not be esteemed in any court of Justice as comeing from Insanity.

"My Will and Pleasure is that I should be buried under ground or sunk with weights to the Bottom of some Waters, that I do not become more obnoxious to the living than I am now, but if buried, that I may be layed on some public highway or place of the greatest resort of the living—such as the State house yard, Gray's Gardens or some Public House that I could hear the Song of the Brown jug on the first day of February every year. I request this that my life may be a lesson of Caution to the living, but beg that I may not be buried on or near any Christian burying ground.

"My further will is that all my just debts be paid and that Misses Hannah Levering collect what is due me from Daniel Longstreth and the Steam Boat company and, after paying herself, that she pay to my other Creditors in equal proportion as far as the money goes.

"But as to my burial my Penury forbids any extravagance. I give two dollars for my funeral expense and one dollar I bequeath to the man who wheals me to the place of interment, the other who shall dig a hole to lay me and cover me up. I also give an Indian Blanket, in the hands of Mrs. Lavering, to tie my body up instead of a coffin.

"All my estate in New England, both real and personal, I give to my Two children, to be equally divided between them.

"My walking stick I give to my worthy friend, Israel Israel, and the whole of my library, with scale and dividers, to his son John.

"And as I have lodged seven or eight Pounds in the Masons funds I trust they will have generosity enough to give everyone present a good Drink so as to make them feel Glad they are alive.

"My further will is that all my estate in Kentucky be sold in that country to the highest bidder and the money disposed of as shall be hereafter directed and that my Writings, which are sealed up, be lodged in the Liberary of Philadelphia and none permited to take them out of said Liberary without giving security for their safe return, giving, in the first place, the Revd. Nathaniel Irwin of Neshaminey, after which, Dr. Wm Thornton, the preference. But my Executors shall strictly forbid to allow of any alteration as to my religious sentiments or more favorable on the first officers of government than what is there recorded; and whatever moneys may be raised from these resources shall be placed on interest or to the purchase of some small estate, the interest or rents of which shall be annually paid on the first day of February to the person who shall go to my grave on said day at 4 oClock in the afternoon in the presence of several witnesses and sing the Song of the Brown jug, and that 'he is gone like a true harted fellow," what shall be shared by him in equal proportion to all present either in Liquor or money as the singer shall direct.

"My last Will is that Mr. Israel Israel, Innkeeper, Major James Moore, who keeps the livery stable at the lower end of town, and Mr. Thomas Bradly, Coppersmith, do see my last will and testament executed."

But there was still solace in liquor and lugubrious songs; and there was yet the teasing hope that he would be able to complete the steamboat. Meanwhile, he sang the song of the brown jug:

> *"With my jug in one hand and my pipe in the other*
> *I'll drink to my neighbor and friend.*
> *All my cares in a whiff of Tobacco I'll smother,*
> *My life I know shortly must end.*
> *While Ceres most kindly refills my brown jug*
> *With brown ale I will make myself mellow*
> *In my old wicar chair I'll set myself snug*
> *Like a jolly and true hearted fellow.*
> *I'll ne'er trouble myself with the cares of my Nation*
> *I've enough of my own for to mind.*
> *All we see in this world is but grief and vexation*

To Death I am shortly resigned.
So we'll drink, laugh and smoke and leave nothing to care
And drop like a pear ripe and mellow.
When cold in my coffin, I'll leave them to say
'He's gone, what a True hearted fellow.'"

XVI

In the summer of 1792 Fitch was bald and bespectacled. Failure had drubbed a pain in his head which he tried to ease by flinging ironic verses at himself.

> *"As for my partners, damn them all!*
> *They took me up to let me fall.*
> *For when my scheme was near perfection*
> *It proved abortive by their defection;*
> *They let it drop for want of Rhineo,*
> *Then swore the cause of failure mineo."*

But now he was finished. Let the world worry along without him; let the flatboats from Fort Pitt be broken up for lumber at New Orleans and the boatmen straggle home through a thousand miles of wilderness; let the pirates board and sack American vessels off the coast of Barbary and let all that great country of pleasant meadows and deep forests along the Ohio and clear down the Mississippi from the Falls of St. Anthony be inaccessible to the pioneer as long as possible.

> *"For full the scope of seven years*
> *Steam Boats excited hopes and fears*
> *In me, but now I see it plain*
> *All further progress is in Vain*
> *And am resolved to quit a Scheming*
> *And be no longer of pattents dreaming."*—

Yet with the barest encouragement he was ready to begin all

Among the many people who had seen the successful experiments of the steamboat in 1790 was Aaron Vail, United States Consul at L'Orient. In his enthusiasm over the invention Vail had signed a contract on March 16, 1791, by which he was "to procure from the government of France either the grant or special contract... in the name of the said John Fitch" for the exclusive privilege of building steamboats. He was also to pay for the construction of at least one boat in France, including the expenses of a mechanic sent to L'Orient by the company, but he was not "compelled to expend a greater sum than two thousand five hundred Spanish milled Dollars." In return for which Vail was to have half the profits from French steamboats, the rest of which was to be divided among the members of the Philadelphia Company until they had been reimbursed for their experiments on the Delaware, when Fitch and Voight were to receive a part equal to whatever shares they might be lucky enough to hold.

On November 20, 1791, the French government acted on Vail's petition and granted letters of patent in Fitch's name for sixteen years. News of Vail's success in the first part of the agreement reached the Company's directors early in 1792. At that time Fitch was still working on the *Perseverance*. Voight was too well settled in his job at the Mint and too embittered from past experiences to be connected again with steamboat building. And as no other mechanics connected with the company were qualified to go, the second part of the agreement, which required the company to send a boatbuilder to France at Vail's expense, was delayed for nearly a year. Then, months after Fitch had given up hope that the rest of the contract would be carried out, after he had walked all around the abyss of suicide and turned away from it and after he had begun to earn a living as a clockmaker, it was finally arranged for him to go to France and build another steamboat.

Meanwhile, the feudal aristocrats who had controlled the

French government under Louis Sixteenth had been overthrown by the merchants and manufacturers with the arms of the oppressed workers and peasants. It was a revolution which had been pleasantly anticipated in the conversation of liberal clubs and fashionable drawing-rooms, the sort of revolution that could be carried on with vague watchwords like "liberty, fraternity, equality," that would place the workers, peasants and small shopkeepers under new rulers.

When the King and his nobles had been thrown down, the bourgeoisie wanted to stop and consolidate their power. But it was not their power that had made the revolution. Since 1789 it had been "a movement of the people to regain possession of the land and to free it from the feudal obligations which burdened it, and while there was all through it a powerful individualist element—the desire to possess land individually—there was also the communist element, the right of the whole nation to the land."[1] And in the summer of 1792, when Lafayette, Brissot de Warville and the other bourgeois spokesmen in the national assembly tried to check the revolution at the overthrow of the king and the establishment of a democracy dominated by wealth as in America and England, the people and their leaders drove the revolution toward a higher democracy.

"Today," Marat cried in the *Ami du People,* "after three years of everlasting speeches from patriotic societies and a deluge of writings ... the people are further from feeling what they ought to do in order to be able to resist their oppressors than they were on the very first day of the Revolution. At that time they followed their natural instincts, their simple good sense which made them find the true way for subduing their implacable foes." But now the people had let the bourgeoisie, the men of property, turn the Revolution against them. "For the Court and its supporters it is an eternal motive for intrigue and corruption; for the legislators, an occasion for prevarication and trickery....

[1] Kropotkin, "The Great Revolution."

Already it is for the rich and avaricious nothing but an opportunity for illicit gains, monopolies, frauds and spoliations, while the people are ruined, and the numberless poor are placed between the fear of perishing from hunger and the necessity of selling themselves.... Let us not be afraid to repeat: we are further from liberty than ever; not only are we slaves, but we are so legally," because the new constitution, like the constitution of the United States, bound the masses of the people to the power of wealth and privilege.

To most of the people in Philadelphia, and in New York from which Fitch sailed in February, 1793, with the French national cockade and a paper bit of stars and stripes decorating his hatband, the Revolution in France was a struggle between the will of the people and the Crown. They rejoiced in the downfall of kings, slavery, bigotry and oppression and in the substitution of reason and democracy. They repeated the jest "Louis Capet is caput" just as their descendants repeated the "Hang the Kaiser" slogan in 1918. And they believed that the overturn of government would be accomplished with as little internal strife as their war for Independence from Great Britain.

During the American Revolution merchants had continued to carry on their trade. Many of them who sent out privateers to capture enemy ships grew rich. There were contracts to furnish supplies for the Continental Army, which meant money for the merchants and manufacturers; there was the billeting and provisioning of the British Army, which meant money for the householders and farmers. Soldiers risked their lives and endured privations, but business went on much as usual. Dr. Ewing, David Rittenhouse and Andrew Ellicott continued to draw their salaries as before. Fitch, though driven out of a good trade in Trenton by the arrival of the British, was enabled to earn a living in Bucks County and, until inflation reduced his wealth to paper, he made several thousand dollars by selling tobacco, beer and dry goods to the troops at Valley Forge. Quite naturally he and the other steamboat company members assumed that conditions in France would be much the same as they had been in America.

But the American Revolution had not challenged the right of private property. When the war had ended the journeymen, apprentices, servants and farmers had gone back home, leaving the Binghams, the Morrises, the Schuylers and Washingtons in control. In France the strong pressure of the masses put private property in jeopardy. And the investor's attitude was that of Gouverneur Morris, America's high minister at Paris, who believed that French "wealth and resources, above all, her marine, must dwindle away" because of the peasants' insurrection, and that the French bourgeoisie would withdraw its money from its own country and export it to England where it would be under "the protection of law and government."

Sailing for France in the spring of 1793 to build a steamboat on the Loire, Fitch went to Paris in hope of assistance from Thomas Paine. By the time he arrived there the deputies to the National Assembly had rejected the American revolution as a "glorious model" for that of France. France had helped America in 1778, but America was not helping France in 1793. The stars and stripes was not a popular symbol, Fitch was informed. Cautiously, and doubtless with some bepuzzlement, he slipped it out of his hatband.

Fitch found Paine living at the edge of the city where he had withdrawn from the three-sided battle raging in Paris. Hated by the rulers of England, of France and by many of them in America because they feared the effects of his liberal ideas on the masses, Paine was also separated from the insurgents and he stood in the middle of the road, utterly honest, utterly fearless, but calling for half-way measures when he spoke—a constitution, banishment of the King. He was living in an old mansion that had belonged to Madame Pompadour as Louis' mistress, at 63 Faubourg St. Denis. The house was occupied by half a dozen other liberal Englishmen and Paine's "apartments consisted of three rooms; the first for wood, water etc.; the next was a bedroom; and beyond it, the sitting room which looked into the garden through a glass door." The garden was stocked with "ducks, turkeys and geese; which, for amusement, we used to feed out of the parlor window on the ground floor. There were some hutches for rabbits, and a sty with two pigs. Beyond was a garden of more than an acre of ground, well laid out, and stocked with excellent fruit trees," oranges, apricots and greengage plums, where Paine "used to find some relief by walking alone after dark, and cursing with hearty good will the authors of that terrible system that had turned the character of the Revolution I had been proud to defend." In that terrific year when the struggle for power kept the guillotine going like a butcher's cleaver and when few men's heads were safe, Paine left off his abstemious habits of a lifetime and found relief in brandy as well as walking in Pompadour's garden. At that time he had had to give up his own inventions, he had been hanged in effigy by the British, had been conspired against by Gouverneur Morris and was soon to be a prisoner of the Committee of Safety; under these circumstances Fitch's visit to Paine was destined to be a failure.

Walking through an ancient city in which executions were taking nearly as many lives as a minor engagement in a modern war, Fitch's curious mind was impressed not with the chaotic struggle, but with a detail. "Sir," he wrote to Dr. Thornton, "I need not describe this machine to you, as I do not expect that ever an Execution will take place in Pennsylvania after the next session of the Legislature. But I must confess I was somewhat disgusted to see the Executioner dressed in the National Uniform and the National Cockade." On reflection, however, he decided that his repugnance "most certainly could proceed from nothing but prejudice of Education, for if it is right to take life at all, this certainly ought to be the most honorable post that a man could fill, as it is the most solemn operation.

"This has brought some reflection into my mind and Queries: what makes the American Executioners disguise themselves as if ashamed of what they was about?

"But, Sir, the Nation of France most certainly know their own Policy better than I can point it out and I now mean to turn my attention to my Little Boat...I propose to set off tomorrow for L'Orient and probably may stop a day or two at Nantes."

Nantes possessed the nearest furnace to L'Orient; on the Loire, where the steamboat was to be built, it had the same position that Philadelphia had on the Delaware—it was the largest, richest port and the most mechanically advanced city in France. But next to Paris and Lyons, Nantes was also the scene of the bloodiest civil war.

"The political barometer of the easy-going mercantile town" of Nantes, Joseph Fouché, that yellow chameleon cleric, informed his constituents in 1792 when they elected him from Nantes to the National Assembly, "where credit is essential and it is the people's wish that business should thrive, there is no taste for radicalism. Since the well-to-do citizens of the seaports have large investments in the colonies they are essentially antagonistic to such fantastical schemes as the abolition of slavery." And he promised, as their deputy, to "protect commerce, to defend property and respect the laws."

That was in 1792. Within a year the National Assembly had abolished the slave trade with the French colonies, on which the wealth of Nantes was based, had confiscated all church property and at the same time had given nothing to the peasants but the opportunity of serving the republic in war on a distant battlefield. This brought both burghers and peasants together in a counter-revolution. Guided by the clergy, whose churches had been closed, and aided by the bourgeoisie, the attack on the supporters of the new government in La Vendée reached one frenzied atrocity after another. At Montaigne they "filled the wells with the bodies of republican soldiers, many of them still alive and only stunned or disabled by blows.... Living men were buried up to the neck, and their captors amused themselves by inflicting all kinds of torture on the unburied heads." "Provided they had time," Michelet reported, "the counter-revolutionaries never took a soldier without killing him under torture; and when the men of Nantes arrived, in April 1793, at Châlons, they saw nailed to a door something which resembled a great bat; this was a republican soldier who for several hours had been nailed there, suffering terrible agonies and unable to die."

The clergy wanted their church lands back, the burghers wanted their slave trade back; "No quarter!" cried Madame de la Roche-Jacquelin, the gentle, cultured wife of one of their leaders, and there was no quarter.

Fitch, thinking only of castings for his engine, stumbled on like a somnambulist. The castings were in Nantes and that is where he went. When he reached the furnace the priests, peasants and burghers were already coming down the slope toward the banks of the Loire and the few hundred soldiers of the first republic were priming their long muskets to defend the town. Fitch at last had to take notice of the civil war, which he did in a mildly irritated letter to Dr. Thornton when he got back to L'Orient on August 11: "I went to Nants to get castings done for the Steam Boat and soon after my arrival the Furnace became a frontier from the insurrection in that part of the country and shortly after the town was beseaged, when I made my escape out of it. Otherwise, I should have wrote you from that place...."

At L'Orient he lodged "Very comfortably" with Aaron Vail and found great delight in the Consul's small daughter, Eliza. But no matter how hospitably Vail treated him, he could offer little hope that a steamboat would be built on the Loire that year. Instead of a steamboat, that river was soon to hold the bodies of thousands of counter-revolutionists drowned in Carrier's "Marriages of the Loire."

For weeks Fitch waited at L'Orient. But Nantes remained the center of the civil war in Brittany. Inland, the crops were trampled or used as forage for the contesting armies. Along the coast, shipping was almost at a standstill. Fall came and the Breton sky grew dun and heavy as a leaky tent. At last Vail suggested that Fitch should go to England and have the engine made there.

With a letter of credit, passage money and an introduction to a Mr. Johnson in London, Fitch set out for England. While the ship was sailing northward, tacking this way and that toward the opening of the Thames, he became so baffled at not knowing where the ship might be in the ever changing winds that his active mind struck upon a solution.

The new invention was "a ready reckoner," similar to the French quarter card, "a new Method of navigation by which a ship's traverse round or to any quarter of the globe may be kept with the same degree of accuracy as by Trigonometry." It reduced the business "to such simplicity as to take off much burthen from masters of vessels" and was so easily understood that "the same may be learned in a few hours by those unacquainted with navigation."

With this new contrivance to engross him, Fitch had a pleasant voyage. He landed in London in the middle of November and took lowly lodgings at 3 Fan Court, Mile's lane, Thames Street. The Ready Reckoner was to be in the form of a chart and, as with his map, he beat and engraved the copper plate himself. The "easy method of working any question necessary to the keeping of a ship's way, induced" him to flatter himself that it was "truly deservable to the greatest proficients as well as to those unskilled who wish to become masters of the art." But in case any navigator found difficulty understanding it, he had an explanatory pamphlet, printed by Gilbert and Gilkerson on Tower Hill, to accompany it. And "any master who does not readily understand it from the plate and the description" might obtain instruction from the author between 10 and 12 o'clock, Sundays excepted, "till they are perfect masters of it at half a guinea each."

But when he went down the busy river, so different from the deserted quay at L'Orient, and saw the captains of the sailing vessels, they listened indifferently or abruptly shook their heads. They knew how to navigate their ships, had learned through long apprenticeship and did not propose to make the business easy. Some of them protested that the Ready Reckoner was a dangerous instrument, that if the crew knew as much as the master there would be insubordination.

Fitch's vehement answer to this left the charge where it stood. He asserted that "Men of no ambition are never to be feared in any plot or mutiny without ambitious leaders" who presumably were already acquainted with the laws of navigation. Also "Men of an ambitious turn, who may have a prospect of an honorable command, undoubtedly would be cautious of setting such an example, which would have a tendency to destroy their views of advancement; but if after good conduct they should attain what they are aiming at, that would become a precedent at a future day to those under their command."

Meanwhile, he had gone to see Johnson, who was to have handled the business of the steamboat company for himself and Vail in London. By this time France was like a diseased harlot to every bourgeois soul in Great Britain, but a harlot with wealth which the British were acquiring for themselves by seizing all neutral vessels bringing provisions to France and declaring a blockade of all French ports. "Without coming forward too much herself, England preferred to subsidize the Allied Powers and to profit by the weakness of France in taking her colonies and ruining her maritime commerce... At the same time England helped the emigres, smuggled in arms and bundles of proclamations to stir up Brittany and La Vendée, and prepared to seize the ports of Saint-Malo, Brest, Nantes, Bourdeaux and Toulon." [1]

As a loyal Britisher Mr. Johnson could not but twitch with pain at the mention of investing money in France. A steamboat on the Loire? Nonsense! What those French revolutionaries needed was not a steamboat, but a dose of good, God-fearing English lead.

Fitch's money was again "tremendously low," but he had Vail's letter of credit. As this was drawn on Johnson and as there was no hope of assistance from Johnson in England, Fitch asked him to advance his passage money back to L'Orient.

At this point Johnson grew apoplectic. Money to go back to that godless, bloody land! Didn't Mr. Fitch know that it was "high treason to negotiate French bills of exchange?" He would advance Fitch passage money to America, but nowhere else.

As this offer meant spending Vail's money without benefiting the steamboat, Fitch rejected it. Putting the letter of credit in his pocket again, he went out into the London streets.

The British blockade of the French ports prevented him from sending "a long, circumstantial letter" to Vail, explaining why he was unable either to accomplish anything on the steamboat in London or to get back to France. Nor could he stay in England, for the British were contemptuous of the Ready Reckoner and he had depended on it to earn a living while working on the steamboat. In this perplexing situation he wrote a letter to Catherine of Russia, "the unlimited monarch of the North," asking exclusive rights to manufacture and sell the Ready Reckoner in her domain. He also "struck out a new method of turning millwork by water, on the same principles of our cranks and paddles" and showed his drawings to "the Great Mr.

---

[1] Kropotkin, "The Great Revolution."

Foulds, the Enginear of the London Water Works," who professed to have "the highest opinion of it."

A letter from Dr. Thornton, to whom he had dedicated the Columbia Ready Reckoner pamphlet, arrived about this time and cheered Fitch a little with the hope that there might be a market for his invention in the United States.

"I cannot but approve of your design," Thornton wrote, "for in my second voyage on the Atlantic I made a chart of the same kind and applied it to the very same use, but mine was neither so extensive nor so comprehensive. It is in my opinion an ingenious method, for which you have a right to much credit. Mine was exhibited, indeed at the time I invented it about seven years ago, to Captain McEvers of this place, when at sea, and he said it was similar to the French quarter card." Robert Leslie, an inventive clockmaker of Philadelphia whom Fitch had known there and later met in London, had also invented "a machine for measuring a ship's way. But," Thornton continued, "let not this tend to a supposition that anything can take from your Discovery. I claim no attention on that score, but shall insist upon it that as you found out this and published it, the world is only obliged to you. I mean immediately to take out the patent for you here, but you only must reap the profit.

"I send this to my friend, Dr. John Coakly Lettsom, F. R. S. & c. &c., one of the best of men, one of my best friends, whom I sincerely regard and respect. I have written to him on your account and I know he will be glad to see you, therefore wait upon him when you receive this. But do not fight Algerines before him. You know what I mean. Regulate your genius.

"The fever [the epidemic of 1793 which drove President Washington and his cabinet from Philadelphia and which was caused by sewage filtering into the city's drinking water] made dreadful havoc here, but there are no remains of it now, February, 1794. I had it, but by going in the country and submitting only to my own rules, I got better. My mother-in-law lost her only sister, Miss Hartley. Mr. Wells had it very ill, but got better. The rest of our friends escaped."

Dr. Thornton further advised him as a mark of his friendship that two copies of his essay on the written elements of language which he had published under the pseudonym of Cadmus and for which he received the Magellanic gold medal from the American Philosophical Society, were waiting for him at W. J. Debretts, bookseller in London. But the letter closed on a maddening note of irony. Fitch was to get "no steam engine made except by Watts and Boulton, and with a copper boiler, without any wood around it, and very strong copper. It will never be a loss, for when worn out it will sell. Attend to no other advice than this, and if the company in France, or one in England, will bear the expense, give one half, as before done in France. You know our company cannot bear expense."

It was for precisely such an engine that Fitch had struggled seven years. No man knew better than himself the weakness of wood against steam, or the value of "very strong copper" even when that metal had worn out. He must have laughed vexatiously to himself when he recollected the hundreds of pairs of sleeve buttons he had made from old copper kettles, and again at Dr. Thornton's caution that the Philadelphia company could not "bear expense." And still again over the dilemma of going to Soho, ordering an engine from Boulton and Watt and taking it to France when it was impossible for him to get there himself.

Fitch stayed in London till the middle of spring in the hope of returning to L'Orient. Then he "went down to the shipping." Vail's letter of credit was still in his pocket, but if he could be of no use to Vail he would not spend his money, and he stubbornly kept it there. By chance the boat was bound for Boston. He signed up as a steerage passenger, under an indentured agreement that he was to work out the cost of his journey after he landed in New England.

XVII

THE summer Fitch landed in Boston he was fifty-one, but he looked like an anachronism, a gaunt, dry character salted with Hugoesque mystery. His long back was bent, he carried his tall walking stick, wore an old cocked hat, knee-breeches, rusty stockings and coarse, silver-buckled shoes. At Mrs. Cooper's Wing's Inn Tavern, where he lodged, he was unknown and cautious not to speak of his various inventions.

Fitch had made his last serious attempt to build a steamboat, but he still had the hope that his Columbia Ready Reckoner or his "new method of turning millwork by water" might be profitable. Not only Mr. Foulds of the London Waterworks had recommended his cranks and paddle device, but "the greatest mechanics of this town," he wrote Thornton from Boston, "have approved the plan and amongst the rest, Mr. Jacob Perkins of Newburyport, with his partner, Mr. Armstrong, who are both famous for philosophical and mechanical arts." Perkins was then working on a machine which would cut and head nails or tacks in a single operation, but it was not patented till the following year. Meanwhile, Fitch had agreed "to convey one fourth of the millwork scheme" to Perkins and Armstrong, "but thro their meanness in bargaining I declined entering into articles of agreement with them. Since then," he added suspiciously, "Mr. Armstrong is gone to the Southern States, it is said to New York, but should it be to Philadelphia, I trust that you will prevent him from taking out a patent for the same...

"I have the highest opinion of it, such as the placing of oars 18 inches lower than a water wheel can be placed, which is equal to an 18-inch head of water, but in a particular manner, for the dead, heavy streams in the Southern states, where a head of water cannot be gained, and in floating mills on the Ohio." Meanwhile, Fitch placed the highest confidence in Dr. Thornton that he would not see him "injured by designing men."

As for the Columbia Ready Reckoner, Fitch had entered into articles of agreement with Osgood Castleton, Esq., for half the profits in New Hampshire, Massachusetts and Rhode Island "and under the patronage of so famed a mathematician, I can hardly doubt but it will be productive of General Good as well as some emolument to myself." A new explanatory pamphlet was to be published, but without the dedication to Thornton, for he had agreed with Castleton that "in this enlightened age to give any one man the preference carries with it something too servile for an American to beg the Patronage of a single individual, although he might be justified in claiming it from his country."

To earn his living Fitch was working on the Boston waterfront. He still had the "long, circumstantial letter" he had written Vail while "lying in the downs" before his ship sailed from England. He had hoped he would "come across some French vessel" at sea "and that if they would not take me again to France, that I could at least forward the letter." But the British blockade had kept the Atlantic clear of the tricolor flag and now, in Boston, Fitch suppressed the letter because "he could not induer the thought of hurting Vail's feelings by an account of my misfortunes and the hard usage I met with in the steerage by being confined and messing with the Seamen whose allowance was infamous, or to inform him that I was brought to the alternative of working in Boston as a Journeyman."

Becoming resigned by the end of September he concluded that "the happiest days of my life is since I came to Boston. My labour is an amusement and affords me a moderate sustinence, and my accomodations are modest and agreeable, and I live retired and unknown, and go every day in the fore and afternoon with my fellow journeymen with the greatest freedom and pleasure to Water. I have no cumber of business on my hands, no vilenous acts to disturb my repose at night." In fact, "the whole burthen which I have on my mind is to discharge the debt of my passage, which I am as yet by no means teased for."

That one cheerful ray in a lifetime of dark, uncomprehending struggle, lasted barely long enough to indicate how pleasant and useful Fitch's days might have been in a society where, instead of a small part living exceedingly well by annihilating the rest, all men worked for "the General Good." Fitch had resolved "never to leave Boston to have the charge of absconding from my creditors imputed to me, therefore it was very uncertain" how long he would have to stay. It was not easy for him to pay off the debt of his passage with journeyman's wages. Even to live at such wages became a grinding task and during the winter he was driven to seek free lodgings.

By the middle of January, 1795, Fitch's position had become intolerable in Boston. He may have been able to pay the cost of his passage, but it is certain that he was unable to save any money and it is likely that he lost his job, for he began to beg assistance to get out of the city. He even wrote to James Nicholson, who had shown an interest in his cattle-boat design, asking for twelve guineas to help him get to Philadelphia. But Nicholson, who had been comptroller of the Pennsylvania treasury until he was charged with misappropriating the funds and who, resigning after a whitewashing investigation, was collecting hundreds of thousands of dollars in a wildcat land speculation, did not reply. Fitch began to think of Windsor.

For there was one place where he could be sure of a welcome, the house of his sister, Sarah, and her husband, Timothy King, the weaver. It was humiliating to go back destitute after twenty-five years, to confront a son who had become a full-grown man, to see his wife and the daughter who had been born after he deserted her. His own flesh and blood, Shaler and Lucy, would be strangers to him if he met them on the street. And yet he had not willfully neglected them. He had always hoped to provide for them. Writing to Shaler from Warminster the summer before he was captured by the Indians he attempted to explain:

"My darling boy, believe me, when I took you in my arms and kissed you for the last time, and took my last farewell, you may be assured that I felt every emotion that it is possible for a tender father to feel. How my heart dissolved in tears, and how my sinews wanted strength, I can better feel than express. Be assured, your father loves you, and that there is nothing would make him more happy than to take you under his parental care."

He had made repeated offers to provide for Shaler and Lucy, but his injured wife had repeatedly rejected them. Again from Bucks County, in December, 1784, he wrote to Shaler:

"Heaven forbid that I should endeavor to raise an irreverent thought in your mind against your mother. But our separation, you may be assured, was no trifling matter to me. There was nothing that I more ardently wished for at the time, than that Heaven would call me to the world of spirits. You, my child, staggered every resolution, and weighed more with me than a mountain of diamonds. Finally I resolved, and then resolved again; and gave you a sacrifice to the world more unwillingly than the patriarch of old."

In this same strain he had written to his daughter, Lucy, and on the dreary Christmas of 1792, to her husband, James Kilbourne. "My dear child," he informed his son-in-law, who apparently had taken the role of peacemaker between his wife's parents, "know that I am a man of tender feelings, however my children may have been educated to form their opinions of me. No man loves his children better than myself, although I never saw but one. Forgive me for not entering into a justifica-

FITCH'S SCREW-PROPELLER STEAMBOAT ON THE COLLECT, NEW YORK, 1796.

FITCH'S MODEL STEAMBOAT, BARDSTOWN, KENTUCKY, 1797-'98.

tion of my conduct; but esteem your mother-in-law and myself as we have both merited; but I require of you that you treat her kindly, because she was once the wife of John Fitch. But much as I love my children," he hastened to add, "any mediation through them would be ineffectual."

And now he was going back to Windsor, strong only in the old rancor which divided him and his wife.

According to Charles Whittlesy, his first biographer, Fitch stayed in Windsor until June, 1796, then set out for Kentucky where he arrived in the late fall or winter. According to a personal memoir in the Documentary History of New York, John Hutchings, as a boy, helped Fitch operate a small steamboat on a freshwater pond called the Collect in New York on which the Tombs prison was later built. Hutchings remembered the boat as a ship's yawl, steered by an oar and driven by a screw propeller. "The cylinder was of wood, barrel shaped on the outside, and strongly hooped, being straight on the inside. The main steam pipe led directly from the boiler top into a copper box, receiver, or valve box, about six inches square. The leading pipes led separately into the bottom or base of the one short cylinder and the longer one, and each piston rod was attached to the extremity of the working beam. This beam was supported by an iron upright; the connecting rod was so arranged as to turn the crank of the propelling shaft, which passed horizontally through the stern of the boat, and was made fast to the propeller or screw. The valves were worked by a simple contrivance attached likewise to the working beam." "The steam was sufficiently high to propel the boat once, twice or thrice around the pond; when more water being introduced into the boiler or pot, and steam generated, she was again ready to start on another expedition." Other witnesses to this exhibition on the Collect were General Anthony Lamb and William H. Westlock, City Surveyor of New York. Hutchings adds that among the passengers was Robert Livingston. And Thompson Westcott, Fitch's second biographer, "conjectured" that at this time overtures were made to him, Fitch, by Chancellor Livingston, whose interest in steam navigation was even, at that early day exceedingly strong.

With regard to all this there is nothing incredible. Livingston knew of Fitch's experiments and of his valuable New York patent. But it is hardly likely that Fitch would have seriously undertaken to build so small a boat in which there could be no practical value when he had already proved his invention. Also, the patent belonged not to Fitch, but to the steamboat company and he was in correspondence at that time with Dr. Thornton who owned most of the shares. Yet neither in the letters between Fitch and Thornton nor in the later letters of Thornton and Robert Fulton, whom Livingston financed, is there any reference to an experiment by Fitch in New York.

According to Daniel Longstreth, the son of Fitch's old friend, Fitch remained in Bucks County for two years. He went there after January, 1795, and he left before the spring of 1797, when he arrived in Bardstown to reclaim the land on which he had laid warrants in 1782.

Barely a year before he arrived in Bardstown, the Indians beyond the north bank of the Ohio had signed a final treaty of peace with the Federal Government. During all those years since Fitch's capture the Indians had continued to fight for their land, driving out white settlers and surveyors and ambushing armies. After a long, relentless campaign of Federal Soldiers and Kentucky militia under General Wayne, they had been beaten into signing the Treaty of Greenville. But in spite of the threats and border raids from across the Ohio, the Kentucky country had developed rapidly. According to a dispatch from Winchester in the Maryland *Gazette* "Emigrants to Kentucky who passed the Muskingum from August first, 1786 to May fifteenth, 1789 numbered 19889 souls, 1067 boats, 8884 horses,

2297 cattle, 1926 sheep, 627 wagons, besides those which have passed in the night unnoticed."

In 1796 there were between one hundred and fifty and two hundred thousand settlers in Kentucky. And when Fitch reached Nelson County, where he had laid his government warrants, he found that the wilderness meadows he had surveyed had been changed within the last twelve years into comfortable farms. The thirteen hundred acres to which he believed he could establish his claims, and he declared "there is no use in law if" he failed, had been divided into "six valuable plantations, with nearly 400 acres of cleared land, with large, commodious houses, barns, outhouses, orchads &c" which "would this day sell for 13,000 Dollars."

"My property here will be much more considerable than I ever expected," he wrote optimistically from Bardstown where he had engaged William Rowan, an attorney, to begin a wholesale prosecution of his claims. Squire Rowan encouraged him and bills were prepared against all the interlopers from "one Wilson who claimed title from Dutch Mary since 1779" to the latest settler.

Meanwhile, Fitch lodged at the tavern of Alexander and Susannah McCowan. The day he arrived he was penniless as usual and he startled the tavern keeper with a strange proposal. He was the owner of a number of farms in the neighborhood, he explained; and Squire Rowan was going to get them back for him, when he would have plenty of money. He had none now, but he didn't expect to live very long. Therefore, if McCowan would board and lodge him and give him a pint of whisky a day, he would leave him a hundred and fifty acres.

To McCowan, Fitch looked healthy enough, but he agreed to the arrangement and a bond was signed between them. It was probably one of the most satisfactory bargains Fitch had ever made. His lawsuits were in the hands of Squire Rowan and he was fixed with Alexander McCowan for life. He found a crony in John Nourse and, for a time, a belated object of parental affection in small Eliza Rowan, the Squire's granddaughter. At Howell's blacksmith shop he secured the right to a bench and began working on a model steamboat, three feet long, with brass machinery "polished in a neat, workmanlike manner" and paddle wheels instead of oars.

That year Fitch drank steadily and was often drunk. At times he lay in his room for days. Sober, he would sit shaking his head and declaring that he would go penniless to his grave, but that America would grow rich from his invention. "The day will come," he must often have repeated, "when some more powerful man will get fame and riches from my invention; but nobody will believe that "poor John Fitch" can do anything worthy of attention."

He believed that whisky would kill him and he wanted to die. There was no use waiting for the lawsuits to end or for the steamboats to come. "I am not getting off fast enough," he told McCowan one morning, "you must add another pint and here is your bond for another hundred and fifty acres."

At the beginning of 1798 he made a will, dividing equally all the property he hoped to possess between his children, Dr. Thornton, William Rowan and Aaron Vail's daughter, Eliza, excepting a thirteenth part which was to go to little Eliza Rowan. And on February first he wrote "I am fast agoing to my Mother Clay."

He was still alive when spring came, but in May he grew sick and unable to sleep. A doctor was called, who prescribed opium pills to ease his pain. On June twenty-fifth he made a new will, which was like the previous one except that it excluded a thirteenth part from Eliza Rowan—who may have died—, included James Nourse among the beneficiaries and gave to William Rowan, "my trusty friend, my Beaver Hat, Shoe, Knee and Stock Buckles, Walking Stick and spectacles." A few days later he began to save the opium pills the doctor had left for him. He had often contemplated suicide and had approached it once. Deism had at least taught him not to be afraid of death. And one night before the middle of July he swallowed a dozen pills at a gulp and washed them down with whisky.

XVIII

JOHN FITCH was buried in Bardstown in an unmarked grave, but he came alive again on March 17, 1811, when the first inland steamboat in history began to descend the Ohio River. The boat was one hundred and twenty feet long, with a twenty foot beam, and a round-bellied hull that sat deep in the water. It had been built at Pittsburgh on the Allegheny side of the town at the foot of Boyd's Hill. Shipwrights and machinists had been brought from New York to construct the boat and the cost of building was $38,000. Named the *New Orleans,* after its port of destination, it went nine miles an hour with the current. Manned by a captain, pilot, engineer and six hands, the *New Orleans* reached Cincinnati the second night of its voyage, passed Bardstown, Louisville, steamed on into the Mississippi, down to the Delta and sported back again to Natchez, then down to New Orleans, carrying cotton and passengers, making money from both.

The boat was supervised by Nicholas Roosevelt, whose family had grown rich from grants of New York land before the Revolution. It was owned by Roosevelt, Chancellor Livingston, De Witt Clinton and Robert Fulton, who had incorporated under the name of the Ohio Steamboat Navigation Company. Basically, the *New Orleans* was the same as the boat Fitch drove on the Delaware in 1790, as the boat he had dreamed of building on the Ohio. The only difference was that there was more money involved and the Mississippi was now open to American navigation.

Yet three years later when Captain Henry M. Shreve launched

the *Enterprise* at Bridgeport on the Monongahela and steamed down to New Orleans the Roosevelt-Livingston-Clinton-Fulton monopolists had the boat seized. At that time the United States was again at war with Great Britain and the Mississippi Delta was a battleground. General Jackson had commandeered the *Enterprise* to bring supplies to the Federal troops in the city, but the monopolists let patriotism stand no more in their way then than they do now; the *Enterprise* was forced out of service, in spite of Jackson's order, while the legal battle was fought through the courts.

How did that group of rich New Yorkers succeed where Fitch had failed? How could they resurrect a proved invention which had become public property and force every man who built a similar boat to pay them royalties? How could they lay their grasping hands upon the method of transportation that was to revolutionize navigation and demand tribute before it could be used?

Robert Fulton claimed to be the inventor of the steamboat. Robert Fulton had been a miniature painter in Philadelphia in 1786 when Fitch was experimenting on the Delaware; he had been living in Paris with Joel Barlow in 1793 when Fitch went there with his plans to show their mutual friend, Paine; he had borrowed from Aaron Vail "all the specifications and drawings of Mr. Fitch, and they had remained in his possession several months;" and he had "examined everything in the United States Patent Office on steam navigation before taking out his own patent."

Robert Fulton claimed to be the inventor of the steamboat, but Chancellor Livingston, his chief backer, knew he was not. As Livingston admitted "the first attempt" to build a steamboat "was made in America" by "Mr. John Fitch" who, "having first obtained from most of the states in the Union a law vesting in him for a long term the exclusive use of steamboats, built one upon the Delaware ... This vessel navigated the river from

Philadelphia to Bordentown for a few weeks, but was found so imperfect and to have so many accidents that it was laid aside after the projector had expended a large sum of money for himself and his associates."

Knowing it was Fitch who had invented the steamboat, Livingston had used the power of his wealth to acquire the New York rights as soon as Fitch died. He accomplished this through the compliance of a friendly legislature, representing that since Fitch was dead, or had left the commonwealth, "it would be for the public advantage to repeal the law" and that as he and his associates had spent vast sums in making steamboats, the "Act for granting and securing to John Fitch the sole right and advantage of making and employing the steamboat by him lately invented" should be repealed and the monopoly transferred to Livingston. This trickery achieved its purpose in 1798 and though the new act specified that within two years Livingston should build a steamboat capable of moving four miles an hour against the stream, the Chancellor had the law extended at his own convenience until he was finally joined by Fulton with a Boulton and Watt engine, when the building of the *Clermont* was begun in 1807.

Nicholas Roosevelt, who until this time had been making steamboat experiments of his own, and who was rich enough successfully to contest Livingston's basically worthless patent, was now bought to silence by an interest in Livingston's company and the monopolists further strengthened themselves, "cleverly" tightening their privileges by the exclusive right to operate a steam ferry between New York and Albany. Thus, if their patent under the regranted Fitch law failed, they were at least assured of a legal weapon to drive any other steamboat from the Hudson which attempted to operate without their consent.

On February 11, 1809 Fulton took out a patent from the United States Patent Office with the flimsy phraseology that he had invented something new in a "method of attaching wheels to the engine of Watt." But this subterfuge aroused the indignation of Dr. Thornton, who had been appointed by Jefferson as the first superintendent of the Federal Patent Office. Not only was the national patent illegal, but the act of New York State was also, for they were both superseded by the Federal patent Fitch had received in 1791. And since its expiration four years earlier, the invention of steamboats had become public property, Thornton wrote vigorously to Fulton.

And with respect to proportions, "if you prosecute anyone for an infraction of your patent rights, it will be by the laws of the United States, and these laws expressly allow the use of all that has been previously known through publication, or that has been in use to be pleaded in defense, from being considered as improvement; and also expressly excludes *different proportions* or mere *variations* of form from being considered as improvements. How then can you defend your claim?"

"The proportions you use are exactly the proportions the Company used of which I held a quarter of the shares many years ago. Our boat was exactly eight feet wide and six feet keel—yours 20 by 150—each equal in length to seven and one half times the breadth. We also used a machine on Watt's and Boulton's Principles. The cylinder I had prepared for a Boat, intended for the Mississippi, of 25 tons burthen, was 3.6 diamater, 4 foot stroke, the Piston to work 30 single strokes a minute. All the proportions, force and velocity depend after this on the Quantity of Steam applied by the Boiler; for the size of the Paddles or buckets of the wheel may be varied with better experience accordingly, but will forever vary according to the force or high power of the steam."

Moreover, Dr. Thornton pointed out to him, his *Clermont* or *Car of Neptune* had never moved faster than five miles an hour in dead water, whereas the Fitch boat had gone, by actual test, eight miles an hour upstream.

Fulton was disturbed. He suggested meeting Dr. Thornton to converse upon "steamboat inventions and experiences. Altho I do not see by what means a boat containing one hundred tons of merchandise can be driven by a steam engine six miles an hour in still water, yet when you assert your perfect confidence in such success there may be something more in your combination than I am aware of." And if Dr. Thornton would build a boat which performed under those conditions "I will contract to reimburse you the cost of the boat and give you 150 thousand dollars for your patent—or if you can convince me of the success by any drawings or demonstrations I will join you in the expense and profits."

Thornton called this bluff at once. "Write the terms," he demanded of Fulton and the boat would be built.

But Fulton preferred palavering. From New York, on August 18, 1811, he prolonged the discussion by quibbling details. As Thornton had informed him, there was nothing patentable about the steamboat, because Fitch had built the first boat and the rights had expired; but "First, your wheels were proposed twenty years ago to Fitch's boat; his patent says nothing of wheels and as proof that you do not consider wheels as good as paddles you say you drove a boat eight miles an hour, and that this cannot be done with wheels." He admitted that "wheels, skulls, paddles etc. were no doubt talked of twenty years ago, but it would be dangerous to let dormant ideas sleep for twenty years and never be useful to the public."

Still dissatisfied with his defense, Fulton became baffled and sarcastic. "Fitch's company had a boat designed for a steamboat, rigged schooner fashion. You told me she was 20 tons burthen, but had she ever an engine on board and what was its power? Was she ever in motion under sail, wind and steam, or is this another thought or project never proved, but being dormant for twenty years proves clearly that it did not present a prospect or hope of utility and cannot now be called up among a thousand thoughts which pass through the minds of ingenious men..."

Disgusted with quibbling, Thornton brought out the whole matter in a pamphlet. After reciting the history of the steamboat company, he charged that Fitch's drawings and specifications had been "subjected to the examination of Mr. Fulton, when in France," by Aaron Vail. This accusation has been strengthened by the support of Nathaniel Cutting, John Dickinson and Noah Webster, all friends of the Vail family. As for the sidewheels of the *Clermont*, "they were known to us, and I often urged their use in our first boat, as can be testified by Mr. Oliver Evans; but the objection to them, on so small a scale, was their waste of power by the fall of the buckets or paddles on the water, and their lift of water in rising, both of which objections would diminish as the wheel increased in size. But sidewheels could not be claimed as a new invention, for their use in navigation had long been known, and published to the world by Dr. John Harris, in his Lexicon Technicum, in 1710, just one hundred years ago.

"If Mr. Fulton should claim the actual application of steam to wheels at the side of a boat, in opposition to the above declaration, I beg leave to offer as a caveat against any such claim, the fireship of Edward Thomason, in the tenth volume of the Reportory of the Arts, which was laid before the Lords of the Admiralty in 1796. This contains wheels at the sides, operated by a steam engine, and was intended to possess the power of moving given distances in all directions, according to the intention of the director; so that without any person being on board it would conduct itself into the enemy's port, and by clockwork at a given moment, explode the combustibles; which plan I also presume might suggest to any person of even less original genius than Mr. Fulton, the mode of letting off Torpedoes, which were invented, during the war for independence, by the late Major Bushness of Connecticut."

Since it had been shown that the New York monopolists were neither improvers nor inventors, "to attempt an exclusive monopoly of these waters is not merely an attempt to deprive others of natural and inherent rights, but without a shadow of reason, to attempt also to deprive them of acquired rights, under the general government; and as if the power and influence of individuals, which seems to have hitherto prevented an interference in this vast monopoly, had encouraged to further acquirements of the rights of their fellow-citizens; and being discontented with the wise and equitable provisions of the congress, in which all other citizens have rested satisfied; they have exhibited an avaricious desire of obtaining an universal monopoly of the waters of the union, by addressing the different legislatures of the states; and were even, in Virginia, on the point of succeeding, and the final question about to be put, when my letter was handed to the Speaker of the House of Representatives, and the bill was immediately negatived. So bold and unprecedented an attempt to infringe the privileges of the citizens at large, if successful, would have terminated in soliciting the congress to grant to a combination of rich merchants Roosevelt, Livingston, Clinton the monopoly of the seas, by the promise of low freights."

But even a devastating pamphlet by the superintendent of the Patent Office was a futile weapon against the wealth and power of the steamboat monopolists. They were empowered to seize and confiscate any vessel impelled by the force of fire or steam that failed to sail without their license and to collect a hundred dollars for each infraction. On the Hudson, the Delaware and the Mississippi they successfully fought any man who dared build a steamboat and operate it without paying them fifty percent of the gross receipts. Until 1820 action was brought against every violator on the Mississippi and until 1824, when Daniel Webster argued the priority of Fitch's right to the invention in Gobbons vs. Ogden before the United States Supreme Court, the monopolists kept control.

Not merely in relation to Fitch, but only in the full, clear light of past steamboat invention can the effrontery of Livingston and Fulton be thoroughly appreciated. How long ago people began to think of steam as a motivating force is not known, but Newcomen's engine, which was the first successful one, did not spring full grown from his imagination. And it was only by the accident, when he was a student at Glasgow University, of being set to work to repair Newcomen's model, that Watt conceived a higher type; and it was only after working many years with others and being financed by Dr. Roebuck, that Watt was enabled to patent the double-acting engine. Even then, the Watt engine had no means of obtaining rotary motion; that was supplied by still another inventor, Matthew Wasbrough, who conceived the use of connecting rod and crank.

Obviously, the steam engine had to be brought to a fair state of performance before a successful steamboat could be made. This was Fitch's first task. That he accomplished it independently of Watt is shown by the fact that he described his engine as double-acting in the *Columbian Magazine* of January, 1786, when Watt's engine was not generally known even in England.

As to the idea of moving a boat by steam, it did not originate with Fitch and certainly not with Fulton. It was foreshadowed in a patent by Jonathan Hulls of England in 1737 and by Genevois in France in 1759, who used paddles that were shaped like duck's feet for his method of propulsion. Experiments were made by Count Auxiron on the Seine in 1774, by De Jouffroy on the Saone in 1782, by Patrick Miller and William Symington on the Firth of Forth in October, 1788, and on the Clyde Canal in 1789, and by Samuel Morey on the Connecticut River in 1790.

When Mr. Sinton splattered past in his fine carriage, making the practical-minded Fitch think how fine it would be if a man could travel thus, but without the expense of keeping a horse, Thomas Paine, John Hall, Oliver Evans and William Henry had all concerned themselves with steam navigation. After Fitch was laid in his unmarked grave and before Fulton built the *Clermont,* a myriad of steamboat projectors were busily at work.

In 1804 Oliver Evans, who had invented a steam mudscow at Philadelphia which he called the Amphibolis Eruktor, "to show that both steam carriages and steam boats were practical ... first put wheels to it, and propelled it by the engine a mile and a half, and then into the Schuylkill" where he "then fixed a paddle wheel at the stern, and propelled it down the Schuylkill and up the Delaware" which was "done in the presence of thousands."

That same year John Cox Stevens drove a steamboat from Hoboken to New York and later "produced, independently of Fulton's plans and experiments, his steamer *Phoenix;* but, precluded by the monopoly which Fulton's success had obtained for him to the waters of New York, Mr. Stevens first employed her as a passenger boat to New Brunswick, and finally conceived the bold purpose of sending her round to Philadelphia by sea."

Fulton's invention, as summed up by Woodcroft, amounted to "a cylinder, with steam acting on each side of the piston, the air pump and detached condenser (Watt's invention); connecting rods, and cranks, to obtain a rotary motion and a flywheel to get over the dead point (Pickand's invention); improved paddle wheels (Miller's invention). In fact, if these inventions, separate or as a combination, were removed out of Fulton's Boat, nothing would be left but the hull."

And when Fulton was granted his monopoly patent by the United States Government it was in the face of nine other American patentees, all of whom had previously been granted rights to steam navigation: John Fitch, Philadelphia, 1791; James Rumsey, Virginia, 1791; Jehosephat Starr, Connecticut, 1797; Edward West, Kentucky, 1802; Dr. William Thornton,

Washington, 1809; Daniel French, New York, 1809; John Stevens, New York, 1810; Samuel Bolton, Philadelphia, 1810; and Michael Morrison, Boston, 1811.

Clearly, the steamboat was not the work of one man. It was a result of the growing intelligence and experience of the race, English, French, Italians, Germans and Americans, applied to meet a progressive need. But of all the men who fretted and labored for its improvement John Fitch worked earliest on the proper principles with the greatest mechanical success and the least financial reward.

Even the dream which had sustained him through years of desperate labor has now an ironic significance, "that future generations, when traversing the mighty Waters of the West, in the manner that I have pointed out, may find my grassy turff, and spread their cupboard on it, and circle round their chearful Knogins of Whiskey, with three times three, till they should suppose a son of misfortune could never occupy the place." And though it might sound "somewhat singular" that "the summit of my everlasting Bliss should extend no further than being surrounded by a set of Drunken Boatmen, as they are generally the honestest part of the community, and more liberal according to what they possess, I will not retract what I have said."

BIBLIOGRAPHY

Manuscripts

Fitch Papers, Autobiography and History of the Steamboat, written for the Rev. Nathaniel Irwin of Bucks Co., Pa. Nov. 12, 1790. (Library Company of Philadelphia.)
Fitch Papers, Diaries, Receipt Books, and Letters, Library of Congress.
Fitch Papers, File C-7, Box 35, Historical Society of Pennsylvania.
Franklin Papers, American Philosophical Society, Philadelphia.
Fulton Papers, Library of Congress.
Longstreth Collection, Historical Society of Pennsylvania.
Records and Papers, Connecticut State Library, Hartford, Conn.
Rumsey Papers, Virginia Archives, Virginia State Library.
Thornton Papers, Library of Congress.
WATSON, John F., Papers and Correspondence, Historical Society of Pennsylvania.

Pamphlets

BARNES, James, "Remarks on Mr. John Fitch's Reply to Mr. James Rumsey's Pamphlet." Library of Congress.
"Explanation of Ship's Traverse at Sea by Columbian Ready Reckoner." American Philosophical Society, Vol. VII, London, 1793.
"John Fitch." Admiral Bunce Section of Navy League of U. S., Hartford, Conn., 1912.
"John Fitch vs. James Rumsey." 1788, Library of Congress.
JOHNSON, Annie Cox, "Memorial to John Fitch." Government Printing Office, 1915, Library of Congress.
MORAY, John, "Last Century's Inventive Steam Pirate." Privately printed, W. Virginia, 1910.
Report of Special Committee appointed by General Assembly, Hartford, 1887.

Rumsey Pamphlets, Documentary History of New York, Vol. II.
THORNTON, William, "Origin of the Steamboat." Washington, 1810, Library of Congress.
WHITTLESEY, Charles, "Justice to the Memory of John Fitch." 1845, Archives of the United States.

Legal Records and Collections

American State Papers Misc., Vol. II, p. 12.
Henning's Statutes, Vol. XI, p. 502.
Hutchins' Papers, Historical Society of Pennsylvania, Vol. III, p. 14.
JOHNSON, New York Reports, Vol. IX, p. 507, Appendix.
Journals of Congress.
Minutes of Provisional Congress and Council of Safety of the State of New Jersey, Trenton, 1789.
New York State Laws, Fulton and Livingston, Vol. II, p. 472, Appendix.
PURDY, Thomas C., Report on Steam Navigation in the U. S., Census Reports, Vol. IV, pp. 653-720.
Virginia—Journal of the House of Delegates, Virginia State Library.

Magazines and Newspapers

BULLOCK, C. S., "Who Built the First Steamboat?" *Cassier's Magazine*, Dec., 1907, Vol. XXXI.
——"The Miracle of the First Steamboat." *Journal of American History*, 1907, Vol. I, pp. 38-48.
CLARK, Allen Cutting, Dr. and Mrs. William Thornton. Columbia Historical Society Records.
"The Delaware River and John Fitch." *Scientific American*, Oct. 9, 1919, Vol. CI.
"Fitch and Fulton." *Hazard's Register of Pennsylvania*, Philadelphia, 1831, Vol. VII.
HAMMOND, F., "John Fitch." *New England Magazine*, Vol. LXXXVIII.
PARSONS, Mira Clark, "John Fitch, Inventor of Steamboats." *Ohio Archæological and Historical Quarterly*, 1900-01, Library of Congress.

Pennsylvania Magazine of History and Biography, Vol. XXIII, pp. 115-116.

WEBSTER, M., "John Fitch." *International Magazine*, Vol. I.

WINSOR, Justin, Remarks (on John Fitch Map), Massachusetts Historical Society Proceedings, Boston, 1892, 2nd Series, Vol. VII.

WOOD, William, Article on John Fitch by a native of East Windsor. *Hartford Times*, April 19, 1883.

Books

BACHE, William, "Historical Sketches of Bristol Borough, Bucks Co." Bristol, Pa., 1853.

BACON, Corra Foster, "The Potomac Route to the West." Washington, 1912.

BALDWIN, Charles Candee, "Early Maps of Ohio and the West." Fairbanks, Benedict & Co., Cleveland, 1885.

BATTLE, J. H., "History of Bucks County, Penn." A. Warner & Co., Philadelphia and Chicago, 1887.

BISHOP, James Leander, "History of American Manufactures." E. Young & Co., Philadelphia, 1861.

BOYD, Thomas, "Light-Horse Harry Lee." Charles Scribner's Sons, New York, 1931.

———, "Simon Girty." Minton, Balch & Co., New York, 1928.

BRISSOT DE WARVILLE, Jacques Pierre, "Nouveau Voyage dans les Etats-Unis." Paris, 1791.

BUCK, Wm. J., "History of Bucks County," Part II. *Bucks County Intelligencer*, 1854.

BUCKMAN, David L., "Old Steamboat Days on the Hudson River." Grafton Press, New York, 1907.

BUTTERFIELD, C. W., "History of the Girtys." R. Clark & Co., Cincinnati, 1890.

CHATTERTON, E. Keble, "Steamboats and Their Story." Cassell & Co., London and New York, 1910.

COLLINS, Vanum Lansing, "Princeton." Oxford University Press, New York, 1924.

CONWAY, Moncure, "Life of Thomas Paine." G. P. Putnam's Sons, New York, 1893.

CUTLER, Rev. Manasseh, Diary.

BIBLIOGRAPHY

DE PEYSTER, Arent Schuyler, "Miscellanies by an Officer." Ed. by J. Watts De Peyster. A. E. Chasmer & Co., New York, 1888.
DOUGLAS, Paul H., "American Apprenticeship and Industrial Education." Columbia University Press, New York, 1921.
DUNBAR, Seymour, "A History of Travel in America." Bobbs-Merrill Co., Indianapolis, 1915.
ELIOT, Jared, "Upon Field Husbandry." Columbia University Press, 1934.
FAŸ, Bernard, "Dr. Franklin." Little, Brown & Co., Boston, 1929.
FORD, W. C., "Writings of Washington." New York, 1900.
HARRISON, Fairfax, "Landmarks in Old Prince William." Privately printed, Richmond, Va., 1924.
HENRY, W. W., "Life of Patrick Henry." Charles Scribner's Sons, New York, 1891.
HOOPES, Penrose R., "Connecticut Clockmakers of the 18th Century." Dodd, Mead & Co., New York, 1913.
ILES, George, "Leading American Inventors." Henry Holt & Co., New York, 1912.
JILLSON, Willard R., "Filson's Kentucke." Facsimile of Wilmington ed., 1784. John P. Norton & Co., Louisville, 1930.
KAEMPFFERT, Waldemar B., "Popular History of American Invention." Charles Scribner's Sons, New York, 1924.
KOCK, Gustav Adolf, "Republican Religion." Henry Holt & Co., New York, 1933.
KROPOTKIN, Peter, "The Great French Revolution." Wm. Heineman, London, 1909.
LATROBE, Benjamin H., Journal of. D. Appleton & Co., New York, 1905.
LLOYD, James T., "Steamboat Directory." D. B. Cooke & Co., Chicago, 1856.
MARSHALL, Christopher, Diary. Edited by William Duane. Joel Munsell, Albany, 1877.
NORTON, Frederick Calvin, "Governors of Connecticut." Hartford, 1895.
PARTON, James, "Great Men and Their Achievements." Arundel Print, New York, 1881.
———, "Life and Times of Benjamin Franklin." Houghton, Mifflin & Co., Boston, 1886.

BIBLIOGRAPHY

PHILLIPS, P. Lee, "The Rare Map of the Northwest, 1785, by John Fitch, Inventor of the Steamboat." W. H. Lowdermilk & Co., Washington, 1916.

PREBLE, George Henry, "Chronological History of the Origin and Development of Steam Navigation." R. L. Hamersly & Co., Philadelphia, 1883.

QUICK, Herbert and Edward, "Mississippi Steamboatin'." Henry Holt & Co., New York, 1927.

READ, David, "Nathan Read." Hurd & Houghton, New York, 1870.

SAKOLSKI, Aaron Morton, "The Great American Land Bubble." Harper & Brothers, New York, 1932.

SIMCOE, John Graves, Correspondence. Ontario Historical Society, Toronto, 1923-31.

SIMPSON, Henry, "Lives of Eminent Philadelphians." W. Brotherhood, Philadelphia, 1859.

SPARKS, Jared, "Life of Franklin," Vol. X.

STILES, Ezra, Literary Diaries of. Edited by Franklin B. Dexter. Charles Scribner's Sons, New York, 1901.

STILES, Henry R., "The History of Ancient Windsor." Charles B. Norton, New York, 1859.

TYLER, "Patrick Henry."

VERHOEFF, Mary, "The Kentucky River Navigation." Filson Club Publication, John P. Norton & Co., Louisville, 1917.

WATSON, John F., "Annals of Philadelphia." Edited by W. P. Hazard. E. S. Stuart, Philadelphia, 1898. Vols. I, II and III.

WEEDEN, W. B., "Economic and Social History of New England." Houghton, Mifflin & Co., Boston, 1890.

WESCOTT, Thompson, "The Life of John Fitch, the Inventor of the Steamboat." J. B. Lippincott & Co., Philadelphia, 1878.

WHITTLESEY, Charles, "Life of John Fitch." Sparks, Vol. XVI, 1854.

WINSOR, Justin, "The Western Movement." Houghton, Mifflin & Co., Boston, 1897.

WOODWARD, W. E., "George Washington." Boni & Liveright, New York, 1926.

ZWEIG, Stefan, "Joseph Fouché." Cassell & Co., London, 1930.

INDEX

American Philosophical Society, 135, 142-143, 155, 157, 165-166, 169, 201, 282
Anderson, Colonel Joshua, 114, 115, 116, 117, 118, 119, 120
Apprenticeship system, the, 15
Arkwright's spinning frame, 214

Bache, Benjamin Franklin, ridicules Fitch's steamboat, 229-230
Baldwin, Jonathan, 137
Barlow, Joel, 294
Barnes, J., brother-in-law of James Rumsey, 197, 198, 203, 204, 206
Beamen, Jonathan, 32
Beauharnais, Countess, 215
Bedinger, Captain Harry, 196, 200
Bernouilli's boat, 155-156
Biddle, Charles, 226, 227, 228
Bingham, William, of Philadelphia, 150, 151, 194, 198
Boileau, Nathaniel, 134, 155
Bolingbroke, 257, 262
Bolton, Samuel, 302
Boston, investment of, by the Continental army in 1775, 48
Boulton, Matthew, and the steam engine, 158
Brissot de Warville, 272
Brooks, Edward, 251
Buckley, Daniel, of Philadelphia, 197, 200
Bucks County, Pa., 55
Bunker Hill, battle of, 46, 48

Cadwallader, Lambert, 137
Canals as means of long distance transportation, 190
Carrier, 278
Cheney, Benjamin, East Hartford clockmaker, Fitch's apprenticeship to, 14-21
Cheney, Deborah, wife of Benjamin Cheney, 18-19

Cheney, Timothy, Connecticut clockmaker, 15, 18, 28, 30; Fitch's apprenticeship to, 21-27
Clermont, Fulton's 295, 296, 298, 301; compared with Fitch's first successful boat, 231
Clinton, De Witt, 190, 293
Clinton, Sir Henry, 54
Clockmakers as craftsmen in the eighteenth century in America, 14-15
Clymer, George, 156, 167, 207, 208
Colles, Christopher, 154, 190
Columbian Magazine, the, 162, 300
Committees of Correspondence, the, 45
Constitutional Convention of 1787, the, 178-179
Continental Army, investment of Boston by, 48; the elimination of democracy in, 48-49
Continental currency, depreciation of, 55-56, 175
Cornbury, Lord, 28, 189
Cornwallis, Lord, 50; surrender of, 91-92
Cowley's steam engine, 132
Coxe, Tench, 152, 170, 179, 214
Crawford, Colonel William, 60
Cutler, Rev. Manasseh, 125, 126
Cutting, Nathaniel, 298

Deism and the Deists in the eighteenth century, 253-264
de Peyster, Major Arent Schuyler, 67, 81, 91-92
Desauglier and the use of steam, 158
Dickinson, John, 298
Dickinson, General Philemon, 47, 51, 52
Dobbs Ferry, N. Y., 111
Documentary History of New York, the, 288

309

INDEX

Donaldson, Arthur, 156, 157, 170, 171
Duer, William, 125-126, 151

East Hartford, Conn, 15, 18
East India Company, the British, 44
Economic conditions of the young United States after the Revolution, 174-175
Edwards, John, 147, 148
Edwards, Timothy, 35
Ellicott, Andrew, 144, 210, 273
Ellsworth, Oliver, 179
Erie Canal, the, 190
Evans, Oliver, 298, 301
Ewing, Dr. John, 114, 121, 126, 136, 137, 181, 201, 210, 225, 273

Federal Gazette, the, 229
Findlay, James, 235, 236
Fitch, Abigail (Church), stepmother of John Fitch, 6, 16, 17
Fitch, Augustus, brother of John Fitch, 6, 7, 28
Fitch, Chloe, sister of John Fitch, 6, 7, 29-30
Fitch family, account of the predecessors of John Fitch in America, 34-35
Fitch, John, his own account of his steamboat invention, and "detail" of his life, deposited with Library Company of Philadelphia, Foreword, and 264-265; early thirst for learning, 3-5; death of his mother, 3, 5-6; incidents of his boyhood, in Windsor, Conn., 3-12; his brothers and sisters, 6; studies surveying, 9-10; brief experience as a sailor, 12-13; apprenticeship to a clockmaker, and his experiences under two masters, 14-27; denied the opportunity to learn the trade and finally buys his freedom, 20-21, 24-27; his situation at this time, 28; establishes a small brasswork business, 30; unsuccessful potash works in Hartland, 31-32; unhappy marriage to Lucy Roberts, 32-34; his heretical notions, 33; ancestors of, 24-35; leaves his wife and Windsor and his wanderings, 35-40; establishes himself in Trenton, N. J., as a silversmith and clock and watch repairer, 40-44; attitude at the beginning of the Revolution, 44, 46; contention over his appointment as an officer in the army, 46-48, 49, 50-51; gunsmith for Committee of Safety, 47; failure to join the army, 52, 53-54; profits as a sutler to the army at Valley Forge, 53; loss of his capital through depreciation of Continental currency, 55-56; first journey down the Ohio, and surveying in the western forests, 62-63; second journey, 63 ff.; his party captured by Indians, 70-72; taken to the British at Detroit and the experiences of the journey, 73-92; taken to Prison Island in the St. Lawrence and his vicissitudes there, 93 ff.; exchanged and his account of his return to the United States by sea from Montreal, 101-109; lands at New York and returns to Warminster, Pa., 111-113; third venture into the west, in 1783, for survey of land claims, 114 ff.; returns over the Alleghenies on foot, 119-120; another surveying expedition the following spring, 120-123; expectations of wealth from his surveys, 124-125; resurveys his claims after passage of Northwest Ordinance of 1784, 125; petitions Congress for appointment as a surveyor in the Northwest Territory, 126; his "Map of the Northwest Parts of the United States of America," 127-128, 134-135, 137, 148; disappointed in hopes of fortune from his surveys and fails appointment as surveyor, 128; beginnings of his experiments with steam navigation, 131 ff.; petitions Congress unsuccessfully for aid in his project, 137-138, 140-141; his efforts to interest Franklin, Washington and others in his steamboat, 141-148; steamboat rights in Virginia, 148; granted a monopoly on steam navigation by the New Jersey Legislature and formation of a stock company, 149 ff.; the subscribers to his company, 153; building an engine and an experimental boat with Henry Voight and their preliminary failure, 157-161; the first successful model, and description of the en-

INDEX

Fitch, John (cont'd)
gine, 162-163; the question of making steamboats profitable, 163-164; efforts to raise funds for the building of a full-sized boat, 164-168; granted exclusive rights in New York, Pennsylvania and Delaware and the building of his first steamboat at Philadelphia, 169-174; exhibition trips of the boat, 180; building of a second boat with greater power and its public trial, 181-187; Rumsey's attack on him and the resulting controversy, 195 ff.; the proofs of Fitch's priority, 199-203, 205-206; Fitch's reply to Rumsey's attack, 203; his third boat and its final successful operation, 211, 217-218, 221 ff.; establishment of regular packet service between Philadelphia and Trenton, 226, 229; financial failure of the steamboat line, 230-232; comparison of his boat with Fulton's *Clermont*, 231; plans for steam navigation in western waters, 232-234; efforts to get a boat built for western rivers, 234-235, 236-237; building of the *Perseverance*, 237; unsuccessful applications for government employment, 240-241; loss of his exclusive rights to navigation of Virginia waters, 241-242; receives permit to enter New Orleans with steamboat and resumes work on the *Perseverance*, 242; Voight's affair with Mary Kraft and Fitch's part in the matter, 242-250; vain endeavors to raise funds to complete the *Perseverance*, 251-252; the end of his experiments on the Delaware, 252; religious beliefs and his Deistical Society, 253-264; ponders suicide and makes his will, 266-268; steamboat patent secured in France and goes there to build another boat, 271, 273, 274; visit to Thomas Paine, 274-275; impressions of the French Revolution, 275-276; unable to build a boat because of the fighting at Nantes, 277-278; goes to England hoping to get an engine built, 278; his "Ready Reckoner and New Method of Navigation," 278-279,
280-281, 283, 284; unable to get an engine built in England or to return to France, sets sail for Boston, 280-282; his "new method of turning millwork by water," 283-284; stay in Boston and return to Windsor, 283-288; letters to his children, 286, 288; reputed screw-propeller boat built by him in New York, 288-289; goes to Kentucky to reclaim lands there and his death and burial at Bardstown, 288, 289-293; new wills made by, 291; Livingston's admission of his claim to the invention of the steamboat, 294-295; his independent building of a workable steam engine, 300

Fitch, Joseph, brother of John Fitch, 6, 7, 8, 9, 10
Fitch, Joseph, father of John Fitch, 3, 4, 5, 8, 9, 12-13, 16, 17-18, 22, 28; second marriage, 6
Fitch, Joseph, great-grandfather of John Fitch, 34, 35
Fitch, Sarah (Shaler), mother of John Fitch, 5-6
Fitch, Sarah Anne, sister of John Fitch, 6, 7, 248, 285; marriage to Timothy King, 16-17
Fitch, Thomas, of Bocking, Essex County, England, ancestor of John Fitch, 34
Fort Pitt, 62
Fort Washington, 50
Fouché, Joseph, 276
Fox, George, 256, 257, 268
Franklin, Benjamin, 141-142, 143, 150-151, 155-157, 162, 165-166, 181, 190, 193, 194, 198, 214, 217; Fitch's interview with, 141-142
French, Daniel, 302
Fulton, Robert, 151, 181, 231, 289, 293; his claims to be the inventor of the steamboat, 294 ff.

Gallatin, Albert, 235, 236, 265
Gardoqui, Don Diego de, Spanish minister, 139, 141
Gates, General Horatio, 194
Gazette, Franklin's, 229
Gazette of the United States, the, 225
George III, 59, 60
Germain, Lord George, 51
Germantown, battle of, 52
Gibbon, 257, 262

INDEX

Gibson, General, 235, 236-237
Grey, General Sir Charles, 52

Hall, John, 149-150, 301
Halyburton, "Rational Inquiry into the Principles of the Modern Deists," 259
Hamilton, Alexander, 170, 178, 214, 236
Hamilton, General Henry, 61, 62
Hand, General Edward, 62
Hargreave's jenny, 214
Hart, Jonathan, 210-211
Hatborough, Pa., 55
Heckewelder, Rev. John, 66-67
Henry, Patrick, 147, 148, 155, 201
Henry, William, 144, 192, 301
Hodder's Arithmetic, 3, 5, 9
Houston, William, 114, 121, 136, 137, 149, 201
Howe, Lord, 50
Howe, Sir William, 52
Hume, 257, 262
Humphreys, Whitehead, 135, 166
Hutchins, Thomas, 126, 128, 153, 173, 211
Hutchins' and McMurray's map of the northwest, 127

Independence Hall, Philadelphia, 178
Indians, troubles with, over settlement of lands west of the Alleghenies, 59, 61, 62; the Williamson massacre, 66, 68-69; assisted by British in their fight against the encroaching Americans, 85; final treaty of peace with, 289
Iron mines in Connecticut, 28
Irvine, General William, 157, 225
Irwin, Rev. Nathaniel, Foreword, 55, 114, 121, 131, 133, 155, 199, 258, 259, 265, 268

Jackson, Andrew, 294
Jay, John, 178
Jefferson, Thomas, 189, 215, 241, 257, 265, 266, 296
Johnson, Dr. Samuel, 179-180
Johnson, Thomas, 144-145, 149, 192, 201-202
Kentucky, emigration to, 289-290
King, Timothy, brother-in-law of John Fitch, 16-17, 20, 28, 220, 248, 285
Knox Henry, 151, 177, 291
Knyphausen, General, 52
Koch, G. Adolph, "Republican Religion," 258 n.
Kraft, Mary, befriends Fitch, 219-220, 238; her affair with Henry Voight and Fitch's part in the matter, 242-250
Kropotkin, "The Great Revolution," 272 n., 280 n.

Lafayette, 272
Lamb, General Anthony, 288
Lee, Light-Horse Harry, 49, 139, 140, 190
Library Company of Philadelphia, the, Fitch's own account of his steamboat invention and "detail" of his life deposited with, Foreword, and 135, 265
Library of Congress, Fitch's documents treasured in, Foreword
Lincoln, General Benjamin, 177
Livingston, Chancellor, 151, 289, 293, 294, 295, 300
Livingston, Walter, 126
Locke, 260
Logan, Indian chief, 61
Long Island, battle of, 50
Longstreth, Daniel, 55, 56, 289
Longstreth, Joseph, 134
L'Orient, France, 277, 278
Louis XVI of France, 272
Loyal Company, the, 59

McMeekin, James, silent partner of Rumsey, 194, 197, 203, 204
Madison, James, 148, 178, 215
Magaw, Samuel, secretary of American Philosophical Society, 143, 194, 198
"Map of the Northwest Parts of the United States of America," Fitch's, 127-128, 134-135, 137, 148
Marat, 272
Mason, Major-General John, 34
Michelet, 277
Mifflin, Thomas, 226, 227, 228
Mississippi River, attitude of east and west toward the free navigation of, at end of eighteenth century, 138-140

INDEX

Molyneaux, William, 45
Morris, Cadwallader, 126
Morris, Gouverneur, 48, 274, 275
Morris, Dr. John, 153
Morris, Robert, 150, 151, 238, 239
Morrison, Michael, 302
Morrow, Charles, brother-in-law of James Rumsey, 197, 198, 203, 204, 206
Murdock, John, and the steam engine, 158

Nantes, 276-277
Navigation Acts, the British, 29
Neshaminy, Pa., 55
Newcomen's steam engine, 132, 134, 158, 300
New England colonies, effect of British revenue laws and restrictions of trade on industry in, 28-29
New England Primer, the, 3
New Orleans, 138, 139, 140
Newton, 260
New York Magazine, the, enthusiastic comment on Fitch's steamboat, 230
Niagara Falls, 127-128
Nicholson, James, 285
Non-importation agreements, 45
Northwest Ordinance of 1784, 125, 128
Northwest Territory, the, 124, 125, 126, 254

Ogleby, James, 131, 132
Ohio Company, the (of Virginia), 59
Ohio Company, the (of 1786), 125
Ohio Steamboat Navigation Company, the, 293
Orrery, Dr. David Rittenhouse's, 135
Osgood, Samuel, 126

Paine, Thomas, 144, 149-150, 151, 192, 274-275, 294, 301
Palmer, Elihu, 259-262
Papen and the condensation of steam, 158
Patterson, Miss Peggy, 134-135, 174
Patterson, Robert, 134-135, 210, 225
Peale, Rembrandt, 180
Pennsylvania Gazette, the, 152
Pennsylvania Packet, the, 135, 229
"Pennsylvania Society for the Encouragement of Manufactures and the Useful Arts," the, 152

Peperill, Sir William, 10
Philadelphia, capture of, by the British, 52; the city at the close of the eighteenth century, 134-136
Philosophia Britannica, Martin's, 133
Pollock, Oliver, 238, 239
Pompadour, Madame, 274, 275
Potomac Company, the, and the Potomac Canal, 189-192
Potts, Stacy, 114, 121, 165
Prichard, William, 135
Princeton College, 39-40
Prison Island in the St. Lawrence River, British prison camp on, during the Revolutionary War, 93 ff.
Putnam, General Rufus, 125

Rahl, Colonel, 50, 52
Randolph, Edmund, 179, 241
"Ready Reckoner and New Method of Navigation," Fitch's, 278-279, 280-281, 283, 284
Revolution, the American, beginnings and early years of, 44-54
Revolution, the French, 271-273, 274, 276-277
Rittenhouse, Dr. David, 135, 157, 167, 181, 210, 225, 251, 273
Roberts, Lucy, marriage to John Fitch, 32-33
Rockwell, Mistress, school-mistress, 6
Roebuck, Dr. John, patron of James Watt, 158, 300
Roosevelt, Nicholas, 293, 295
Rousseau, 257
Rumseian Society, the, 192, 194, 195, 198, 203, 204, 206, 207
Rumsey, James, and his mechanical boat, 144-145, 146-147, 156, 157, 181, 188; a protégé of Washington, 190-192; superintendent of the Potomac Canal construction, 190-192; efforts to apply steam to navigation and the trial of his boat, 192-194; his influential patrons and formation of the Rumseian Society, 194-195; attack on Fitch and attempt to acquire the patents granted to him, 195 ff.; the controversy that followed, 198-209
St. Clair, General Arthur, 194, 198
Sakolski, "Great American Land Bubble," 60 n.
Salmon's Geography, 3, 4, 5, 9, 265
Samuel, Bunford, Foreword

INDEX

Savary's steam engine, 132
Say, Dr. Benjamin, 153, 169, 171, 182, 184, 186, 187, 216, 225, 251
Say, Thomas, 153
Schuyler, General Philip, 132, 154
Screw propeller boat reputed to have been built by Fitch, 288-289
Sergeant, Jonathan, 114, 121, 126
Shays' Rebellion, 177-178
Shreve, Captain Henry M., 293
Smeaton and the steam engine, 158
Smith, Dr. Samuel, 137
Society for Political Inquiry, the, 150-151
Southern, John, and the steam engine, 158
Stages as prospective competitors with the steamboat, 163-164
Starr, Jehosephat, 301
Steamboat, the beginnings of Fitch's experiments, 131 ff.; Fitch's first successful model and description of the engine, 162-163; building of Fitch's first practicable craft, 172-174; Fitch's second boat, 181-187; Rumsey's boat and its trial, 193-194; Rumsey's attack on Fitch and the resulting controversy, 195 ff.; Fitch's third boat and its final successful operation, 211, 217-218, 221 ff.; establishment of a monopoly by Livingston and Fulton and their associates, 293 ff.; first steamboats in the Ohio and Mississippi, 293-294; various claims to the invention of, and their merits, 294 ff.; Fulton's claim to be the inventor of, 294 ff.; Livingston's admission of Fitch's invention of, 294-295; early patentees and experimenters, 300-301
Steam engines, early, 132-133; the various contributors to their development, 158-159; Fitch's accomplishment, 300
Stevens, John Cox, 301, 302
Stockton, Richard, 153, 173, 216, 242, 251
Sugar Act, the British, of 1764, 29, 44
Taylor, John, 215
Thornton, Dr. William, and his part in Fitch's experiments, 214-216, 217, 221, 223, 226, 227, 242, 268, 275, 277, 281-282, 283, 284, 289; controversy with Fulton over his claim to be the inventor of the steamboat as against Fitch's, 296-299
Tobacco, shipped from Connecticut to West Indies in eighteenth century, 4
Trenton, N. J., Fitch's establishment as silversmith at, 40-41; battle of, 52

"United Company of Philadelphia for the Promotion of American Manufactures," 135, 179

Vail, Aaron, U. S. Consul at L'Orient, France, 277, 278; secures Fitch steamboat patent in France, 271; lends Fitch's drawings to Fulton, 294, 298
Valley Forge, 52, 53, 54, 273
Voight, Henry, works with Fitch in his steamboat building, 154-155, 157, 158-163, 164, 165, 167, 169, 171, 172-174, 181, 183, 184, 186, 187, 210-213, 217, 222, 223, 225, 226, 240; appointed chief coiner in the United States Mint, 241; his affair with Mary Kraft and the resulting rupture with Fitch, 242-250; his revenge on Fitch, 251-252; joins Fitch in his views on religion, 255, 256
Voltaire, 257
von Guericke and the vacuum engine, 158

Warminster, Pa., 55, 112
Wasbrough, Matthew, and the steam engine, 158, 300
Washington Augustine, 59
Washington, George, 48, 49, 50, 52, 54, 59, 60, 91, 92, 139, 140, 150, 176, 177, 178, 180-181, 195, 196, 198, 199-200, 236, 254, 257, 258, 265, 281; Fitch's interview with, 145-147; and his Potomac Canal plans, 188 ff.; partizanship towards Rumsey, 190-192
Washington, Lawrence, 59
Watt, James, and the steam engine, 158, 159, 214, 300
Watts, Dr., 260
Wayne, General Anthony, 85, 176, 177, 289

INDEX

Webster, Daniel, 299
Webster, Noah, 298
Wells, Richard, 164, 169, 171, 173, 182, 184, 186, 187, 198, 201, 207, 216, 223
Wesley, 258, 259
West, Edward, 301
Westcott, Thompson, Fitch's second biographer, 289
Western lands, settlement of, beyond the Alleghenies, and resentment of the Indians at, 59-62; system of disposal of, 124-126; importance of free navigation of the Mississippi to development of, and cross purposes of east and west as to their trade, 138-140
Westlock, William H., 288
Whisky Rebellion, the, 235-236
Whittlesey, Charles, first biographer of Fitch, 288

Wilkinson, General James, 232
Wilkinson, John, and the steam engine, 158, 172
Williamson, Colonel David, Indian massacre by his command, 66, 68-69
Williamson, Hugh, 200
Willing, Thomas, partner of Robert Morris, 150
Windsor, Conn., boyhood home of John Fitch, 3, 4, 12, 28, 34-35, 288
Wolcott, colonial governor of Connecticut, 4, 9, 10, 11, 30, 105
Woodward, Wm. E., "Life of Washington," 48 *n*.

Yarnell, Peter, Quaker, 258
Yorktown, surrender of Cornwallis at, 91-92
Young, Seth, Connecticut clockmaker, 15

B
F 545

1304 4